ELIZABETH I

ELIZABETH I

AUTOGRAPH
COMPOSITIONS AND
FOREIGN LANGUAGE
ORIGINALS

Edited by
Janel Mueller and
Leah S. Marcus

THE UNIVERSITY OF CHICAGO PRESS
Chicago & London

JANEL MUELLER is professor of English and the William Rainey Harper Professor in the College at the University of Chicago, now serving as Dean of the Division of the Humanities. She has been the editor of the journal *Modern Philology* and is the author of *The Native Tongue and the Word* (University of Chicago Press, 1984).

LEAH S. MARCUS is the Edwin Mims Professor of English at Vanderbilt University. Her books include *Childhood and Cultural Despair* (1978), *The Politics of Mirth* (University of Chicago Press, 1986), *Puzzling Shakespeare* (1988), and *Unediting the Renaissance* (1996).

The University of Chicago Press, Chicago 60637
The University of Chicago Press, Ltd., London
© 2003 by The University of Chicago
All rights reserved. Published 2003
Printed in the United States of America

12 11 10 09 08 07 06 05 04 03   1 2 3 4 5
ISBN: 0-226-50470-0 (cloth)

Library of Congress Cataloging-in-Publication Data

Elizabeth I, Queen of England, 1533–1603.
   [Selections. 2003]
   Elizabeth I : autograph compositions and foreign language originals / edited by Janel Mueller and Leah S. Marcus.
     p.   cm.
   Includes bibliographical references and index.
   ISBN 0-226-50470-0 (alk. paper)
   1. Great Britain—History—Elizabeth, 1558–1603—Sources. 2. Elizabeth I, Queen of England, 1533–1603—Correspondence. 3. Queens—Great Britain—Correspondence. I. Title: Autograph compositions and foreign language originals. II. Mueller, Janel M., 1938–. III. Marcus, Leah S. (Leah Sinanoglou). IV Title.
DA350 .A25 2003
942.05′5′092—dc21

                    2002008739

CONTENTS

I   AUTOGRAPH COMPOSITIONS

ILLUSTRATIONS

PREFACE

This volume assembles all of the originals of Queen Elizabeth I's texts that figure in our companion volume, *Elizabeth I: Collected Works*.[1] As used here, "originals" include Elizabeth's compositions that survive in her own handwriting, whether in English or in foreign languages, and her foreign language compositions that have been preserved by other hands. The term "originals" applies exclusively to the queen; we do not include King James's original handwritten letters from the correspondence that the two monarchs began in 1585. We arrange the compositions in this volume chronologically, in two parts: first Elizabeth's autograph texts, then her non-English, non-autograph texts.

The texts in this volume take the form of transcriptions, not photographic reproductions — except for the few illustrations labeled "figures" and easily recognized as such. Our transcriptions offer typographical representations — that is, print simulations or approximations — of their handwritten or early printed originals preserved in various archives. In the interests of accessibility and utility for our readers, our transcriptions expand all contracted forms into full words or phrases. Using standard resources of contemporary print technology, we have designed our transcriptions of the autograph texts to convey many of the significant and the idiosyncratic features of Elizabeth's compositions. Signifi-

---

1. The notes to this volume employ the abbreviated reference *CW*. For other abbreviated forms of reference — e.g., BL, PRO — carried over from our first volume, see the listing in *CW*, pp. ix–x.

cant features include additions or revisions to the main body of her text and how she entered these—whether side by side on the same line, or above the line of writing, or in a page margin, or squeezed in to the left of her signature, as several postscripts to letters are. Characteristic or idiosyncratic features of her autograph texts include spellings, letter-forms (majuscule or miniscule), punctuation marks (or their absence), and an array of special features involving paragraph breaks (or their absence), the positionings of her signature or of salutations or closing phrases or postscripts in the letters, and the embellished capital letters and certain retraced opening words in the prayers of the girdle prayer book that she compiled during Monsieur's courtship.

We have not been concerned to reproduce line breaks and page breaks in the body of Elizabeth's handwritten prose because these are usually arbitrary. Where a line break or page break happens to coincide with the end of a sentence or phrase, there is sometimes some indication that Elizabeth treats the break as the equivalent of a punctuation mark and supplies no punctuation there. However, since her characteristic practice is to punctuate very lightly, we have left these possibly significant breaks unmarked. We do, of course, reproduce the line breaks in the versicles of Elizabeth's prayers as well as the line and stanza breaks in her poetry because these are essential formal features of such compositions.

Our transcriptions of Elizabeth's non-autograph, foreign language texts replicate their spelling, punctuation, and paragraph units as these appear in sixteenth-century manuscript copies or printed editions—again, with contracted forms expanded in full. One departure from our policy of faithful replication will be self-evident. To insure easy cross-referencing, the headings and numberings of Elizabeth's speeches, letters, poems, and prayers have been carried over from *Collected Works* into this volume. Moreover, we have not undertaken to signal self-emendations or other textual interventions in the writing practices of copyists or in the typesetting procedures of compositors in the printing house. The sufficiently demanding object of our close textual attention in these transcriptions has been the writing performed by Elizabeth herself. Hence, the "original" aspect of the non-autograph, foreign language texts is the "original language," the language other than English, in its sixteenth-century state in which Elizabeth composed, and that is what our transcriptions replicate.

Accordingly, in part 2, comprising texts in hands other than hers, we are careful to record local corrections that Elizabeth wrote into scribal copies of Letters 46, 47, 52, and 87, Version 1. At junctures where the absence of diacritical marks or the spelling form or the word grouping leaves the sense doubtful—whether French, Latin, Italian, Greek, or Spanish—we have provided an explanatory note. In the extreme and fortunately unique case of Prayers 27 and 28, in Greek, where the compositor ran out of the letters *nu* and *kappa* and respectively substituted *mu* and *chi,* we have restored the texts to intelligible form.

Proportionally, the body of material in this volume comprises more than a quarter of the total presented in *Elizabeth I: Collected Works.* Since that volume offers these texts in modern English spelling and punctuation, it might be asked what justifies inclusion of these so-called originals in the modes of presentation that we adopt here. Our principal answer is that these materials afford rich and varied possibilities for a more immediate access to Queen Elizabeth as author than can be gained from the modern English versions alone. This greater immediacy of access leads in two related directions. First, there is the opportunity to observe Elizabeth's compositional habits through the material traces of the languages she knew and used—her choices of vocabulary and phrasing, her vagaries of spelling and punctuating, her sometimes heavy revisions and redraftings. The chronological arrangement of materials within the two sections of this volume is particularly intended to facilitate a developmental approach to Elizabeth's literary output. Second, readers have the opportunity to weigh for themselves certain of the critical challenges and choices that we as editors confronted in transcribing Elizabeth's original texts for this volume and in modernizing and translating them for the *Collected Works.*

We can be more specific about how the materials in this volume can enhance readers' appreciation and understanding. Let us begin with handwriting—always the most immediate and most distinctive means of accessing an author as well as a central site for editorial attention and decisions. From a developmental perspective, Elizabeth's handwriting encodes a fascinating story. To sketch it requires neither a technical account of her handwriting nor the fullness of documentation that a facsimile edition would provide; several of our illustrations in this volume and *Collected Works* are entirely adequate for the purpose. The gist of this story and the core of its interest lie in the remarkable process of transformation and adaptation to which Elizabeth subjected her handwriting after she became queen. We invite our readers to engage with the strategies by which she contrived to cope with the time pressures and the material conditions of producing written texts in her era and her position.

Like her older sister Mary and her younger brother Edward, Elizabeth was taught to write exclusively in the newer style of handwriting known as italic.[2] They were the first children of English royalty to be given this training, which signaled openness to humanist influences and served as a display mode for the New Learning and its adherents. Figure 2 in our first volume (*CW*, p. 8) reproduces one of the earliest specimens of Elizabeth's italic: the opening of a Latin letter to Henry VIII, written when she was twelve. In what even today remains its ready decipherability, italic handwriting contrasts with the older, so-called secretary hand—an intricate yet versatile system of writing developed by scribes in royal and papal courts during the later Middle Ages. Many sixteenth-century men of affairs used italic for their signatures or for inscriptional purposes, otherwise relying on the efficiency of secretary hand and its numerous contracted and abbreviated forms. By contrast, from Elizabeth's generation onward, italic was the hand in which girls of high birth—and schoolboys generally—were taught to write English. Her style of handwriting sets her off from the mature women who were the intimates of her girlhood: her nurse, Lady Margaret Bryan; her governess, Katherine Ashley; and her stepmother, Queen Katherine Parr—all of whose scripts heavily employ secretary and other older letterforms. As a symbolic mode, Elizabeth's italic can be grouped with other accomplishments of hers—needlework, intricate figure-dancing, the playing of the lute and virginals—as one of the humane arts that graced and expressed the cultivated life that was largely her lot as a child and teenager.

Predictably enough, Elizabeth's girlish italic is carefully penned, and imitative. The earliest originals in her handwriting cannot be reliably distinguished from ones in the hand of Jean Bellemain (d. 1552), the French tutor whom she shared with Prince Edward. She seems to have learned from him the letterforms and the sparing embellishments that are characteristic of both their hands. Bellemain's italic is illustrated here in figure 1 (the opening of a dedicatory letter he wrote to Elizabeth) and,

---

2. On the introduction of italic in England through humanist and courtly connections, see Anthony G. Petti, *English Literary Hands from Chaucer to Dryden* (Cambridge, Mass.: Harvard University Press, 1977), pp. 18–20. Because of these very connections, alternative early names for "italic" handwriting—confusingly, from our perspective—were "roman" and "roman letters."

FIGURE 1   Jean Bellemain's dedicatory epistle to Princess Elizabeth, prefacing his French translation of St. Basil's Greek epistle *On the Single Life;* BL, MS Royal 16.E.1, fol. 1r. Reproduced by permission of the British Library.

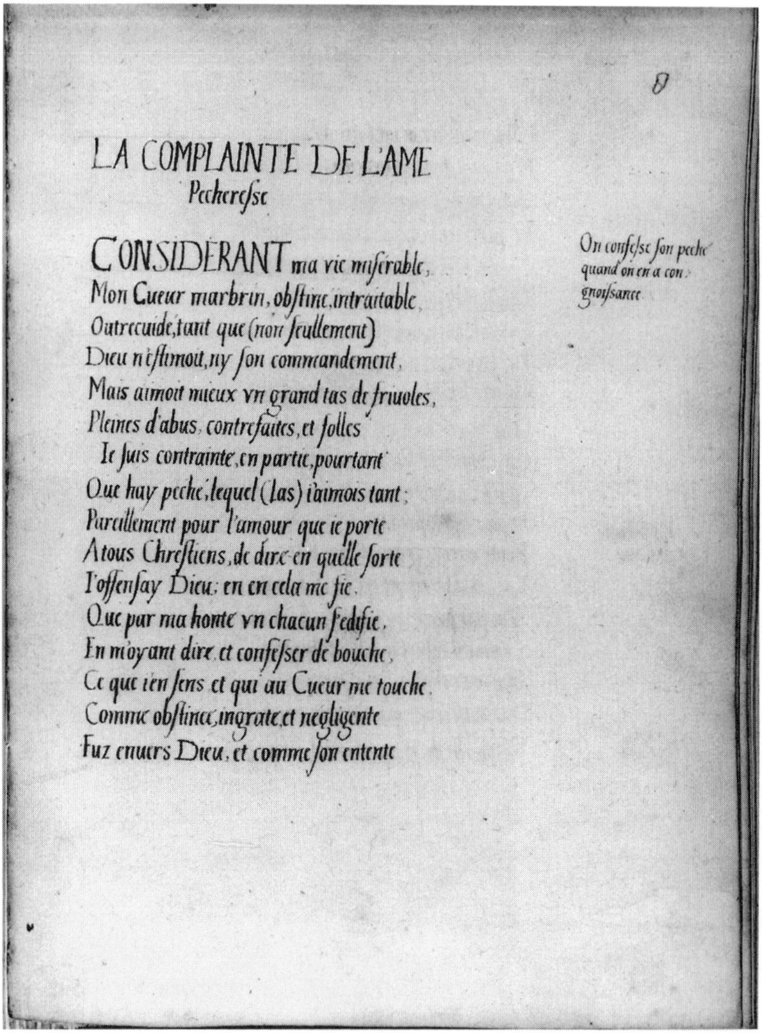

LA COMPLAINTE DE L'AME
Pecheresse

CONSIDERANT ma vie miserable,
Mon Cueur marbrin, obstiné, intraitable,
Outrecuidé, tant que (non seullement)
Dieu n'estimoit, ny son commandement,
Mais aimoit mieux vn grand tas de friuoles,
Pleines d'abus, contrefaites, et folles
Ie suis contrainte, en partie, pourtant
Que hay peché, lequel (las) i'aimois tant :
Pareillement pour l'amour que ie porte
A tous Chrestiens, de dire en quelle sorte
I'offensay Dieu : en en cela me sie.
Que par ma honte vn chacun s'edifie,
En m'oyant dire et confesser de bouche,
Ce que i'en sens et qui au Cueur me touche.
Comme obstinée, ingrate, et negligente
Fuz enuers Dieu, et comme son entente

On confesse son peché
quand on en a con-
gnoissance.

FIGURE 2   Princess Elizabeth and/or Jean Bellemain, French verse translation of Queen
Katherine Parr's *Lamentation of a Sinner*, opening; BL, MS Royal 16.E.28, fol. 8r.
Reproduced by permission of the British Library.

possibly, in figure 2 (the opening of a French verse translation of Queen Katherine Parr's *Lamentation of a Sinner*, a fair copy in either Bellemain's or Elizabeth's italic). During her mid to later teens, Elizabeth's handwriting is more flowing and more embellished: figures 3 and 4—letters to Lord Protector Edward Seymour and to Queen Mary, written in 1549 and 1554 respectively—illustrate these tendencies clearly. Her signature becomes more decorative, acquiring a series of elaborations that culminate in the well-known, full-blown complement of under-flourishes and swag lines that become her queenly trademark. Elizabeth's penchant for artful ornamentation may trace to the influence of her Latin and Greek tutor and future Latin secretary, Roger Ascham, famed as much for his exceptional calligraphy as for his Christian humanism. He paid Elizabeth fulsome tribute as a scholar in *The Schoolmaster* (1572).[3]

However, demands for speed or prolonged use at a single sitting could make casualties of the beauty and legibility of sixteenth-century italic. This is what subsequent specimens of Elizabeth's handwriting reveal. After November 1558 the necessity of adapting her italic to the exigencies of reigning over England launched a forty-five-year course of eclecticism and improvisation whose written remains are both utterly unique and personally revealing. Tracking Elizabeth's specialization of her handwriting allows the reader to register, at close range in the material record, one way in which she managed her time and energies under the then prevailing system of personal monarchy.

Her key adaptations are superbly on view in figure 5—a confidential Latin memorandum sent to her principal minister, Sir William Cecil, in September 1564, requesting advice on some delicate negotiations with Mary, Queen of Scots. For this memorandum Elizabeth reused a sheet of paper on which she had begun a letter to Catherine de Médicis, queen mother of France, in her fluid, lightly embellished, easily legible italic. That salutation is canceled, and Elizabeth begins her message to Cecil. Abruptly, italic calligraphy proves to be no longer the staple script that it was for Princess Elizabeth. Her new contrivance is the handwriting of the memorandum proper: a loosely shaped, sketchy series of letterforms that can be set down quickly—which a court secretary soon would notate as "Queen Elizabeth's running hand." Figure 5 illustrates the diffi-

3. Roger Ascham, *The Schoolmaster*, ed. Laurence V. Ryan (Charlottesville: University of Virginia Press for Folger Shakespeare Library, 1965), pp. 56, 87.

culty of this rapid (and eclectic) italic.[4] The indistinguishability of several letterforms—notably, *n* and vocalic or consonantal *u; b* and sigma-shaped *s*—is a major source of difficulty, and the category of minimal differences among letterforms will enlarge to include, still more problematically, *e* and *i.* With time, too, key letters undergo more and more radical deformations: *m*'s and *n*'s often become mere wavy lines, *a*'s may sometimes look like caret marks, sometimes like *o*'s. Figure 16 in our first volume (*CW*, p. 379) offers a typical example of Elizabeth's hasty italic in its long-term, mature state—what she herself terms "this Skribling" in the next-to-last line of that text.

The great preponderance of Elizabeth's autograph compositions after she became queen are in this idiosyncratic italic handwriting that she made her own vehicle. Significantly, though, she did not abandon her earlier italic script but produced fresh instances of its beauty and legibility whenever she took special care in writing out a text. One short example, dating from about 1565, is the English epigram "No Crooked Leg," which she inscribed in her French psalter, now preserved in the Windsor Castle Library. This careful, legible, optionally embellished mode of writing is standardly called a "set" or "formal" hand. However, our terminology takes account of the specific circumstances in which Elizabeth as queen used this mode. We call it her inscriptional italic, used for expressions of affection, familiarity, and gratitude; fine examples are found at the foot and the head, respectively, of two letters to the earl and countess of Shrewsbury (see *CW*, pp. 213, 228). The most extensive later text in Elizabeth's inscriptional italic appears to be her girdle prayer book from circa 1579–82, recently challenged as being in a copyist's hand.[5] Regrettably, the present whereabouts of the original of this collection of six prayers, two in English and one each in French, Italian, Latin, and Greek, are unknown; a photostatic copy in the British Library constitutes the

---

4. For a succinct technical description and a facsimile of Elizabeth's rapid italic, see Jean F. Preston and Laetitia Yeandle, *English Handwriting, 1400–1650* (Binghamton, N.Y.: Medieval and Renaissance Texts and Studies, 1992), pp. 64–65.

5. British Library (hereafter BL), MS Facsimile 218, sigs. 3r–36r. See the description of this text in our source note in *CW*, pp. 311–12. In July 2001, at a U.K. conference on "Standards of Manuscript Description," H. R. Woudhuysen expressed doubt that the hand of this text is Elizabeth's, and Marcus concurs that it is problematic to regard the hand as hers. Mueller, however, finds insufficient reasons for altering the attribution at present. Pending further information, we retain the girdle prayer book here among Elizabeth's autograph texts. See also the source note to prayers 30–35, p. 44, in this volume.

only record of this text at present. By contrast, such compositional efforts as her French stanzaic verses and her prayer on the defeat of the Spanish Armada survive in her hasty italic (*CW*, pp. 412, 422).

For the most part, these two diverging kinds of the queen's italic handwriting call for the differentiation that we have been signaling. But there is one significant feature, common to both kinds, that begins to make its appearance as early as the mid-1560s. This is Elizabeth's practice of substituting majuscule for miniscule letterforms—most commonly, *V* for *v*, *W* for *w*, *C* for *c*, *S* for *s*, and *L* for *l*. While the majority of such substitutions are word-initial, through the 1570s, 1580s, and 1590s Elizabeth increasingly inserts capital letters in other locations inside words—for example, *L*'s, *V*'s, and *W*'s as flourishes in the middle or at the end of a word (e.g., SkotLand, faithfulL, traveL, iVeL, loVinge, SoVeraigne, trouVe, oWne, boWels).

Compounding idiosyncrasy with a measure of uncertainty, Elizabeth's majuscule *V*'s and *W*'s are not always clear instances of capital letters; we transcribers have faced some difficult judgment calls. Even by the standards of her age, her *v*'s and *w*'s tend to be outsized. Hence, our tendency is to capitalize them, especially in cases where some letterforms are far larger and more protuberant than others. If our transcriptions fall short of perfect consistency across Elizabeth's entire autograph corpus, we have made every effort at local consistency in representing her capitalization practices—that is, consistency within a given text or within texts from the same period. The impression, in particular, that her handwriting of the 1580s and 1590s makes ever freer use of capital letterforms tallies closely with the features of the original texts in the archive.

How should we construe her increasingly heavy use of majuscule letterforms in her later compositions? The question itself breaks new critical ground, and the answers are not immediately clear. At first glance the word-medial and word-final occurrences of capital letters might seem to indicate that Elizabeth had dispensed with the distinction between majuscules and miniscules. But a closer look at the contexts of word-medial and word-final capital letters suggests an emphatic or highlighting function for a number of them because they typically occur in the closing phrase of a letter or an inscription, just before the queen's elaborate signature, or in key words in her French stanzaic verses. Often, too, as will be seen in many of the texts in this volume, the semantic contexts of word-initial capital letters suggest that these may have similar functions. Accordingly, to the extent that we find the identifying marks of capital letterforms—for, as noted, there is some systemic ambiguity about *V/v* and *W/w* in italic, an ambiguity that extends also to *C/c, K/k, L/l, S/s,* and *U/u*—our transcriptions of these autograph "originals" reproduce the queen's capitalization practices as a potentially expressive aspect of her written style.

If Elizabeth's handwriting merits attention for the access it offers to her on an authorial and personal front, it also requires notice on the other front we have signaled—the access that readers can have to our work as editors. In transcribing her non-inscriptional autograph originals written after November 1558, the challenge remains constant: Elizabeth's adaptation of italic to hasty writing in extended sessions poses problems of construal that cannot always be definitely resolved. While it is often hard to tell whether a sketchy letterform in isolation is, say, an *i* or an *e*, an *n* or a *u*, it is far more demanding to confront these ambiguous letterforms in a textual context, for such ambiguities must be interpreted one way or the other if there is to be a transcription at all. Figure 7 in *Elizabeth I: Collected Works* (p. 104) illustrates a notorious ambiguity at the opening of Speech 10, where the fourth word clearly ends "-elL" but begins with what could be a rounded *w* or an undotted *i* plus *u* with a consonantal value. Is the word "welL" or "iuelL" (evil)? The contrast in meaning is total. Construing the immediate context straightforwardly and unironically—which is itself an interpretive choice—yields the phrasing which we present in our transcription: "I loue so iuelL counterfaitting and hate so much dissemulation. . . ."

Due to the ambiguities of the letterforms *n* and consonantal or vocalic *u* in sixteenth-century handwriting, Elizabeth's French letters pose a particularly severe problem of transcription: the context may not sufficiently determine whether the reading is "nous" or "uous" when these pronouns are serving as direct or indirect objects. (As grammatical subjects, of course, these pronouns are rendered unambiguous by the different endings of their verbs.) For example, Letter 47 urges the last serious suitor for Elizabeth's hand, the French prince François Hercule de Valois, duke of Alençon (whom she always addresses as "Monsieur"), to beware of machinations against their relationship by certain ill-willed parties— "telz que font les gens a croyre qu'estes si presumtible et si remuant quilz n/uous pourront facilement detourner de n/uos plus cheres quand ilz n/uous ont a part." The text of this letter that we have transcribed is a secretary's copy of the queen's original sent to Monsieur. This "file" copy contains a correction in Elizabeth's hand but no clarification of the "nous"/

"uous" ambiguity. Did she mean to say "those who make the people be-
lieve that you are so presumptuous and fickle that they can easily make
us withdraw our favor from our dearest ones when they have us apart"?
Or did she mean ". . . so presumptuous and fickle that they can easily
make you withdraw your favor from your dearest ones when they have
you apart"? Since certainty in deciding between objective "nous" and
"uous" can be elusive, readers who use these original texts in our transcriptions should be on the alert for instances of this crucial ambiguity
affecting the French letters to Monsieur.

We have been focusing thus far on the highly individuated written remains of Elizabeth I as the most immediate and the most lasting records
we have of her historical singularity. We now address some possibilities
and challenges presented by spelling, phrasal and sentential units, and
material traces of authorial judgments that show through in her revisions
of her texts. But as we turn to the authorial front, to Elizabeth's precocity
and mastery in language, a paradox confronts us: What meaning can a
kind of "immediate access" have with regard to forms and expressions
now more than four centuries old? Without some prior exposure to the
far less prescriptive and standardized conditions of writing, spelling, and
punctuating in modern European vernaculars in the later sixteenth century, a present-day reader who plunged into the middle of this volume of
"originals" might find Elizabeth's compositions odd or even inept. To
admit this possibility is to concede that certain levels of understanding
of her authorial practices require historical information and perspective
that we cannot provide here. Yet these original texts will agreeably sur-
prise readers who are prepared to read not just with their eyes but also
with their ears, sounding out words and phrases, finding meaning and
nuance that resonate in the linguistic forms current for Elizabeth and her
age. Charged with circumstantial specificity, these original texts have
unique value and importance as both starting points and mainstays for
literary analysis and appreciation of Elizabeth's writings.

At the level of the word and the phrase, the possibilities of access
to Elizabeth as an author can lead a reader in at least two directions:
the study of her manuscript revisions to track her political and rhetorical strategies of self-representation at key junctures, and the study of
her spelling, vocabulary, and phrasing for clues to how she spoke. As to
the first, analyses of Elizabeth as a verbally self-cognizant and self-
determining presence within her texts have already begun to appear, and
we hope to foster this promising line of study with the transcriptions of

original texts presented in this volume.[6] Readers will quickly find sites for interpreting Elizabeth's thought processes through the cancellations, insertions, and rephrasings that we have replicated typographically here, most notably in Speech 6 (answering the Lords' petition that she marry, April 10, 1563); Speech 10 (upbraiding the Commons at the dissolution of Parliament, January 2, 1567); Speeches 17 and 18 (her first and second replies to the Parliamentary petitions urging the execution of Mary, Queen of Scots, November 12 and 24, 1586); and Letter 90 (draft and final versions of a letter to James VI of Scotland in May 1594).

Compared to the study of textual traces left by authorial revision, the search to discover how Elizabeth might actually have spoken is more intrinsically problematic. *Elizabeth I: Collected Works* makes one form of this point in laying out the governing paradigm for our understanding of the textual relations among various versions of Elizabeth's public speeches: we hypothesize that an extemporaneous oral presentation typically came first, and text(s) recording the oral presentation followed. Under such circumstances Elizabeth's verbatim utterance remains fugitive and irrecoverable—although, in order to circulate at all, the reported versions of her speeches would have had to meet some standards of conformity to what she said. Analogously, the study of the phrasing, vocabulary, and spelling of even her original texts will at best grant access on a sliding scale to how Elizabeth might actually have spoken.

With regard to matters of grammar and syntax, present-day readers and editors can tread on fairly firm ground. Thanks to close descriptive scholarship performed by historians of English on the syntactic constructions and colloquial features of sixteenth- and earlier seventeenth-century texts (particularly those of Shakespeare), it is often clear that what from a twentieth-century perspective may seem to be grammatical irregularities were frequently either vestiges of still older states of English or freedoms of expression available to all native speakers at that era.[7] For example, since possessive constructions did not obligatorily

6. See Allison Heisch, "Queen Elizabeth I: Parliamentary Rhetoric and the Exercise of Power," *Signs* 1 (1975): 31–55; Frances Teague, "Queen Elizabeth in Her Speeches," in *Gloriana's Face: Women, Public and Private, in the English Renaissance,* ed. S. P. Cerasano and Marion Wynne-Davies (Detroit: Wayne State University Press, 1992), pp. 63–78; and Susan Frye, *Elizabeth I: The Competition for Representation* (New York: Oxford University Press, 1993).

7. See especially E. A. Abbott, *A Shakespearean Grammar,* 3rd ed. (London: Macmillan, 1870); H. C. Wyld, *A History of Modern Colloquial English,* 3rd ed. (Oxford: Basil Blackwell, 1936); Frederikus T. Visser, *An Historical Syntax of the English Language* (Leiden: E. J. Brill, 1963).

end in apostrophe plus *s*, Elizabeth, like her contemporaries, could say and write "my honor sake," "a Princess hede." Because there were also less stringent conditions on number agreement in her English, she and her contemporaries could pair plural with singular forms in subject-verb constructions or intermix singular and plural pronouns with the same referent—for example, "ten Wisar hedz knoWes how to Win" (Letter 85), "other regard them selues" (Speech 9, Additional Document D). In general, such grammatical liberties are readily intelligible; it is important not to class them as errors or singularities. But one pervasive feature of the English of Elizabeth and her contemporaries can cause difficulties of understanding. This is the frequency of ellipsis—omission of some lexical item or function-word that is left to be inferred from, or implied by, the immediate context. Nouns, pronouns, main verbs, auxiliaries, adverbs, prepositions—all may be subject to ellipsis. The following examples, where a caret marks the site of the omitted element, will illustrate selectively:

>   conveniently   executed
> wiche if ∧ presently coulde   haue bine ~~finisshed~~ had not bine differd. (Speech 6—ellipsis of subject pronoun "they")
>
> the princes opinion and good WylL ought in good ordar ∧ haue bine felt in other sort than in so publik a place ∧ ~~ons to~~ be vttered (Speech 10—two ellipses of infinitive marker "to")
>
> yow profes so constant defence of your Country ~~and~~ togither ∧ myne from alL spaniardz or strangers (Letter 78—ellipsis of preposition "with")

If the grammar and syntax of Elizabeth's English compositions yield fairly straightforward access to her and her contemporaries' usage in speaking and writing, other questions—what the relation of her speech may have been to her spellings or her word forms, for example—must be approached with more caution. A number of Elizabeth's characteristic English spellings do seem to suggest that, as she wrote out a word in a sequence of letters that she had learned for it from her reading or other training, she also sounded the word out. In effect, the sound factor appears to color spelling but not determine it completely. Frequent word endings in *-ar*, for example, suggest an open vowel sound and (perhaps) a consonant trilled on the back of the palate: "Sistar," "sinistar," "troublars," "whisperars," "rular," "lookars on," "bearar," "ministar," "sufferars," "desiars," "Iniurars"—the list could be almost indefinitely extended. Another sound value, enhanced sibilance of endings of possessives and plurals, may be indicated by her choice of a -*z* spelling rather than an -*s* one: "Godz," "frendz," "foez," "hartz," "grauntz," "mindz," and the like.[8] There are intermittent signs, too, that the consonantal values of *g, ng,* and *gt* may have been close to that of hard *k* in Elizabeth's speech: hence, her spellings "brinkers up," "lenken" (lengthen), "slidik" (sliding), "sucgestion," "thinkes" (things), "Vacabond."[9] And, as suggested by such spellings as "hit" (it) and "habilite," she may have aspirated some initial vowels and dropped initial *h* elsewhere ("Atfilde"), employing a speech feature now linked to the London Cockney dialect, which Ben Jonson's comedies begin to parody lightly towards the end of her reign.[10] Since the difficulties of deciphering her handwriting are considerable, it is fortunate that ambiguities arising from spelling (as opposed to letterforms) are proportionately rare in Elizabeth's writings: witness "oubeit" (howbeit or albeit) in Letter 2, "fraughted" (freighted or fraught) in Letter 72, "happelie" (happily or haply) in Speech 17, Version 2; "Waite" (wait or weight) in Letter 75. One exception is her frequent spelling of "they" as "the." This particular spelling, however, was widespread in earlier sixteenth-century English texts; it is a staple in Queen Katherine Parr's writings, among many others.

A century ago F. J. Furnivall publicized what remains one of the most striking practices in Elizabeth's spelling from first to last: her frequent use of *i* to render the English sound *ee* (long *e*) in certain words, coupled with her use of alternative spellings in *i* or *e/ee* for certain others. Furnivall compared Elizabeth's *i* spellings of the sound value of *ee* with those of her contemporaries and found them anomalous; as a start on the problem of analysis he tabulated all relevant instances in a late set of her English translations.[11] The present volume, however, offers many additional examples. Words where *i* renders *ee* uniquely include "betwin" and

---

8. Such word endings are a consistent context for Elizabeth's spellings with -*z*, indicating that this letter form in her English had the sound value of modern *z* (or *zed*), not the older *yogh.*

9. Perhaps some of these features trace to the Buckinghamshire dialect native to Lady Margaret Bryan (d. 1552), Elizabeth's governess in infancy and early childhood, who probably taught her to speak English. Lady Margaret had previously served as Princess Mary's governess. It also seems possible that Katherine Ashley, Lady Bryan's successor, had some influence on Elizabeth's spelling practices.

10. See A. C. Partridge, *Tudor to Augustan English: A Study in Syntax and Style from Caxton to Johnson* (London: André Deutsch, 1969), chap. 2.

11. F. J. Furnivall, "Note on Q. Elizabeth's Use of I for Our Long E," in Caroline Pemberton, ed., *Queen Elizabeth's Englishings of Boethius De Consolatione Philosophiae, 1593, Plutarch De*

"betwine"; "hide" and "hidy"; "Spidy"; "Wide" and "Wided." Words with spellings in both *i* and *e* include "bine" and "bene"; "besiching" and "beseching"; "dides" and "dedes"; "kipe" and "kepe"; "excide" and "exceed." There is a further complication: *i* can also take its more usual English sound values in Elizabeth's spelling—for example, the pronoun "I," "Stike" (stick), "Wisching." From his perspective staked exclusively in sixteenth-century English usage and orthography, Furnivall found the sound values of *i* and *e* in Elizabeth's compositions simply inexplicable. With a writer as multilingual as she, however, a broader perspective on spelling practices in her era may be in order.

It is clear that Elizabeth's practice of writing *i* in place of *ee* in certain English words gives *i* the sound value it regularly takes in French and Italian (and in Latin as well). The facility with which she could shift from one language to another, kept in regular use throughout her reign, may have motivated this particular spelling practice as her means of registering her awareness of a shared sound feature amid the welter of differences that seemed so predominant in European vernaculars at her day—and continues to seem so in ours. If tenable, this account of her idiosyncratic substitution of *i* for *ee* would yield its own kind of immediate access—not to Elizabeth's pronunciation of English per se but to a particular perception she had about a sound similarity in several languages that she knew well. Readers of her foreign language compositions will observe that the principle of sound coloration noted in her English spellings also applies when she writes in another living vernacular like French or Italian but does not apply when she writes in the more codified mediums of Latin or Greek. In annotating her foreign language texts we have tried to anticipate where spelling or phrasing might need glossing to be comprehensible to a reader. Most broadly, our presentation of her original texts in this volume aims to draw readers into appreciating and assessing the rich cognitive and compositional implications of her multilingualism, even and especially in her English texts.

The mention of Elizabeth's multilingualism brings the foreign language materials in this volume directly to the fore. One kind of access they offer is almost too obvious to state. Yet the fact remains that no prior edition of any of Elizabeth's writings has given readers the opportunity to place English translations of her compositions in foreign languages

---

Curiositate, 1598, Horace De Arte Poetica, 1598, Early English Text Society, original series 113 (London: Kegan Paul, Trench, Trübner, and Ellis, 1899), pp. xvi–xvii.

side by side with her originals. Our policy in translating Elizabeth has been to adhere as closely to her word choices and syntactic units as considerations of sense and grammaticality permit. This policy takes its warrant and its precedent from her own characteristic practices in writing another language (also, it might be added, in translating to or from English): her vocabulary and phrasing are recurrently patterned on the forms and word order of English, leaving the flavor of her native language as an implicit norm and a recurrent effect of her expression. In addition, her foreign language vocabulary and idioms—particularly in comparatively extemporaneous productions like speeches and letters— exhibit a certain constrictedness, even repetitiveness, while remaining serviceable to her subtlety and nuance of discourse.

Yet for readers who can and will follow the course of Elizabeth's Latin compositions in this volume, there awaits the discovery of a considerably more complicated sequence of developments—a story of progression from high stylistic cultivation to colloquial pungency, the latter quite cognizantly registered in comments by the mature queen. This story begins with Elizabeth's girlish Latin compositions under the supervision of Roger Ascham, where classical norms of erudition cast a long shadow. Her Latin letters to Edward especially bear the marks of rigorous schoolroom workouts with such mechanics as the familiar and formal pronouns of direct address, the whole gamut of verb tenses as further conditioned by active and passive voice and indicative and subjunctive moods, as well as the elegancies of Ciceronian idiom—especially the celebrated phrasal reiterations for rhetorical emphasis, as in Letter 7: "cum recordor (quotidie autem recordor)." The curious fact that this very letter was ascribed to Ascham himself in an edition of 1703 supplies circumstantial evidence that Elizabeth's proficiency in Latin under his tutelage could pass for work by the master himself. However, on the showing of later compositions on secular subjects in this volume, extemporaneous speech in Latin elicited from Elizabeth a marked change of style—far more direct, succinct phrasing and sentence structure, far simpler vocabulary and verb forms—as witnessed by her 1564 speech at Cambridge University, her 1566 and 1593 speeches at Oxford University, and her extemporaneous retort to the Polish ambassador in 1597 (Speeches 7, 8, 20, and 22).[12] In general, it seems that the carefully pre-

---

12. As published in 1563 and 1569, Elizabeth's Latin prayers present a transitional stage between high style and colloquial style. Although the sentence units of these prayers are com-

meditated Ciceronian epistles required for the conduct of diplomacy were left to the devising of her Latin secretaries after Elizabeth became queen.[13] Her more colloquial Latin is so discernible in the university speeches that their manuscript history reveals a scholarly (or pedantic) one-upmanship developing among later academic copyists, who take liberties with phrasing—especially with verb tenses and moods—to make the queen sound more orotund, more eloquent in Cicero's manner. At Oxford in 1593 she herself remarked: "Addatur etiam huius linguae desuetudo, quae talis et tam frequens fuit, vt in triginta sex annis, trigesies nec tot vsam fuisse memini."[14] By her own explicit standards of accounting, the question of her competence in Latin became a question of the compositional techniques that she kept actively in use through the years. The pair of techniques that proves most important is easy to identify and integral to her prose style, in whatever language she writes.

There is, first, an at once conceptual and syntactic procedure for the composition of sentences (or paragraphs) that blends the formal values of static balance and dynamic progression. The basic patterns produced by applying this procedure are traditionally termed "periodic construction." In one typical pattern this procedure will put in place an envelope structure of two symmetrical members—an antithesis, or a pair of correlatives, or a comparative or degree construction—and then fill the envelope out with linear, sequential phrases or clauses, which cross-cut and complicate the larger equipoise of the pairing. Alternatively, the envelope structure may consist of a series of clauses and phrases joined end to end but interspersed with local responsions of paired elements embedded within the larger, linear series. An example taken from a mid-1548 letter to Edward will illustrate this periodic construction in one of the patterns taught by Ascham. The correlative conjunctions are set in boldface to highlight their balancing function as a container for the additive phrases and clauses:

---

plex, capacious, and many membered, her frequent echoes of the Vulgate—especially of the Psalms—produce briefer, simpler, and more direct phrasing, thus anticipating the direction taken by her Latin style in her secular compositions.

13. For an edition of forty Latin letters, instruments of Elizabeth's diplomacy preserved in various Continental libraries, see E. I. Kouri, ed., *Elizabethan England and Europe, Bulletin of the Institute of Historical Research,* Special Supplement 12 (London, 1982).

14. "Let there be added besides a disuse of this language, which has been such and so constant that in thirty-six years I scarcely remember using it thirty times" (*CW,* p. 327). *Trigesies* is a variant spelling of *tricesies,* itself a variant form of *tricies.*

Nam etsi non ignorarem tantam tuorum erga me beneficiorum esse magnitudinem, vt illorum partem vel minimam referenda gratia consequendi spes prorsus omnis adimeretur, in **hoc tamen** omnes mihi neruos contendendos esse putaui, vt iustam meritamque gratiam voluntate memoriaque mente persoluerem.[15]

The same bivalent form of composition—at once static in its counterpoised elements and dynamic in its trailing elements—is on view in a more straightforward example from Elizabeth's 1564 Latin speech at Cambridge:

Etsi foeminilis pudor, (subditi fidelissimi, et Academia clarissima) rudem et incultum sermonem prohibet, in tanta doctissimorum hominum turba narrare: **tamen** nobilium meorum intercessio, et beneuolentia erga academiam proferre inuitant.[16]

The other compositional technique that continues to signify eloquence in Elizabeth's secular Latin is the ready availability of *sententiae* and *exempla*—maxims and illustrative anecdotes. What such a storehouse of sagacity and received lore could yield has been well characterized in scholarship addressing the broader cultural and rhetorical applications of humanism: the mental address, the promptness and aptness of response, the exercise of public authority evinced and confirmed by utterance rich in pithy distillations of ethical commonplaces, psychological truths, and political wisdom.[17] Again and again in her writings, Elizabeth is found assessing a situation, action, or emotion in terms of the classical maxim or the proverbial saying or the Bible verse that it exemplifies; if there is no such encapsulation at hand, she proceeds to fashion the new "sentence" that the present occasion requires. At two critical junctures in her speeches she offers her own testimony to the need to consider her words well and to make a pause for reflection a reflex of her

---

15. "For although I have not been ignorant that the magnitude of your favors to me is such that all hope is absolutely taken away of repaying even the least part of them, I have nevertheless thought that I should strain every sinew in this case to render just and merited thanks with a goodwill and a remembering mind" (*CW*, p. 21).

16. "Although feminine modesty, most faithful subjects and most celebrated university, prohibits the delivery of a rude and uncultivated speech in such a gathering of most learned men, yet the intercession of my nobles and my own goodwill toward the university incite me to produce one" (*CW*, p. 87).

17. See especially Mary Thomas Crane, *Framing Authority: Sayings, Self, and Society in Sixteenth-Century England* (Princeton: Princeton University Press, 1993).

public comportment, invoking, as a model for herself, the philosopher in Plutarch who recited the letters of the alphabet before he answered a weighty question.[18] The copiousness and diversity of Elizabeth's quotations of others' wise words in notable phrasings defy any brief characterization and, in any case, are on frequent view in context in the pages of this volume. Within the specific compass of her classical erudition, she will be found invoking Homer, Pindar, Demosthenes (in Latin), Ennius, Cicero, Virgil, Horace, Suetonius, Publilius Syrus, as well as the stock referents of classical history and mythology—Alcibiades, Alexander the Great, Julius Caesar, Clotho, Lethe, Prometheus and Epimetheus. As a further insight, her recurrent mistakes and approximations in these citations suggest that she is working from memory.

Elizabeth's classically grounded eloquence assumes its fullest importance through the adaptability she demonstrates for hybrid, high-style sentence structures and the sententious mode across a wide domain of applications: vernacular as well as Latin, verse as well as prose. Since the modernizing of texts in our preceding volume recurrently affects not just punctuation but the segmenting of phrases and sentences, it is distinctively the presentation of texts in this volume, in their original spelling and punctuation, that offers access to the norms and forms of Elizabeth's compositional practices. Again, a few examples will illustrate rather than exhaust the subject. She adapts the hybrid, high-style sentence to familiar English expression as early as her last letter to Queen Katherine Parr; witness the run of "although . . . yet" correlatives embedded with add-on constructions in three consecutive sentences from the beginning (Letter 10). Her opening two rhyme units of "No Crooked Leg" (Poem 4) develop as an apparently straightforward linear envelope, but by midpoint in line 3, the particle "so" initiates the syntactic conversion into a comparison, "so . . . as," developed in the closing two rhyme units. This even apportionment brings into balance the combination of asymmetrical and symmetrical units in the whole poem, which itself consists of nothing but sententious formulations. Elizabeth's second response to the Parliamentary petitions for the execution of Mary, Queen of Scots (Speech 18), opens with a set-off sententious formulation of her own composition and follows with three more sententious utterances in antithetical symmetry replete with end rhyme—"rare" . . .

18. See *CW,* pp. 71, 198, 204. Repeated examples are rare with Elizabeth; when they occur, they signal their importance.

"care"—on the two balanced clauses of the fourth sentence—before attaining periodic form with the fifth sentence. This complex construction consists of twinned symmetrical envelopes ("such . . . that" and "such . . . as") with trailing phrases and clauses as the offsetting filler for both. Speech 22, the extemporaneous Latin response to the Polish ambassador in 1597, likewise exhibits a predominantly symmetrical envelope structure of antitheses that modulate into the different symmetry of degree and result constructions: "talia verba . . . sin vero tale . . . mihi videris libros multos perlegisse; libros tamen principum ne attigisse," with the responsion of clausal end rhyme. Through these proliferating phrases, Elizabeth threads serial reflections on the King of Poland's youth and inexperience and his ambassador's ignorance of both principles and policies of statecraft to produce a verbal counterweave of assured decorum and authority. Robert Cecil said he never heard her in better form.[19]

An ability to deal in one or more languages other than English will furthermore allow readers access to one of the most conspicuous features of Elizabeth's piety: her identification of religious exercise with linguistic exercise, resulting in an extensive body of prayers in several languages by a first-person feminine subject who styles herself both England's queen and the Lord's handmaid. These include the English, French, Italian, Latin, and Greek prayers of the miniature girdle prayer book (circa 1579–82) as well as the Latin devotions and prayers of *Precationes priuatae. Regiae E.R.* (London, 1563) and the sustained concluding section of *Christian Prayers and Meditations in English, French, Italian, Spanish, Greeke, and Latine* (London, 1569).

The developmental narrative implicit here begins before and beyond the materials of this volume, with Princess Elizabeth's ideas for good New Year's gifts, in the form of multiple translations of religious works prepared for Henry VIII in 1545 (French, Latin, and Italian versions of Queen Katherine Parr's *Lamentation of a Sinner*) and for Queen Katherine herself in 1544 and 1545 (English translations of Marguerite de Navarre's *Miroir de l'âme pécheresse* and of the first chapter of Calvin's *Institution de la Religion Chrestienne* in its 1541 Geneva edition). The potentialities for spiritual audacity and linguistic veiling in which the young Elizabeth would have been steeped by working so closely with these texts seem to accrue to the foreign languages themselves in her religious uses of them after she became queen. All of her boldest addresses

19. See *CW*, p. 335.

to God are couched in languages other than English. Nowhere in English, for example, does she permit herself the abjection she expresses in French when she confesses "mes pechez noirs et sanglants" ("my black and bloody sins") in Prayer 31. Nowhere in English does she question God's ways with her as sharply as she does in her Latin prayer on her nearly fatal case of smallpox in 1562, where she concedes the rationale of her chastisement at God's hands but denies any discernible rationale for the fright lately suffered by her people: "iam inquam, nuper ancillam tuam, vel admonendi salabriter vel iusti puniendi, atque ita eam corrigendi, emendandique gratia, periculosissimo, adeoque letali pene huic corpori morbo me affecisti: sed et animum pariter meum multis angoribus grauiter perculisti: totum praeterea populum Anglicum cuius quies atque securitas, post te proxime, in meae Ancillae tuae incolumitate sita est, meo periculo vehementer preteruisti, attonitumque reddidisti."[20]

It even appears possible that Elizabeth coded her choice of one or another language in composing her prayers to specific thematic concerns—for example, the Greek prayer (Prayer 34) in the girdle prayer book first meditates on Elizabeth's own sins in Pauline vocabulary of δόλερα (snares) and πταίσματα (stumblings) before adducing examples of Christ's merciful dealings with sinners in the synoptic gospels and finally ending with a plea for Christ's help as βοηθὸς κὶ ἀντιλήπτυρ (ally and partaker), prose counterparts of much earlier Homeric terms. Her mixed diction infuses epic heroism into fighting the good fight as a Christian. For their part, the Italian prayers in *Christian Prayers and Meditations* and the girdle prayer book may have as a primary and unifying objective the vindication of Elizabeth on fronts where her position or beliefs oppose papal authority: her assurance that only God can remit sin (Prayer 16), her vocation as defender of true religion (Prayer 18), her acknowledgment that she rules by God's permission and direction alone (Prayer 19), her tribute to God as the only supreme authority ruling in earth or heaven (Prayer 32). To the extent that such thematic interpretation may illuminate the choice of the language in which Elizabeth

20. "I say now, as Thy handmaid of late, whether for the sake of healthfully warning or justly punishing me and thus correcting and amending me, Thou hast affected me in this body with a most dangerous and nearly mortal illness. But Thou hast likewise gravely pierced my soul with many torments; and besides, all the English people, whose peace and safety is grounded in my sound condition as Thy handmaid nearest after Thee, Thou hast strongly disregarded in my danger, and left the people stunned" (*CW,* p. 140; rev. trans.).

composes her later religious works, an especially careful examination of French will be in order—as the medium for Calvinist doctrines of human sinfulness and depravity ("mes transgressions et mes pechez noirs et sanglants" in Prayer 31; cf. the opening of Prayer 10); for rejoicing that England has been spared religious wars and for extending her protection to those in exile for their religion, presumably Huguenots (Prayers 12, 13, and 31); and for projecting Elizabeth's rule of England as the confirmation of God's unique favor and full approbation (Prayer 15). If Elizabeth's French prayers voice a consistent set of hopes and convictions on the subject of European Protestantism and her role as its champion, these in turn may help to explicate the dream vision of her French stanzaic verses (Poem 15). This typically Protestant (because nonscalar) progress of a soul struggling with crises of the government it exercises and the salvation it seeks finally locates its first-person speaker in a place of celestial light and a state of perfect equilibrium.[21] Can the composition of these verses have been Elizabeth's other linguistic and spiritual means of coping with Henry IV's conversion to Catholicism in 1593, besides the English translation of Boethius's *De consolatione philosophiae* that her court intimates observed her make?[22]

We hope, as a final point, that these little-known and virtually undiscussed materials, now available in this volume, will advance understanding of Elizabeth as a religious writer and, by extension, help to illuminate her enactment, especially her authorial exercise, of her other major public role: that of Supreme Governor of the Church of England. In fact, a standing invitation in that direction seems to have been issued to readers with the publication of *Christian Prayers and Meditations* in 1569, which carries imprints of her royal arms on both sets of its endpapers. This volume showcases Elizabeth as an at once model Christian and ideal Christian monarch with its woodcut frontispiece of her in her private chapel, on her knees in prayer in full regalia, except for her crown which she has laid on her lectern next to her prayer book, while her sword of state lies on the carpet, its hilt propped against her kneeling-cushion (see figure 6). By now, the time to cultivate a fuller and deeper

---

21. On the "great vacillations in . . . emotional temper" that characterize English Protestant meditations on the total divide between human sinfulness and freely imparted salvation, see Barbara Kiefer Lewalski, *Protestant Poetics and the Seventeenth-Century Religious Lyric* (Princeton: Princeton University Press, 1979), quotation from p. 23.

22. For an original-spelling transcription of this translation, see Pemberton, *Elizabeth's Englishings*, pp. 1–120.

understanding of Elizabeth I has surely arrived—not just in her religious dimension or in the broader panoply of access that we have been indicating for the original texts contained in this volume, but across the whole spectrum of her authorial production. That is at once the conviction and the objective informing our edition.

This preface was drafted by Mueller and revised with the benefit of vigorous critique by Marcus, Mary Beth Rose, Anne Lake Prescott, and Alan Thomas of the University of Chicago Press. Sean Gilsdorf, also of the University of Chicago Press, and Joshua Scodel rendered timely help with the Latin texts. A similar procedure has governed the preparation of the texts and annotations in this volume: Mueller made most of the initial transcriptions, which she used as teaching materials between 1993 and 1998; these have been closely rechecked by Marcus, who also formulated the specifics of our principle of direct transcription in its final form and vetted the notes. The commentary and notes also benefited from a close vetting by Prescott, though remaining errors are, of course, our chagrin and our responsibility. An errata list for *Elizabeth I: Collected Works* immediately follows this preface.

We refer our readers to the full listing of archival sources that concludes the preface to *Elizabeth I: Collected Works* (p. xxiii), and which applies also to this volume. Further acknowledgments and thanks are due to Carol Mescall, Rights Manager, Reproduction Permissions Department of the British Library, for permission to reproduce photographs of Lansdowne 1236, fol. 35; Royal 16.E.1, fol. 1r; and Royal 16.E.28, fol. 8r; Christina Mackwell, Senior Assistant Librarian of Lambeth Palace Library, for permission to reproduce a photograph of the frontispiece of Queen Elizabeth's own copy of *Christian Prayers and Meditations* (STC 6428), preserved at Lambeth; the Photoreproduction and Permissions Office of the Public Record Office, Kew, for permission to reproduce photographs of State Papers Domestic, Mary I, 11/4/2, fol. 3v; and State Papers, Scotland, Elizabeth, 1564, 52/9/65, fol. 113r; and the supervisory staff of the Western Manuscripts Reading Room of the Bibliothèque Nationale, Paris, for permission to transcribe and print the text that is our Letter 92, Version 2. For their ingenuity in producing this volume, Russell Harper and Renate Gokl of the University of Chicago Press have our admiring thanks. Gratitude also goes to Gregory Kneidel of the University of Connecticut at Hartford, who at key points during his postdoctoral year at the University of Chicago aided the preparation and printing out of the computer files for this multilingual volume.

ELIZABETH I:

COLLECTED WORKS

ERRATA

The following errata have been corrected in the first paperback edition

p. 15, note 1: Read "Bodleian Library, University of Oxford, MS Additional C.92 (formerly MS Arch. F.c.8)"

p. 20, line 3 from bottom: Read "a most lucky deliverance"

p. 31, note 1: Read "Bodleian Library, University of Oxford, MS Ashmole 1729, art. 6 (formerly MS Arch. F.c.39)"

p. 41, heading to Letter 22: Read "March 17, 1554"

p. 42, line 6: Read "once again kneeling with humbleness"

p. 103, line 3 from bottom: Read "of themselves substantives? I say no more"

p. 131, last line: Read "Your most loving sovereign, *Elizabeth R*"

p. 256, Letter 52, last line: Read "to understand, etc."

p. 298, note 1: Read "Bodleian Library, University of Oxford, MS Additional C.92 (formerly MS Arch. F.c.8, fol. 26)"

p. 363, Letter 82, line 8: Read "that I have become desirous rather to use him in this respect than to lack so faithful a servant—indeed you yourself—to whom"

p. 368, note 1: Read "in Elizabeth's hand with address in another hand"

p. 380, note 22: Read "Hatfield reads 'foreigners' help' and omits the following phrase" [apostrophe after "foreigners" mistakenly omitted in paperback]

p. 409, note 1: Read "MS Additional 15227, fol. 81v (circa 1623–30)"
p. 426, note 1: Read "in Elizabeth's hand or a close imitation of it"

The following corrections will be made in any future edition(s)

p. 7, line 1: Read "a man or woman"
p. 9, Letter 3, line 16: Read "childish unripeness of mind"
p. 10, lines 7–8: Read "your daughter, who should be not only an imitator of your
    virtues but also an inheritor of them"
p. 13, Letter 5, line 6: Read "other, most just causes"
p. 15, line 5: Read "a dream of a shadow"
p. 16, lines 16–17: Read "I now desire at least in words to give thanks to your
    majesty, since I cannot in deed"
p. 19, note 1: Read "MS Rulers of England, Box III, Part I, art. 6"
p. 21, Letter 11, line 7: Read "just and necessary reasons"
p. 42, line 8: Read "so bold to desire"
p. 42, note 4: Read "two days"
p. 101, line 9 from bottom: Read "she hath cause to credit"
p. 115, Letter 26, line 3: Read "since I have not given her any answer for all this
    time"
p. 116, line 2 from bottom: Read "that you both are a noble princess and were a
    loyal wife"
p. 140, lines 7–9: Read "whether for the sake of healthfully warning or justly
    punishing me and thus correcting and amending me by grace"
p. 230, note 4: Read "The water from St. Anne's Well, Buxton, had been credited
    since medieval times with special healing properties. We thank Paul
    Hemelryk for this information."
p. 232, Letter 43, line 2: Read "If the importunate request of this gentleman were"
p. 363, Letter 82, line 8: Read "indeed to you yourself"
p. 441, line 20: Read "Devereux, Robert, earl of Essex"
p. 442, line 2: Read "Essex. *See* Devereux, Robert"
p. 446, line 1: Read "Valerius Maximus, 88n"

ELIZABETH I

I

AUTOGRAPH COMPOSITIONS

LETTER 1 ⇌ PRINCESS ELIZABETH TO QUEEN KATHERINE PARR, JULY 31, 1544[1]

|L'inimica fortuna inuidiosa d'ogni bene, et voluitrice de cose humane [me]
|priuò per un'anno intero della Illustrissima presentia vostra, et non ess[endo]
|anchora contenta di questo, vn'altra uolta me spoglio del mede[simo]
|bene: la qual cosa a me saria intollerabile, s'io non pensassi be[n tosto]
|di goderla. Et in questo mio exilio certamente conosco la cle[mentia de]
|sua altezza hauer hauuto cura, et sollicitudine, della sanità m[ia tanto,]
|quanto fatto haurebbe la maiestà del Re. Per la qual cosa n[on solamente]
|sono tenuta de seruirla, ma etiandio da figlial amore reuer[irla. Onde]
|intendendo vostra Illustrissima Altezza non me hauer domentica[ta ogni]
|Volta che alla maiestà del Re ha scritto: il che a me ap[ertineva]
|quella prieghare. Pero infino a qua non hebbi ardire à [scrivergli,]
|per il che al presente uostra Eccellentissima altezza humilmente [priegho,]
|che scriuendo a sua maistà si degni de raccommend[armeli, prie-]
|gando sempre sua dolce benedettione, similmente pri[ghando]
[i]l signore Iddio gli mandi successo bonissimo acquis[tando]
[vittoria de] soui[2] inimici, accioche piu presto possia uostra a[ltezza,]

---

1. *Source:* BL, MS Cotton Otho, C.X, fol. 235. A recto leaf, damaged by the fire of 1742 in Sir Robert Cotton's library. The Bodleian copy, MS Smith 68, art. 49, a poor transcript overall, was made before the fire; it serves to supply destroyed portions, enclosed here in square brackets. The vertical line | marks the intact left margin of the page.
2. **soui** suoi.

[et io insie]me con Lei rallegrarsi del suo felice retorno. N[on altro]
[priegho id]dio che conserui sua Illustrissima altezza alla cui gr[atia]
[humilmente b]asciando le mani m'offero et raccomm[ando.]
[Da Santo] Iacobo alli 3i di Iulio.

[Vostra obedientissima filiogla³ et fidelissima serva. Elyzabetta.]

LETTER 2 ❧ PRINCESS ELIZABETH TO QUEEN KATHERINE,
PREFACING HER NEW YEAR'S GIFT OF AN ENGLISH TRANSLATION
OF MARGUERITE OF NAVARRE'S *MIROIR DE L'ÂME PÉCHERESSE*,
DECEMBER 31, 1544¹

TO OVR MOSTE NOBLE AND
vertuous quene KATHERIN, Eliza
beth, her humble daughter wisheth
perpetuall felicitie and euerlasting ioye.

NOT ONELY knowing the affectuous wille, and feruent zeale, the wich
your highnes hath towardes all godly lerning, as also my duetie
towardes you (most gracious and souuerayne) princes but knowing
also: that pusilanimite and ydlenes, are most repugnante vnto a
reasonable creature: and that (as the philosopher sayeth) euen as an
instrument of yron or of other metayle, waxeth soone rusty, onles it be
continualy occupied, Euen so shall the witte of a man, or woman, waxe
dull, and vnapte to do, or vnderstand any thing perfittely, onles it be
always occupied vpon some maner of study. Wiche thinges
consydered, hath moued so small a portion, as god hath lente me. to
proue what i could do. And therfore haue i (as for a seye, or beginninge
(folowing the right notable sayeng of the prouerbe afore sayd)²
translated this lytell boke out of frenche ryme, in to englishe prose:
ioyning the sentences together as well as the capacitie of my symple
witte, and small lerning coulde extende themselues. The wich booke is

---

3. **filiogla** figliola.
1. *Source:* Bodleian Library, University of Oxford, MS Cherry 36, fols. 2r–4v. On parchment, bound in worn blue-green fabric covers embroidered by Elizabeth with pansies in the corners, ornamental edging, and intertwined initials *KP* on front and back.
2. Elizabeth fails to close the outer set of parentheses.

intytled, or named the miroir or glasse, of the synnefull soule where in
~~sh~~ is conteyned, how she (beholding and contempling what she is) doth
perceyue how, of herselfe, and of her owne strenght, she can do nothing
that good is, or preuayleth for her saluacion: onles it be through the
grace of god: whose mother daughter, syster, and wife, by the scriptures
she proueth herselfe to be. Trusting also, that through his
incomprehensible loue, grace, and mercy, she (beynge called frome
synne to repentaunce) doth faythfully hope to be saued. And althoughe
i knowe that as for my parte, wich i haue wrought in it: ~~the~~ (as well
spirituall, as manuall) there is nothinge done as it shulde be: nor els
worthy to come, in youre graces handes, but rather all vnperfytte and
vncorecte: yet do i truste also that oubeit[3] it is like a worke wich is but
newe begonne, and shapen: that the fyle of youre excellent witte, and
godly lerninge, in the redinge of it (if so it vouchesauue your highnes to
do) shall rubbe out, polishe, and mende (or els cause to mende) the
wordes (or rather the order of my writting) the wich i knowe in many
places to be rude, and nothing done as it shuld be. But i hope, that after
to haue ben in youre graces handes: there shall be nothinge in it worthy
of reprehension and that in the meane whyle no other, (but your
highnes onely) shal rede it, or se it, lesse[4] my fauttes be knowen of
many. Than shall they be better excused (as my confidence is in youre
graces accoustumed beneuolence) than if i shuld bestowe a whole yere
in writtinge, or inuentinge wayes for to excuse them. Prayenge god
almighty the maker, and creatoure of all thinges to garaunte vnto youre
highnes thesam newe yeres daye, a lucky and a prosperous yere, with
prosperous yssue, and continuance of many yeres in good helhte and
contynuall ioye, and all to his honnoure, praise, and glory. Frome
asherige, the laste daye of the yeare of our lord god. 1544.

3. **oubeit** howbeit (however) or albeit (although); the spelling allows either alternative.
4. **lesse** lest.

LETTER 3 ❧ PRINCESS ELIZABETH TO KING HENRY VIII,
PREFACING HER TRILINGUAL TRANSLATION OF QUEEN
KATHERINE'S *PRAYERS OR MEDITATIONS*, DECEMBER 30, 1545[1]

ILLVSTRISSIMO AC
potentissimo ʀegi, Henrico octa-
uo, Angliae Franciae Hiberniaeque
regi, fidei defensori, et secundum
christum, ecclesiae anglicanae et hi-
bernicae supremo capiti. Elizabeta
Maiestatis Suis humillima filia, omnem
foelicitatem precatur, et benedicti-
onem suam suplex
petit.

Quemadmodum immortalis animus, ~~im~~mortali corpore praestat, ita
sapiens quisque iudicat animi res gestas pluris aestimandas, et maiori
laude dignas esse, vlla corporis actione. Cum itaque maiestas tua tantae
excellentiae sit, vt nulli, aut pauci tecum sint comparandi in regijs, et
amplis ornamentis. et ego obstricta sum tibi, lege regni, vt domino, lege
naturae vt domino, et patri meo lege diuina, vt amplissimo domino, et
singulari, ac benignissimo patri, et omnibus legibus et officijs, varijs ac
pluribus modis obstricta sim maiestati tuae: libenter querebam (id
quod officium meum fuit) quo pacto amplitudini tuae prestantissimum
munus offerrem, quod tum facultas, tum industria mea inuenire possent.
In quo solum vereor, ne tenera, et inchoata studia, et puerilis ingenij
immaturitas, minuant illius rei laudem, et commendationem, quam
perfecta ingenia. in argumento diuinissimo pertractarunt. Nam nihil
acceptius esse debet regi, quem philosophi deum in terris esse sentiunt,
qûum[2] illud opus animi, quod nos in coelum tollit, et in terra coelestes,
atque in carne diuinos facit: et quum perpetuis ac infinitis miserijs
implicati simus, tunc etiam beatos nos, et foelices reddit. Quod quum
tam pium sit, et pio studio atque magna industria Reginae illustrissimae
fuerit anglicè collectum, et propterea ab omnibus magis expetendum, et

---

1. *Source:* BL, MS Royal 7.D.X, sigs. 2r–5r. On parchment, bound in crimson fabric embroidered by Elizabeth with pansies in the corners, ornamental edging, and the elaborately
intertwined initials *HR* and *KP* front and back. For a photographic reproduction of this letter's first page, see *CW,* p. 8.
2. **qûum** quam.

a maiestate tua in maiori precio habendum sit: accommodatissimum
mihi visum est, vt hoc, quod argumento suo rege, collectione vero
regina dignissimum est, a me filia tua in alias linguas conuerteretur;
quae non modo virtutum tuarum imitatrix, sed illarum etiam haeres
esse debeam. In quo quicquid meum non est, amplissima laude dignum
est, quemadmodum totus liber est tum argumento pius, tum ingeniose
collectus, et aptissimo ordine dispositus. Quicquid vero meum est, si in
eo aliquis error insit, tamenpropter ignorationem, aetatem, breue
tempus studij, et voluntatem, veniam meretur: et si mediocre sit, etiam
si nullam laudem mereatur, tamen si bene accipiatur, me vehementer
excitabit vt quantum annis cresco, tantum etiam scientia, et dei timore
crescam, itaque fiet vt illum religiosius colam, et maiestatem tuam
officiosius obseruem. Quamobrem non dubito, quin paterna tua
bonitas, et regia prudentia, hunc internum animi mei laborem non
minoris aestimabit, quam aliud vllum ornamentum, et sentiet diuinum
hoc opus, quod est pluris aestimandum, quia à serenissima regina
coniuge tua, colligebatur, paulo in maiori precio habendum esse, quia
abs filia[3] tua conuertebatur. Ille rex regum, in cuius manu corda regum
sunt, ita gubernet animum tuum, et vitam tueatur, vt in vera pietate, ac
religione diu sub maiestatis tuae imperio ~~diu~~ viuamus Harfordiae 30 die
decembris 1545

LETTER 4 𐑭 PRINCESS ELIZABETH TO QUEEN KATHERINE,
PREFACING HER ENGLISH TRANSLATION OF CHAPTER 1 OF JOHN
CALVIN'S *INSTITUTION DE LA RELIGION CHRESTIENNE* (GENEVA,
1541), DECEMBER 30, 1545[1]

A treshaulte, tresillustre,
et magnanime princesse Catherine,
Royne d'angleterre, france, et irelande.
Elizabeth sa treshumble fille rend salut et deue obéissance.

3. **abs filia** Elizabeth makes several uses of this phrase. "Abs" ordinarily precedes only "c,"
"q," and "t."

1. *Source:* Edinburgh, Scottish Record Office, MS RH 13/78, fols. 1r–7r. On parchment,
bound in pale blue-green fabric covers richly embroidered, in silver threads, with the same
pansies, edging, and intertwined initials used by Elizabeth for the companion volume given
to her father.

IADIS de toute ancienneté (tresnoble, treséxcellente, et souueraine
princesse) la coustume a tousiours obtenu, que pour garder la mémoire
des choses notables qui e estoient faittes au temps passé, et pareillement
pour en eslargir la renommee, plusieurs hommes ingénieux (affin
aussy qu'ilz applicassent leur sens, et industrie, et qu'on vist qu'ilz
excédassent en toute maniére d'artifice ingénieux le reste de tous
autres animaux) se sont en plusieurs lieux, et en diuerses maniéres
amuséz a rédiger, et réduire en mémoire les choses faictes en leur
temps, lesquelles leur sembloient plus dignes de commémoration ou
souuenance: Et pour ce faire (a cause que la proprieté, et nécessaire
vsance des lettres, et la manière d'éscrire n'estoit encor inuentee,) ilz
auoient accoustumé de rédiger, et produire leurs actes plus
mémorables auec certains caractéres, figures, ymages, ou éffigies,
d'hommes, bestes oyséaux poissons, arbres, ou herbes, grossement, et
lourdement entailléz: car il ne leur challoit comme ce fust qu'ilz
besongnassent, pourueu que la mémoire de leur intention fust éslargie,
éspandue, et obseruee par tout le monde. Puis nous voyons maintenant
comme depuis la création du monde tout ainsi que les iours, ᵉᵗ moys, se
sont augmentéz, et multipliéz semblablement, ainsi peu a peu, l'ésprit
de l'homme, par succession de temps, est plus ingenieux et inuentif
plus aorné, et poly, qu'il n'estoit au parauant. Et pourtant ont inuenté
les vns de esleuer en bosse, fondre ou grauer en or, argent, cuyure ou
autres metaulx: les autres en pierre, marbre, boys, cire paste endurcie
ou autres matiéres, les statues de noz predecesseurs, leur grandeur,
hauteur, grosseur, proportion, corpulence, et corsage: leur
phizionomie, taint, couleur, et regard: leur maintien, port, contenance:
leurs faitz, et géstes: en quoy faisant les paintres excellens ne méritent
moindre louange. Mais tous ensemble ne peurent oncq, et ne peuent
encor réprésenter ou déclarer par leurs ouurages, l'ésprit, ou engin, le
parler, ou entendeme nt d'aucun personage. Et pourtant par sur tous les
susditz artz et sciences, l'inuention des lettres me semble la plus
spirituelle, excellente, et ingénieuse: car par l'ordre d'icelles, non
seulement les susdictes qualitéz corporelles peuent estre déclarees;
mais qui plus est l'ymage de l'esprit et engin, et entendeme nt auec le
parler, et intention de lhomme, peut estre parfaitement congneu: voire,
graué, et protraict si pres du naif, et naturel, qu'il semble proprement
que les parolles, qui pieça furent dittes, et pronuncees, ayent encor la
mesme viguer quelles auoient alors. Ainsy que nous voyons que dieu
par sa parolle, et éscriture peut estre veu, ouy, et congneu quel il est

(entant qu'il est licite, et nécessaire pour nostre saluation) lequel
autrement ne peut estre congneu, ny veu, a cause que de soymesme il
est inuisible, et inpalpable, quant a nous, et ne se peut veoir, ny toucher.
Et pourtant n'y a il paintre, graueur, ~~ou~~ ymagier, ou autre, tant
ingenieux, et subtil soit il qui puisse au vray monstrer, ou produire
aucun ymage ou semblance de son essentielle diuinité, nomplus, et
moins ꝗ qu'il pourroit faire de l'ésprit d'aucune autre créature.

Doncq est l'art de paindre grauer, ou tailler l'ymage, et effigie des
choses corporelles, visibles, et palpables; et au contraire, léscriture,[2] est
l'ymage, et éffigie des choses spirituelles, inuisibles, et inpalpables. Et
pourtant, ie, d'un instinct naturel, suiuant' noz susdictz prédécesseurs
me suis ingérée, et entremise de traduire en nostre langue maternelle
vn petit liure, duquel ainsi que saint paul dit, l'argument ou subiect
surpasse la capacité de toute créature: et toutesfois est de viguer si
tresgrande qu'il n'y a créature viuante, telle qu'elle soit, qui n'en ait le
sentiment en soy: lequel certes requerroit plus grand' éloquence, ou
aornement de parolles et sentences, que ie ne luy sçaurois applicquer.
Mais veu que de la source dont est sorty ce liure, la maiésté de la
matiére surpasse toute éloquence humaine, estant priuilégee, et ayant
telle force en soy, qu'une seule sentence a pouoir de rauir, inspirer, et
donner congnoissance aux plus idiotz, et ignorans qui soient viuans,
en quelle sorte dieu veult estre congneu, veu, et ouy: pourtant ie pense
que de soymesme est suffisante, et n'a que faire d'aucun adueu,
support, ou ayde humaine. Quoy considéré (suiuant principallement
l'intention de mon autheur,) me suis enhardie, et aduenturee de le
translater mot, pour mot, et nompas que ce soit vn oeuure parfaict:
mais me confiant que vostre ♄ hautesse aura plus d'ésgard au zéle, et
desir qu'i'ay de vous complaire, que n'auréz a la capacité de mon simple
pouoir, et sçauoir: et que de vostre grace le voudréz estimer de prouenir
d'une pareille intention commes des desusditz,[3] auquelz il ne challoit
comme ce fust qu'ilz besongnassent, poureu que leur intention fust
congneuë. Parquoy i'éspere qu'en cas pareil vostre hautesse
m'excusera, et que de vostre gracieux accoustumé bon acueil le
receuréz en tesmoignage que pour chose qui soit en ce monde, ne
voudroye tumber in aucuns arréraiges de mon deuoir enuers vostre
grace: mais plustost, a mon povoir, comme la moindre, tenir la lumiére,

---

2. **léscriture** "Scripture" or "writing" generally; the context is ambiguous.
3. **desusditz** dessus-dits.

et ésclairer, pour, et affin d'estre aiuttrice[4] au feruent zéle, et parfaite
amour qu'auéz enuers iceluy dieu qui tout créa. Lequel
tresafectueusement ie suply' de vous vouloir si tresparfaitement
accroistre en la congnoissance de soy, que l'organe de vostre royale voix
puisse estre le vray instrument de sa parolle, affin de seruir de miroir, et
lumiere à tous vraiz crestiens, et chrestiennes. Du chasteau de harford
ce pén'ultime iour de l'an, 1545

LETTER 5 ❧ PRINCESS ELIZABETH TO KING EDWARD VI,
FEBRUARY 14, 1547[1]

[Addressed] Excelentissimo et Nobilissimo Regi Edouardo Sexto

Quod ante hoc tempus nullas ad tuam Maiestatem literas dederim, Rex
Serenissime et Illustrissime, nullasque pro singulari illa humanitate
fraternoque amore coram mihi exhibitis gratias egerim, Id queso ne aut
beneficiorum obliuioni, quae absit, aut sequitiei,[2] que minime decet,
sed alijs causis iustissimis attribuendum esse existimet.[3] Nam dum ad
tuam Maiestatem scribere saepe conarer, corporis valetudo aliquantum
aduersa maxime vero capitis dolor ab incepto reuocauit. Quo nomine
spero tuam Celsitudinem meum erga se animum literarum vice
accepturam esse. Qui quidem animus non tam ex ore quam ex corde
profectus debitam quandam erga tuam Maiestatem obseruantiam et
fidem declarabit. Verum haec ego re ipsa et factis potius quam uerbis a
te cognosci cupio. Quod ut fiat ego omnibus viribus contendam.
Quemadmodum enim aurum ubi igni excoctum et a scoria probe
expurgatum fuerit, tum demum certo dignoscitur, sic opera
cuiuscunque hominis animum certissimo arguunt. Porro quod
reliquum est ago tuae Maiestati gratias quam possum maximas quod

---

4. **aiuttrice** an approximate French—and exact Italian—cognate of Latin *adiutrix*,
"helper," "aide" (gendered feminine).

1. *Source:* BL, MS Harley 6986, art. 11, fol. 19r, with traces of seal. The assignment of the year
follows the BL's Harleian Catalogue.

2. **sequitiei** sequitur? A form parallel to "obliuioni" is lacking in the correlative pair
"aut . . . aut."

3. **existimet** Second person address shifts to third person, with "tua Maiestas" as the un-
derstood subject.

non tantum praesentem praesens omnibus humanitatis officijs prosecuta sit, verumetiam nunc absens suum erga me absentem animum annulo misso testatum fecerit. Ex quo intelligere potui promissi memoriam tuae Maiestati refricare minime opus fuisse non solum quia vt ne facerem tua Celsitudo iusserit verumetiam propter ~~monstratam~~ ostensam mihi beneuolentiam de qua non dubitaui antea. Deus conseruet tuam Maiestatem diu incolumem et eandem (vt facere cepit). ad maximarum virtutum incrementa prouehat. Enfeldiae, 14 februarij.

Maiestatis tuae humillima serua et soror.
Elizabeta

LETTER 6 ❧ PRINCESS ELIZABETH TO KING EDWARD VI UPON HIS RECOVERY FROM SICKNESS, SEPTEMBER 20, 1547[1]

[Addressed] Illustrissimo et Nobilissimo Regi Edouardo Sexto.

Quòd tanto temporis intervallo tàm raras a me literas acceperis, Rex Illustrissime, quibus vel gratias agerem pro beneficijs, vel saltem debitam meam erga te observantiam testatam facerem, Spero facile me veniam impetraturam: praesertim cum nulla admissa sit cessatio obliuione quadam tui, cuius nunquam obliuisci vel possum, vel debeo. Nunc vero cum tuam Maiestatem in locis non procul Londino sitis uersari intelligam, rumpendum mihi silentium esse duxi, vt testificarer neque de debito meo erga te cultu quicquam esse remissum, neque tua incolumitate quicquam mihi esse posse optabilius. quam firmam et integram esse ex quorundam sermone cognoui. Ego sanè dum singula Dei Optimi Maximi beneficia mente recolo, hoc unum ex omnibus maximum fuisse iudico, quod te Londini ex proximo morbo tam subitò et clementer restituit. In quem quidem te dei quadam prouidentia lapsum esse arbitror, quemadmodum proximis literis ad tuam Maiestatem scripsi, vt, omni morborum materia pulsa, tu huiusce regni habenis tractandis quamdiutissimè seruareris. Nihil ~~enim~~ aequè

---

1. *Source:* BL, MS Harley 6986, art. 15, fol. 21r, with traces of seal. The assignment of the year follows the British Library's Harleian Catalogue.

incertum aut minus diuturnum quàm vita hominis, nimirum qui
Pindari[2] testimonio nihil sit aliud, quam vmbrae somnium. Et homine,
vt ait homerus,[3] nihil terra alit fragilius. Cum itaque cuiusque hominis
vita tot tantisque casibus non modo sit exposita, sed etiam vincatur,
singulari quadam diuinae prouidentiae clementia et morbum
preteritum abs te depulsum, et in istis locorum (quos a morbis non
plane immunes fuisse cognoui) et aeris mutationibus tam crebris ab
omnibus omnium morborum periculis te seruatum esse iudicamus.
Cui prouidentiae Maiestatis tuae tutelam committo, simulque rogo vt
eandem quamdiutissime incolumem seruet. Ashrigiae 20 Septembris.

Maiestatis tuae humillima soror.

Elizabeta

LETTER 7 ❧ PRINCESS ELIZABETH TO KING EDWARD VI,
FEBRUARY 2, 1548[1]

[Addressed] Illustrissimo et Nobilissimo Regi Edouardo Sexto

Amoris erga me tui argumenta nulla vel plura, vel illustriora dari
potuerunt Rex serenissime et Illustrissime: quàm cum proximè fructu
iucundissimae consuetudinis tuae perfruerer. Cuius sanè cum recordor
(quotidie autem recordor) quasi tecum esse et collocutione[u]m tuarum
humanitate praesens ipsa frui planè videor. Caeterum cum in mentem
veniunt innumerabilia tua illa in me ~~officia~~ beneficia, quibus isthuc[2]
aduenientem excepisti, discedentemque abs te dimisisti, non facile
habeo commemorare quantopere in diversas partes distrahatur
animus, ancipitemque cogitandi curam adferat. Nam vt ex
beneficiorum erga me tuorum magnitudine amorem in me tuum
propensum maximeque fraternum perspiciens non parum inde gaudij
laetitiaeque concepi, ita rursus meritorum erga me tuorum

---

2. Pindar *Pythian Ode* VIII, last two lines.
3. Homer *Iliad* XIV.446–47.
1. *Source:* Bodleian Library, University of Oxford, MS Add. C.92 (formerly MS Arch. F.c.8),
fol. 12; this letter was once pasted onto the flyleaf of King James I's works in a MS that he himself presented to the Bodleian. On the later attribution of this letter to Elizabeth's tutor,
Roger Ascham, which we discount, see our source note in *CW*, p. 15.
2. **isthuc** istuc

multitudinem aequa iustaque lance expendens doleo, quòd intelligam
me eorum vim ne cogitanda quidem nedum referenda gratia vllo
vnquam tempore consequi posse. Ne tamen tua Maiestas tot tantaque
in me benefacta aut male locata, aut potius (vt Ciceronis ex Ennio
sumptis vtar verbis[3]) malefacta esse arbitraretur, aut denique parum
me memorem gratamque esse indicaret,[4] volui nunc saltem, cum re
non possem, verbis tuae Maiestati gratias agere. Quod quidem ipsum
citius a me vel literas vel nuncio misso factum fuisset, nisi opusculum
quoddam, quod etiam ad tuam Maiestatem mittere cupiebam,
propositum meum interuertisset. Id quod cum propter angustiam
temporis, quod mihi vel aqua citius effluxisse video, ad calcem (vti me
facturam opinabar) a me ipsa perduci minime potuerit, spero nunc
hasce literas quantumuis rudes meam absentis causam apud tuam
Maiestatem acturas esse, simulaque animum erga te meum
quomodocunque saltem declaraturas. Nam vt id plaenè abundéque
satis ~~vel~~ mutis vocibus a me fiat, minime fieri posse existimo.
praesertim cum (vt tua non ignorat Maiestas) meae naturae quasi sit
proprium, non modo non tantum verbis dicere, quantum mente
cogitare, verumetiam non plus dicere quàm cogitare. Quorum
posterius (plus dicere puto) quemadmodum pauci detestantur, ita
multi vbique vsurpant, maxime verò in aulis principum et Regum:
quibus, id vince[5] cauendum est, ne plures intra cubicula sua κόλακασ
quàm extra aulam suam κόρακασ[6] habere videantur. Qua quidem de
re hoc loco satis. Illud tantum precor vt Deus conseruet tuam
Maiestatem quam diutissime incolumem ad nominis sui gloriam
regnique vtilitatem. Hatfildiae 2⁰ februᵃrij.

> Maiestatis tuae humilima soror
> et serua
> Elizabeth

---

3. Cicero *De officiis* II.18, citing Ennius *Scenica,* no. 24: "nam praeclare Ennius, bene facta
male locata malefacta arbitror."

4. **indicaret** alternatively, iudicaret (ambiguous n/u), with the reading "lest [your
Majesty] judged."

5. **vince** word and sense unclear; possibly a miswriting of "hince" (causal form of "hinc"),
"hence."

6. **κόλακασ . . . κόρακασ** In both words Elizabeth writes a non-terminal sigma form in
terminal position. The sound likeness of the Greek words for "flatterers" and "crows" yields a
pun which antiquity ascribed both to Diogenes and to Palladas. Athenaeus *Epigrammata*

LETTER 8 &ᴥ PRINCESS ELIZABETH TO DOWAGER QUEEN
KATHERINE, CIRCA JUNE 1548[1]

[Addressed] To the Quenes hithnis.

Althougth I coulde not be plentiful in giuinge thankes for the manifolde
kindenis receyue[2] at your hithnis hande at my departure, yet I am some
thinge to be borne with al, for truly I was replete with sorowe to departe
frome your highnis, especially leuinge you vndoubful of helthe, and
albeit I answered litel I wayed it more dipper whan you sayd you wolde
warne me of al euelles that you shulde hire of me, for if your grace had
not a good opinion of me you wolde not haue offered frindeship to me
that way, that al men iuge the contrarye, but what may I more say than
thanke God for prouidinge suche frendes to me, desiringe God to
enriche me with ther longe life, and me grace to be in hart no les
thankeful to receyue it, than I nowe am glad in writinge to shewe it. and
althougth I haue plentye of matter, hire I wil staye for I Knowe you ar
not quiet to rede. Frome Cheston this present saterday.

Your hithnis humble doughter
Elizabeth

LETTER 9 &ᴥ PRINCESS ELIZABETH TO THOMAS SEYMOUR,
LORD HIGH ADMIRAL, SUMMER 1548[1]

[Addressed] To my Lorde Admirall

My Lorde you neded not to sende an excuse to me, for I coulde not
mistruste the not fulfillinge of your promes to prosede for want of good
wyl, but only the oportunite serueth not, wherfore I shal desier you to

---

VI.65, records Diogenes's maxim likening the two as devourers, respectively, of the living and
the dead; the *Greek Anthology,* XI.323, contains Palladas's epigram remarking that the one-
letter spelling difference scarcely obscures the sameness of the two predators (*Anthologia
Graeca, Buch IX–XI,* ed. Herman Beckby [Munich: Ernst Heimeran Verlag, 1957], pp. 702–3).

1. *Source:* PRO, State Papers Domestic, Edward VI 10/2, fol. 84c. For a photographic reproduction, see *CW,* p. 18.

2. **receyue** receyued (wear to the paper has obliterated the word ending).

1. *Source:* J. Pierpont Morgan Library, MS Rulers of England, Box III, Part I, art. 6. A single
sheet with embellished double rule at top and bottom in red ink. The date is conjecturally
supplied by the Morgan Library Catalogue.

thinke that a greater matter than this coulde not make me impute any
vnkindenis in you for I am a frende not wonne with trifels, nor lost
with the leke. This² I commit you and al your affaires in Gods hande
who Kepe you from al euel. I pray you make my humbel
commendations to the Quenes hithnis.

Your assured frende to my power.
Elizabeth

LETTER 10 ʕ PRINCESS ELIZABETH TO DOWAGER QUEEN
KATHERINE, JULY 31, 1548¹

Although your hithnys letters be most ioyfull to me in absens, yet
consyderinge what paine hit ys to you to write ~~and~~ your grace beinge
so great with childe, and so sikely your commendacyon wer ynough in
my Lordes lettar. I muche reioyce at youre helthe with the wel likinge
of the country, with my humbel thankes that your grace wisshed me
with you til I ware wery of that cuntrye, your hithnys were like to be
combered if I shulde not depart tyl I were we[ary] beinge with you,
although hit were in the worst soile in the wor[ld,] your presence wolde
make it pleasant. I can not reproue my Lo[rd for] not doinge your
commendacyons in his lettar for he did hit: and al[though] he had not,
yet I wil not complaine on him for that he shalbe diligen[t to] giue me
knolege frome time to time how his busy childe dothe, a[nd if] I were
at his birth no dowt I wolde se him beaton for the trobe[l he has] put
you to. Master Denny and my Lady with humbel th[anks] prayeth most
intirely ᶠᵒʳ ʸᵒᵘʳ ᵍʳᵃᶜᵉ prainge the almyghtty God to sende [you a
most²] lucky deliuerance, And my mystres wisseth no les giu[ing your
Highnes] most humbel thankes for her commendacions. Wri[tten with
very little] leysor this last day of Iuly.

[Your humble daughter]
[Elizabeth]

2. **This** Thus.
1. *Source:* BL, MS Cotton Otho, C.X, fol. 236v; like Letter 1, this one shows fire damage from
1742. Lost readings (enclosed in square brackets) are restored from the eighteenth-century
copy, Bodleian, MS Smith 68, art. 50.
2. **most** mistakenly omitted in *CW*, p. 20.

LETTER 11 ❧ PRINCESS ELIZABETH TO KING EDWARD VI,
SUMMER OR FALL 1548[1]

[Addressed] Nobilissimo et Serenissimo Regi Edouardo Sexto

Tametsi nihil aeque studuerim, Rex Serenissime, quàm vt
ingratitudinis non modo notam verumetiam suspicionem vel
minimam effugerem, metuo tamen ne in illam incidisse videri possim,
quae tot a tua Maiestate beneficijs semper affecta nullas tanto temporis
interuallo literas dederim, e quibus animi saltem grati signa
cognosceres. Cuius rei causae cum sint iustae ac necessariae, spero
simulque confido Maiestatem tuam me ab omni ingratitudinis crimine
facilé liberaturam esse. Valetudo enim capitis et oculorum aduersa
accessit, quae ita me grauiter ab aduentu in hanc domum molestauit,
vt, dum saepe ad tuam Maiestatem scribere conarer, in hunc vsque
diem semper a proposito institutoque reuocata sim. Quae valetudo
cum Dei Optimi Maximi ope et auxilio nunc semet aliqua'ntu'm[2]
remiserit, existimaui scribendi officium minimè diutius a me
differendum esse, quo tua Maiestas intelligeret quiduis potius quam
animum erga se gratum beneficiorumque memorem hactenus mihi
defuisse. Nam etsi non ignorarem tantam tuorum erga me
beneficiorum esse magnitudinem, vt illorum partem vel minimam
referenda gratia consequendi spes prorsus omnis adimeretur, in hoc
tamen omnes mihi neruos contendendos esse putaui, vt iustam
meritamque gratiam voluntate memoriaque mente persoluerem. In
quo quidem cum nihil sit a me hactenus vnquam praetermissum, spero
tuam Maiestatem hoc meum scribendi gratiaeque agendae hucusque
intermissum officium non modo in aequam partem accepturam,
verumetiam debitam sibi gratiam animo semper et voluntate a me
fuisse habitam, existimaturam esse. Dominus Iesus qui omnia

---

1. *Source:* Bodleian Library, University of Oxford, MS Smith 19, art. 1, fol. 1. Dating is conjectural, based on close similarity between features of Elizabeth's hand here and in the July
31, 1548, letter to Katherine Parr.

2. **aliqua'ntu'm** Although she writes out the whole word, Elizabeth also twice inserts the
apostrophe-like mark often used in period texts as an abbreviation for an appropriate Latin
word ending. See the ninth contraction mark listed in Jean F. Preston and Laetitia Yeandle,
English Handwriting, 1400–1650 (Binghamton, N.Y.: Medieval and Renaissance Texts and
Studies, 1992), p. xii.

conseruat et tuetur, tuam Excellentiam isto regno, magnis virtutibus, multisque annis, perpetuo augeat. Enfildiae

Maiestatis tuae humilissi^{ma} serua et soror.
Elizabeta

LETTER 13 ❧ PRINCESS ELIZABETH TO EDWARD SEYMOUR, LORD PROTECTOR, JANUARY 28, 1549[1]

My Lorde your great gentilnis, and good wil towarde me as wel in this thinge as in other thinges I do understande, for the wiche euen as I ougthe, so I do giue you most humble thankes. And wheras your Lordshipe willeth and counselleth me, as a ernest frende, to declare what I knowe in this matter, and also to write what I haue declared to Master Tirwit I shal most willingely do it. I declared vnto him first that after that the Coferar had declared vnto me what my Lorde Admiral answered for Alins matter, and for Diram place, that it was appointed to be a minte, he tolde me that my Lorde Admiral did offer me his house for my time beinge with the Kinges Maiestie. And further sayd and asked me wether if the counsel did consente that I shulde haue my Lord Admiral wether I wolde consente to it or no. I answered that I wolde not tel him what my minde was, and I inquired further of him what he mente to aske me that question or who bad him say so, he answered me and said, no bodye bad him say so, but that he parseued (as he thogth) by my Lorde Admirals inquiringe wither my patente were sealed or no, and debatinge what he spente in his house, and inquiringe what was spente in my house, that he was giuen that way rather than otherwise. And as concerninge Kat Aschilye she neuer auised me vnto it but said alwais (whan any talked of my mariage) that she wolde neuer haue me marye nether in inglande nor out of inglande without the consent of the Kinges Maiestie, your graces, and the counsels, and after the Quene was departed whan I asked of her what newes she harde from London, she answered merilye, the say ther that your grace shal haue my Lorde

---

1. *Source:* Hatfield House, Cecil Papers, 133/4/2. The endorsement reads "my ladie Elizabeth. xxviii January."

Admiral, and that he wil come shortely to woue you. And moreouer I
said unto him that the Coferar sent a letter hither that my Lorde sayd
that he wolde come this waye as he went doune to the countrye, than I
bad her write as she thogth best, and bade her shewe it me whan she
had done, so she write that she thoght it not best for feare of iuspicion,[2]
and so it wente forthe, and my Lord Admiral after he harde that asked
of the Coferar whie he mighte not come as wel to me as to my Sister,
and than I desired Kat Aschilye to write againe (lest my Lorde migth
thinke that she knewe more in it than he) that she knewe nothinge in it
but suspicion. And also I tolde Master Tirwit that to the effect of the
matter I neuer consentid unto any suche thinge without the counsels
consent therunto. And as for Kat Aschilye or the Coferar the neuer
tolde me that the wolde practise it. Thes be the thinges wiche I bothe
declared to master Tirwit and also wherof my conscience berethe me
witnis, wiche I wolde not for al erthely thinges offende in any thinge for
I knowe I haue a soule to saue as wele as other fokes haue wherfore I wil
aboue al thinge haue respect unto this same. If ther be any more thinges
wiche I can remembre I wil ether write it my selfe, or cause maister
Tirwit to write it. Maister Tirwit and others haue tolde me that ther
goeth rumors abrode wiche be greatly bothe agenste myne honor, and
honesti wiche aboue al other thinkes I estime, wiche be these, that I
~~shulde~~ am in the tower and with childe by my Lord Admiral, My Lord
these ar shameful schanlders, for the wiche besides the great desier I
haue to se the Kinges Maiestie I shal most hartely desire your Lordship
that I may come to the court after your first determination, that I may
shewe my selfe there as I am. Writen in hast frome Atfelde this 28 of
Ianuarye.

                          Your assured frende to my litel power.
                                              Elizabeth

---

2. **iuspicion** suspicion.

LETTER 14 ᶜᵉ᷇ PRINCESS ELIZABETH TO EDWARD SEYMOUR,
LORD PROTECTOR, FEBRUARY 6, 1549[1]

[Addressed] To my verey good Lorde my Lorde Protector.

My Lorde I have reseued your gentil letter and also your message by
Master Tirwit for the wiche two thinges especially (althogth for manye
other thinges) I can not giue your Lordeshipe souficiente thankes, and
wheras your grace doth wil me to credit Master Tirwit I haue done so,
and wil do so as longe as he willeth me (as he doth ~~not~~) to nothinge but
to that wiche is for mine honor, and honestie, and euen as I sayd to him,
and did write to your Lordship, so I do write now againe that whan ther
doeth any more thinges hapen in my minde wiche I haue forgotten I
assure your grace I wil declare them most willingelye for I wolde not (as
I truste you haue not) so yuel a oppinion of me that I wolde concile any
thinge that I knewe, for it wher[2] to no purpos and surely forgetfulnis
may wel cause me to hide thinges but vndouttedly els I wil declare al
that I knowe. From Hatfelde the 6 of Februarye.

Your assured frende to my litel power.
Elizabeth

LETTER 15 ᶜᵉ᷇ PRINCESS ELIZABETH TO EDWARD SEYMOUR,
LORD PROTECTOR, FEBRUARY 21, 1549[1]

[Addressed] To my verey good Lorde my Lorde Protector.

My Lorde hauinge reseuede your Lordeships letters I parceue in them
your goodwil towarde me bicause you declare to me plainlie your
mynde in this thinge and againe for that you wolde not wische that I
shulde do any thinge that shulde not seme good vnto the counsel for
the wiche thinge I giue you most hartie thankes. And wheras I do
understande that you do take in iuel parte the letters that I did write

---

1. *Source:* Bodleian Library, University of Oxford, MS Ashmole 1729, art. 6 (formerly Arch.
F.c.39), with remnants of seal. Reproduced in facsimile as no. 22 in *Humanistic Script of the
Fifteenth and Sixteenth Centuries* (Oxford: Bodleian Library, 1960).

2. **wher** were.

1. *Source:* BL, MS Lansdowne 1236, fol. 33, with traces of seals.

unto your Lordeshipe I am verye sorie that you shulde take them so for
my mynde was to declare unto you plainlie as I thogth in that thinge
wiche I did also the more willingelye bicause (as I write to you) you
desired me to be plaine with you in al thinges. And as concerninge that
pointe that you write that I seme to stande in my none[2] witte in beinge
so wel assured of my none selfe, I did assure me of my selfe nomore
than I trust the trueth shal trie, And to say that wiche I knewe of my
selfe I did not thinke shulde haue displeased the counsel or your grace.
And surelye the cause whie that I was sorye that ther shulde be anye
suche aboute me was bicause that I thogth the people wil say that I
deserued throwgth my lewde demenure to haue suche a one, and not
that I mislike anye thinge that your Lordeshipe, or the counsel shal
thinke good for I knowe that you and the counsel ar charged with me,
or that I tak apon me to rule my selfe for I knowe the ar most disceued
that trusteth most in them selues, wherfore I trust you shal neuer finde
that faute in me, to the wiche thinge I do not se that your grace has
made anye directe answere at this time, and seinge the make so iuel
reportes alreadie shalbe but a increasinge of ther iuel tonges, howbeit
you did write that if I wolde bringe forthe anye that had reported it you
and the counsel wolde se it redreste wiche thinge thogth I can easelye
do it I wolde be lothe to do it for bicause it is my none cause, and againe
that shulde be but a bridinge of a iuel name of me that I am glade to
ponesse them, and so get the iuel wil of the people, wiche thinge I
wolde be lothe to haue. But if it mougth so seme good vnto your
Lordeshipe and the reste of the counsel to sende forthe a proclamation
in to the counntries that the refraine ther tonges declaringe how the
tales be but lies it shulde make bothe the people thinke that you and the
counsel haue great regarde that no suche rumors shulde be spreade of
anye of the Kinges Maiesties Sisters as I am thougth vnwordie, and also
I shulde thinke my selfe to receue suche frendeshipe at your handes as
you haue promised me, althogth your Lordeship hathe shewed me
greate alreadie. Howbeit I am aschamed to aske it anye more bicause I
se you ar not so wel minded therunto. And as concerninge that you saye
that I giue folkes occasion to thinke in refusing the good to vpholde the
iuel I am not of so simple vnderstandinge, nor I wolde that your grace
shulde haue so iuel a opinion of me that I haue so litel respecte to my

2. **my none** mine own.

none honestie that I wolde mainteine it if I had souficiente promis of
the same, and so your grace shal proue me whan it comes to the pointe.
And thus I bid you farewel, desiringe god alwais to assiste you in al your
affaires. Writen in hast. Frome Hatfelde this 21 of Februarye.

Your assured frende to my litel power.
Elizabeth

LETTER 16 ও PRINCESS ELIZABETH TO EDWARD SEYMOUR,
LORD PROTECTOR, MARCH 7, 1549[1]

[Addressed] To my verey good Lorde my Lorde Protector.

My Lorde I haue a requeste to make vnto your grace wiche feare has
made me omitte til this time for two causes, the one bicause I sawe that
my request for the rumors wiche were sprede abrode of me toke so litel
place wiche thinge whan I considered I thogth I shulde litel profit in any
other sute; howbeit now I vnderstande that ther is a proclamacion for
them (for the wiche I giue your grace and the rest of the counsel most
humble thankes) I am the bolder to speake for a nother thinge. And the
other was bicause parauenture your Lordeship, and the rest of the
counsel wil thinke that I fauor her iuel doinge for whome I shal speake
for, wiche is for Kateryn Aschiley, that it wolde please your grace and the
rest of the counsel to be good vnto her wiche thinge I do not to fauor her
in any iuel (for that I wolde be sorye to do) but for thes consideracions
wiche folowe the wiche hope dothe teache me in sainge that I ougth not
to doute but that your grace and the rest of the counsel wil thinke that I
do it for thre other consideracions, first bicause that she hathe bene with
me a longe time, and manye years, and hathe taken great labor, and
paine in brinkinge of me vp in lerninge and honestie, and therfore I
ougth of very dewtye speke for her, for Saint Gregorie sayeth that we ar
more bounde to them that bringeth us up wel than to our parents, for
our parents do that wiche is natural for them, that is bringeth us into this
worlde but our brinkers up ar a cause to make us liue wel in it.[2] The

<hr>

1. *Source:* BL, MS Lansdowne 1236, fol. 35r, with traces of seals.
2. Probable allusion to Saint Gregory of Nazianzus's famous funeral oration on Saint Basil
the Great (Discourse 43, chaps. 12–13; J.-P. Migne, ed., *Patrologia Graeca* 36:509A–513A).

seconde is bicause I thinke that whatsoeuer she hathe done in my Lorde
Admirals matter as concerninge the marijnge of me she dide it bicause
knowinge him to be one of the counsel she thogth he wolde not go
aboute any suche thinge without he had the counsels consent therunto,
for I haue harde her manye times say that she wolde neuer haue me
mary[3] in any place without your Graces and the counsels consente. The
thirde cause is bicause that it shal and doth make men thinke that I am
not clere of the dide myselfe, but that it is pardoned in me bicause of my
youthe, bicause that she I loued so wel is in suche a place. Thus hope
preuailinge more with me than feare hathe wone the battel, and I haue at
this time gone furth with it. Wiche I pray God be taken no other wais
that[4] it is mente. Writen in hast. Frome Hatfilde this 7 day of Marche.

[Insert squeezed in between body of letter and signature:]

Also if I may be so bolde not offendinge I beseche your grace and the
rest of the counsel to be good to master Aschiley her husbonde wiche
bicause he is my kindesman I wold be glad he shulde dow

> Your assured frende to my litel power.
> Elizabeth

LETTER 17 ◁ PRINCESS ELIZABETH TO KING EDWARD VI, WITH A PRESENT OF HER PORTRAIT, MAY 15, 1549[1]

Like as the richeman that dayly gathereth riches to riches, and to one bag
of of mony layeth a greate sort til it come to infinit, so methinkes your
Maiestie not beinge suffised withe many benefits and gentilnes shewed to
me afore this time, dothe now increase them in askinge and desiring
wher you may bid and commaunde, requiring a thinge not worthy the
desiringe for it selfe, but made worthy for your higthnes request. My
pictur I mene in wiche if the inward good mynde towarde your grace
migth as wel be declared, as the outwarde face and countenaunce shal be
seen I wold nor haue taried the commandement but preuent[2] it, nor haue

3. This insertion is added in the left margin.
4. **that** than.
1. *Source:* BL, MS Cotton Vespasian F.III, fol. 48.
2. **preuent** prevented (grammatical ending left off), in Latinate sense of "anticipated."

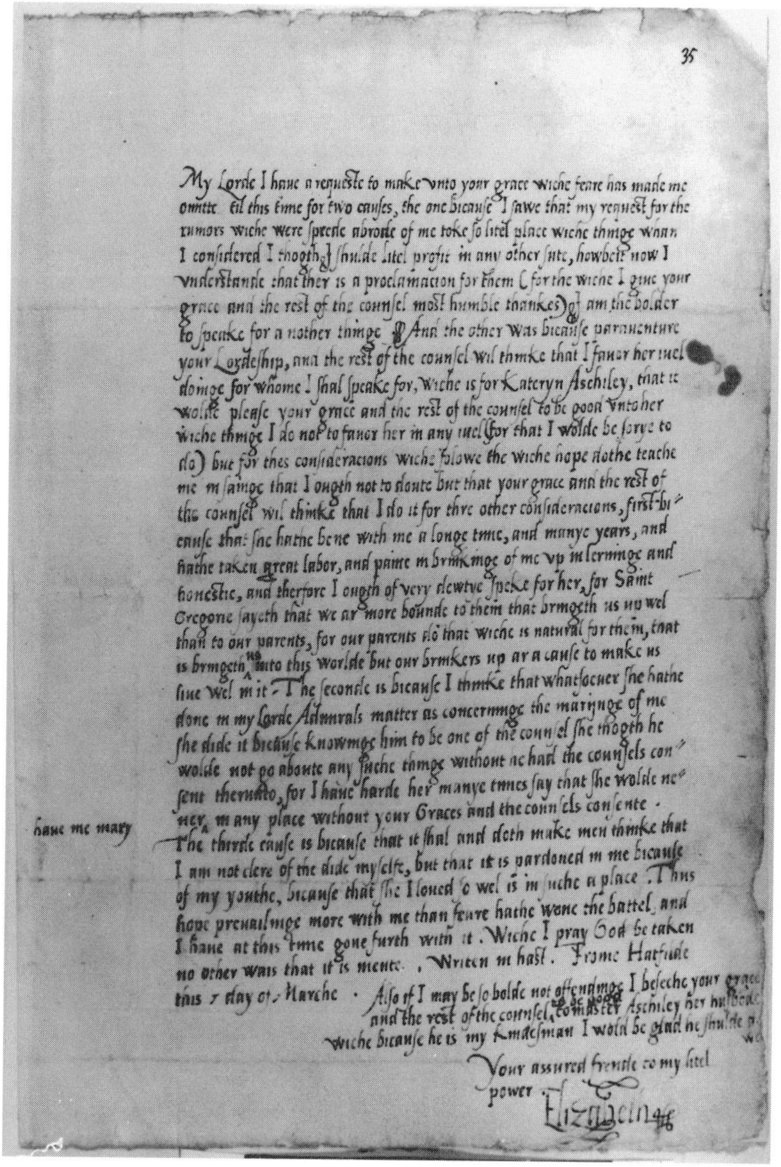

35

My Lorde I haue a requeste to make vnto your grace wiche feare has made me
omitte til this time for two causes, the one bicause I sawe that my request for the
rumors wiche were sprede abrode of me toke so litel place wiche thinge wan
I considered I thogth I shulde litel profit in any other sute, howbeit now I
vnderstande that ther is a proclamacion for them (for the wiche I giue your
grace and the rest of the counsel most humble thankes) I am the bolder
to speake for a nother thinge And the other was bicause parauenture
your Lordeship, and the rest of the counsel wil thinke that I fauor her iuel
doinge for whome I shal speake for, wiche is for Kateryn Aschiley, that it
wolde please your grace and the rest of the counsel to be good vnto her
wiche thinge I do not to fauor her in any iuel (for that I wolde be sorye to
do) but for thes consideracions wiche folowe the wiche hope dothe teache
me in sainge that I ougth not to doute but that your grace and the rest of
the counsel wil thinke that I do it for thre other consideracions, first bicause that she hathe bene with me a longe time, and manye years, and
hathe taken great labor, and paine in bringinge of me vp in lerninge and
honestie, and therfore I ougth of very dewtye speke for her, for Saint
Gregorie sayeth that we ar more bounde to them that bringeth us vp wel
than to our parents, for our parents do that wiche is natural for them, that
is bringeth us into this worlde but our brinkers vp ar a cause to make us
liue wel in it. The seconde is bicause I thinke that whatsoeuer she hathe
done in my Lorde Admirals matter as concerninge the mariage of me
she dide it bicause knowinge him to be one of the counsel she thogth he
wolde not go aboute any suche thinge without he had the counsels consent therunto, for I haue harde her manye times say that she wolde neuer haue me mary in any place without your Graces and the counsels consente.
The thirde cause is bicause that it shal and doth make men thinke that
I am not clere of the dide myselfe, but that it is pardoned in me bicause
of my youthe, bicause that she I loued so wel is in suche a place. Thus
hope preuailinge more with me than feare hathe wone the battel, and
I haue at this time gone furth with it. Wiche I pray God be taken
no other wais that it is mente. Writen in hast. Frome Hatfilde
this 7 day of Marche.

Also if I may be so bolde not offendinge I beseche your grace
and the rest of the counsel to be good to master Aschiley her husbande
wiche bicause he is my kinsman I wold be glad he shulde w[...]

Your assured frende to my litel
power. Elizabeth

FIGURE 3 Letter 16, to Edward Seymour, Lord Protector, March 7, 1549; BL, MS Lansdowne 1236, fol. 35. Reproduced by permission of the British Library.

bine the last to graunt but the first to offer it. For the face, I graunt, I might
wel blusche to offer, but the mynde I shal neuer be asshamed to present.
For thogth from the grace of the pictur the coulers may fade by time; may
give by wether may be spotted by chance, yet the other nor time with her
swift winges shal ouertake, nor the mistie cloudes with ther loweringes
may darken, nor chance with her slipery fote may ouerthrow. Of this
althogth yet the profe coulde not be greate bicause the occasions hathe
bine but smal, notwithstandinge as a dog hathe a day, so may I
perchaunce haue time to declare it ᶦⁿ dides wher now I do write them but
in wordes. And further I shal most humbly beseche your Maiestie that
whan you shal loke on my pictur you wil witsafe³ to thinke that as you
haue but the outwarde shadow of the body afore you, so my inward
minde wischeth that the body it selfe wer oftner in your presence
howbeit bicause bothe my so beinge I thinke coulde do your Maiestie
litel pleasur thogth my selfe great good, and againe bicause I se as yet not
the time agreing therunto I shal lerne to folow this sainge of Orace, Feras
non culpes quod vitari non potest.⁴ And thus I wil (troblinge your
Maiestie I fere) ende with my most humble thanke Besechinge God
longe to preserue you to his honour to your comfort, to the realmes
profit, and to my ioy. From Hatfilde this 15 day of May.

> Your Maiesties most humbly sistar and seruant.
> Elizabeth

LETTER 18 ⮞ PRINCESS ELIZABETH TO KING EDWARD VI,
APRIL 21, 1552¹

[Addressed] To the most Noble Kinge Edward the Sixt.

What cause I had of sory whan I harde first of your Maiesties siknes al
men migth gesse, but none but my selfe coulde fele, wiche to declare wer

---

3. **witsafe** vouchsafe.

4. Presently ascribed to Publilius Syrus; see his *Sententiae,* ed. Wilhelm Meyer (Leipzig:
B. G. Teubner, 1880), p. 30. This maxim is I.ii.14 of Erasmus's *Adagia* (*Collected Works of
Erasmus,* vol. 31, *Adages I.i.1 to I.v.100,* trans. Margaret Mann Phillips [Toronto: University of
Toronto Press, 1982], pp. 246–47).

1. *Source:* Department of Printing and Graphic Arts, Houghton Library, Harvard University, pf MS Typ 686, written on a folded folio sheet with highly decorated capitals. Dating is
conjectural, based on Edward's bout with smallpox and measles in April 1552.

or migth seme a point of flatery and therfore to write it I omit. But as the
sorow coulde not be litel, bicause the occasions wer many so is the ioy
gret to hire of the good escape out of the perillous diseases. And that I am
fully satisfied and wel assured of the same by your graces owne hande I
must nides giue you my most humble thankes assuring your Maiestie
that a precious iewel at a nother time could not so wel haue contented as
your lettar in this case hathe comforted me. For nowe do I say with Saint
Austin that a disease is to be counted no siknes that shal cause a bettar
helthe whan it is past than was assured afore it came.[2] for afore you had
them euery man thogth that that shulde not be eschued of you that was
not scaped of many. but sins you haue had them dout of ~~it~~ them is past
and hope is giuen to al men that it was a purgation by thes menes for
other wors diseases wiche migth happen this year. Moreouer I considar
that as a good father that loues his childe derely dothe punis him
scharpely, So God favoring your Maiestie gretly hathe chastened you
straitly, and as a father dothe it for the further good of his childe, so hathe
God prepared this for the bettar helthe of your grace. And in this hope I
commit your Maiestie to his handes. most humbly crauing pardon of
your grace that I did write no soner desiring you to attribute the faute to
my iuel hed, and not to my slothful hande. From Hatfilde this 21 of April.

Your Maiesties most humble sistar to commande.

Elizabeth

LETTER 19 ᙜ PRINCESS ELIZABETH TO PRINCESS MARY,
OCTOBER 27, 1552[1]

[Addressed] To my welbeloued sistar Marye.

Good Sistar as to hire of your siknes is vnpleasant to me, so is it
nothinge feareful, for that I vnderstande it is your olde gest that is
wont oft to viset you, whose comminge thogth it be oft, yet is it neuer
welcome, but notwithstanding it is comforttable for that Jacula praevisa
minus feriunt.[2] And ~~me~~ as I do vnderstande your nede of Iane Russels

2. See Saint Augustine, *Confessions,* bk. 5; *Enarratio in Psalmum XXXVII,* sec. 5.
1. *Source:* BL, MS Lansdowne 1236, fol. 39, with traces of seals. Assignment of the year is
conjectural.
2. "darts foreseen smite less" (proverbial).

seruice, so am I sory that it is by my mans occasion letted, wiche if I
had knowen afore, I wold haue caused his wil, giue place to nide of her
seruice, for as it is her duty to obey his commandement, so is it his part
to attende your pleasure, And as I confesse it wer miter for him to go to
her, sins she attendes vppon you, so indide he required the same, but
for that diuers of his felowes had busines abrode, that made his tarijnge
at home / Good Sistar thogth I haue good cause to thanke you for your
oft sendinge to me, yet I haue more occasion to rendre you my harty
thankes for your gentil writinge, wiche how painful it is to you, I may
wel gesse by my selfe, and you may wel se by my writinge so oft, how
pleasant it is to me. / And thus I ende to troble you desiring God to
sende you as wel to do, as you can thinke and I wische or I desire or
pray. From Hasherige scribled this 27th of October.

Your louinge sistar. Elizabeth

LETTER 20 ☙ PRINCESS ELIZABETH TO KING EDWARD VI,
CIRCA SPRING 1553[1]

[Addressed] To the Kinges most Excellent Maiestie.

Like as a shipman in stormy wether plukes downe the sailes tarijnge for
bettar winde, so did I, most noble Kinge, in my vnfortuna[te] chanche
a thurday[2] pluk downe the hie sailes of my ioy and comfor[t] and do
trust one day that as troblesome waues haue repulse[d] me bakwarde,
so a gentil winde wil bringe me forwarde to my hauen. Two chief
occasions moued me muche and griued me gretly, the one for that I
douted your Maiestie[s] helthe, the other bicause for al my longe
tarijnge I wente without that I came for, of the first I am ~~well~~ releued in
a parte, bothe that I vnderstode of your helthe and also that your
Maiesties loginge is far from my Lorde Marques chamber, Of my other
grief I am not eased, but the best is that whatsoeuer other folkes wil
suspect, I intende not to feare your graces goodwil, wiche as I knowe

---

1. *Source:* BL, MS Harley 6986, art. 16, fol. 23r, with traces of seals. Dating is conjectural,
based on the references to Edward's illness and to the anxiety aroused by the proximity of
the "lord marquis" (presumably Henry Grey, father of Lady Jane Grey). Square brackets enclose editorially supplied elements that have worn away at the right margin of the MS.
   2. **a thurday** on Thursday.

that I neuer disarued to faint, so I trust wil stil stike by me[.] For if your
graces aduis that I shulde retourne (whos wil is a commandemente)
had not bine, I wold not haue made the halfe of my way, the ende of my
iourney. And thus as one desirous to hire of your Maiesties helth thogth
vnfortunat[3] to se it I shal pray God for euer to preserue you. From
Hatfilde this present saterday.

> Your Maiesties humble sista[r] to commandemente.
>   Elizabeth

LETTER 22 ₰ PRINCESS ELIZABETH TO QUEEN MARY,
MARCH 17, 1554[1]

If any euer did try this olde saynge that a kinges worde was more than a
nother mans othe I most humbly beseche your Maiestie to verefie it in
me and to remember your last promis and my last demaunde that I be
not condemned without answer and due profe wiche it semes that now
I am for that without cause prouid I am by your counsel frome you
commanded to go vnto the tower a place more wonted for a false
traitor, than a tru subiect wiche thogth I knowe I deserue it not, yet in
the face of al this realme aperes that it is prouid wiche I pray god I may
dy the shamefullist dethe that euer any died afore I may mene any
suche thinge, and to this present hower I protest afor God (who shal
iuge my trueth) whatsoeuer malice shal deuis)[2] that I neuer practised
conciled nor consentid to any thinge that migth be preiudicial to your
parson any way or daungerous to the statt by any mene / and therfor I
humbly beseche your maiestie to let me answer afore your selfe and not
suffer me to trust your counselors yea and that afore I go to the tower
(if it be possible) if not afor I be further condemned; howbeit I trust
assuredly your highnes wyl giue me leue to do it afor I be go for that
thus shamfully I may not be cried out on as now I shal be yea and
without cause: let consciens moue your hithnes to take some bettar way
with me than to make me be condemned in al mens sigth afor my
desert knowen. Also I most humbly beseche your higthnes to pardon

---

3. **vnfortunat** i.e., not fortunate enough.
1. *Source:* PRO, State Papers Domestic, Mary I 11/4/2, fol. 3.
2. Elizabeth inserts an extra closing parenthesis.

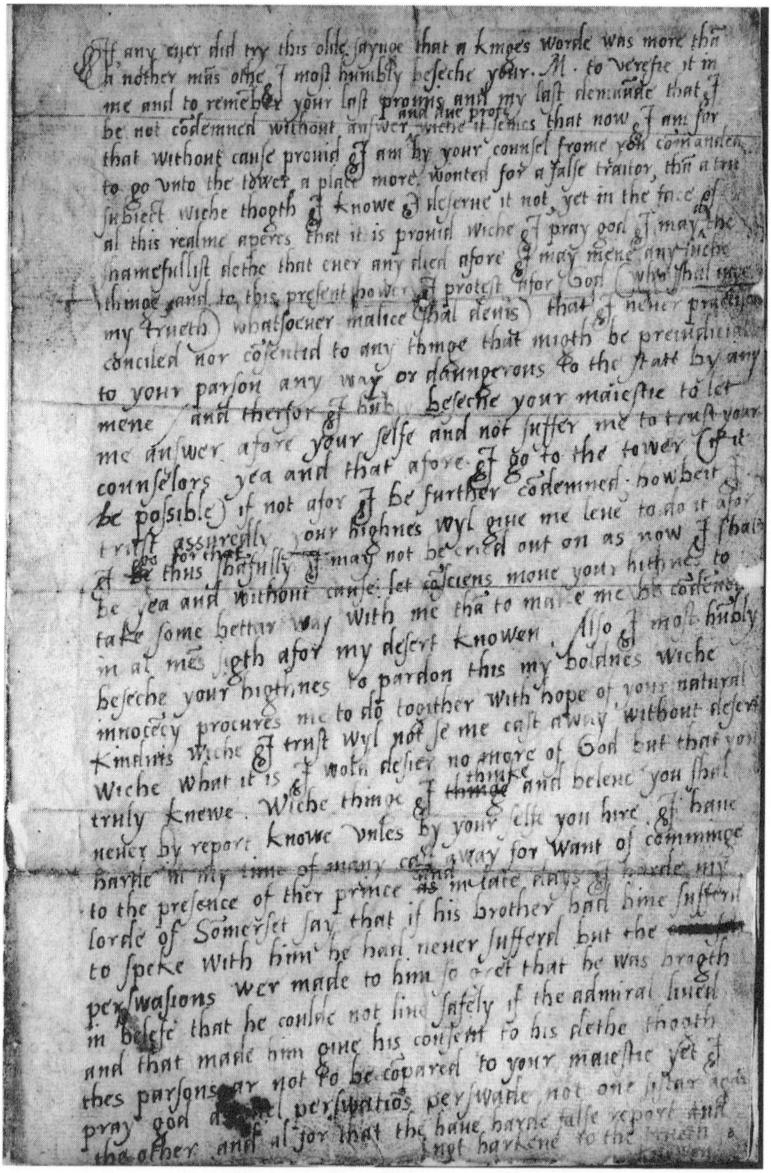

FIGURE 4   Letter 22, to Queen Mary, March 17, 1554, PRO, State Papers Domestic, Mary I, 11/4/2, fol. 3. Reproduced by permission of the Public Record Office, the National Archives, England.

therfor ons agam with hublches of my hart, bicause' J am not
suffera to bow the knees of my body J hubly crane to speke
with your higthms wiche J wolde not be so bold to desier
if J knewe not my selfe most clere as J knowe my selfe most
trn. and as for the traitor Wiat he migth parauentur writ
me a lettar but on my faithe J neuer receued any from him and
as for the copie of my lettar sent to the freche kinge J pray
God coforme me eternally if euer J sent him worde, message
toke or lettar by any menes, and to this wad my truith
J wil stande it my dethe.

J humbly crane but only one worde
of answer fro your selfe.

your highnes most faithful subiect that
hathe bine from the begininge, and wylbe
to my ende. Elizabeth

this my boldnes wiche innocency procures me to do togither with hope
of your natural kindnis wiche I trust wyl not se me cast away without
desert Wiche What it is I wold desier no more of God but that you truly
knewe. Wiche thinge I ~~thinge~~ thinke and beleue you shal neuer by
report knowe vnles by your selfe you hire. I haue harde in my time of
many cast away for want of comminge to the presence of ther prince ~~as~~
and in late days I harde my lorde of Sommerset say that if his brother
had bine sufferd to speke with him he had neuer sufferd but the ~~causes~~
perswasions wer made to him so gret that he was brogth in belefe that
he coulde not liue safely if the admiral liued and that made him giue his
consent to his dethe thogth thes parsons ar not to be compared to your
maiestie yet I pray god as iuel perswations perswade not one sistar
again[3] the other and al for that the haue harde false report and not
harkene to the trueth knowen therfor ons again kneling[4] with
humblenes of my hart, bicause I am not sufferd to bow the knees of my
body I humbly craue to speke with your higthnis wiche I wolde not be
so bold to desier if I knewe not my selfe most clere as I knowe my selfe
most tru. and as for the traitor Wiat he migth parauentur writ me a
lettar but on my faithe I neuer receued any from him and as for the
copie of my lettar sent to the frenche kinge I pray God confound me
eternally if euer I sent him word, message token or lettar by any menes,
and to this ~~and~~ my truith I wil stande in to my dethe.

[Diagonal lines fill the interval between the body of the letter and its ending, to
prevent unwanted insertions.]

I humbly craue but only one worde
of answer from your selfe

> Your highnes most faithful subiect that
> hathe bine from the beginnjnge, and wylbe
> to my ende.
>   Elizabeth

---

3. **again** against (a trimmed page edge has obliterated the word ending). The eighteenth-
century copy of this letter in Dr. Thomas Birch's papers (BL, MS Harley 7190, art. 2, fols. 125r–
126r) reads "against" at this point.

4. **kneling** above-the-line insertion mistakenly omitted in *CW*, p. 42. Fig. 4 does not
show the insertion because the top edge of the MS was not included in the photograph.

LETTER 23 ᐳ PRINCESS ELIZABETH TO QUEEN MARY,
AUGUST 2, 1556[1]

[Addressed] To the Quene's most Excelent Maiestie

Whan I revolue in mynde (most Noble Quine) the olde loue of
Painenams[2] to ther prince, and the reuerent fere of Romaines to ther
Senate, I can but muse for my parte; and blusche for thers, to se the
rebellious hartes and deuellis intentes of Christians in names, but Iues
indide, towarde ther oincted Kinge Wiche me thinkes if the had feared
God thogh the coulde not haue loued the state, the shulde for drede of
ther owne plage haue refrainned that wikkednes wiche ther bounden
duty to your Maiestie hathe not restrained: But Whan I cal to
remembrance that the deuel, tanquam leo rugiens circumit querens
quem deuorare potest[3] I do the les marveille though he haue gotten
such nouices into his professed house, as vessels (without Gods grace)
more apt to serue his palace than mite to inhabite inglische lande. I am
the bolddar to cal them his impes for that saint Poule sayeth seditiosi
filij sunt diaboli,[4] and sins I haue so good a buklar I fere the les to enter
into ther iugement. Of this I assure your Maiestie though it be my parte
aboue the rest to bewaille suche thinges though my name had not bine
in them, yet it vexeth me to muche than[5] the deuel owen me suche a
hate as to put me in any part of his mischevous instigations, Whom as I
profes him my foe, that is al christians ennemye, so wische I he had
some otherway inuented to spite me, but sins it hathe pleased God thus
to bewray ther malice afore the finische ther purpos I most humbly
thanke him bothe that he hathe euer thus preserved your Maiestie
throw his ayde muche like a lambe from the hornes of thes basans
bulles, And also sturs vp the hartes of your louinge subiects to resist
them and deliuar you, to his honor, and ther shame The intelligence of
wiche prociding from your Maiestie, deserueth more humble thankes
than with my pen I can rendre. Wiche as infinite I wil leue to number.
And amonge erthely thinges I chiefly wische this one that ther wer as
good surgions for makinge anatomies of hartes that might sheW my

1. *Source:* BL, MS Lansdowne 1236, fol. 37.
2. **Painenams** pagans.
3. "as a roaring lion goes about, seeking whom he may devour"; except for *circumit* in place
of *circuit,* an exact quotation of I Peter 5:8 in the Vulgate.
4. "The seditious are the children of the devil"; a loose paraphrase of Ephesians 2:2.
5. **than** that.

thoghtes to your Maiestie, as ther ar expert fisitians of the bodies able to expres the inwarde griues of ther maladies to ther pacient: For than I doute not, but knoWe wel, that whatsoeuer other shulde sugiect ᵇʸ malice yet your Maiestie shulde be sure by knowelege, ˢᵒ that the more suche misty cloudes offuscats the clere light of my truith, the more my tried thoghtes shulde glistar to the dimming of ther hidden malice. But sins wisches ar vain and desiars oft failes I must craue that my dides may supplye, that my thoghtes can not declare, and the be not misdeamed ther as the facts haue bine so wel tried: And like as I haue bine your faithful subiect from the beginninge of your raigne, so shal no wicked parsons cause me to change to the ende of my lief. And thus I commit your Maiestie to Gods tuicion whom I beseche longe time to preserue, ending with the new remembrance of my olde sute more for that it shulde not be forgotten, than for that I thinke it not remembrd. from Hatfilde this present sonday the seconde day of August.

> Your Maiesties obedient subiect and humble sistar.
> Elizabeth

SPEECH 6 ⧼⧽ QUEEN ELIZABETH'S ANSWER TO THE LORDS'
PETITION THAT SHE MARRY, APRIL 10, 1563, DELIVERED BY LORD
KEEPER NICHOLAS BACON[1]

S ~~his muche~~
~~muche~~ ~~A duar d~~ no
Sins Ther can be ~~never~~
~~A duer~~ dewar det than princes word: ~~ougth no man craue~~ ~~wiche for to~~
    that   the
to kipe   vnspotted for my part ~~I w~~ as one that ~~S~~ wold be lothe that ~~that~~
leste thing that
~~wiche~~ kipes the marchants credit from crase shulde be the cause that
        speche
princes ~~sainge~~ shulde merite blame and so ther honor quaile ~~and since~~

---

1. *Source:* BL, MS Lansdowne 94, art. 15B, fol. 30. Draft in a larger hand, much revised at another sitting in darker ink and smaller writing; for a photographic reproduction, see *CW*, p. 78. William Cecil's endorsement reads "10 April 1563. The Queen's spech in the Parliament, vttred by the Lord Kepar." Our formatting replicates as closely as possible the specifics of revision, but to facilitate reading, words or phrases inserted above a line of text have been brought 2.5 points closer to the line below. Elizabeth's actual compositions are much denser, with insertions squeezed tightly between the lines (see *CW*, fig. 5, p. 78).

~~vnto the peticion~~
an answer therfor I Wil make ~~answer at my behest~~ and this it is ~~The gret~~
peticions that ~~both hows~~ presented me
The two ~~longe scroles~~ that you ~~made~~ gave in many Wordes exprest
conteined thes two thinges in some as of your cares the gretest my
mariage and my successar. Of wiche two the last I thinke is best be
toched and of the other a silent thoght may serue for I had thoght it had
                                                        trees blossomes
bene so desired as ~~not~~ none others ~~fruict~~ shuld haue ~~mached~~ bine
minded   hope of my fruigt
~~mencioned~~ er ~~that~~   had bine denied you / ^

[Addition in left margin careted for insertion here:]

                                        I am
^ And by the way if any here dowte that ~~am~~ as it wer by ~~m~~ vowe or
determination bent neuer to trade that life put oute that heresie your
belefe is awry for I[2] as I thinke it best for a privat woman so do I strive
                                                        se
with my selfe to thinke it not mete for a prin~~ne~~ and if I can bend my wyl
to your nides I wyl not resist ~~in th~~ suche a mynde

[Main text resumes:]

~~and by the way~~
but to the laste thinke not that you had nided this desier if I had seen a
                            ripe
time so fit and it so ~~mete~~ to be ~~p~~ denounced. The gretenes of the cause
therfor and nide of your retournes dothe make me say that wiche I
think the wise may easely ges that as a short tyme for so longe a
continuance ought not passe by rote as many telleth tales euen so as
cause by conference with the lerned shal showe anie matter worthy
                                    ~~as manie menne~~ more
vtterance for your beholfes so shal I   gladly pursue your
                        than with   ~~whiche I craue than~~
good aftir my dayes ~~than with~~ my prayers ~~mi~~ be a meane to lingar my
liuing threde / And this moche more than I had thogth wil I ~~f~~ adde for
                                                        menes
your comfort. I haue good record in this place that other ~~wais~~

2. I inserted halfway below the line of writing.

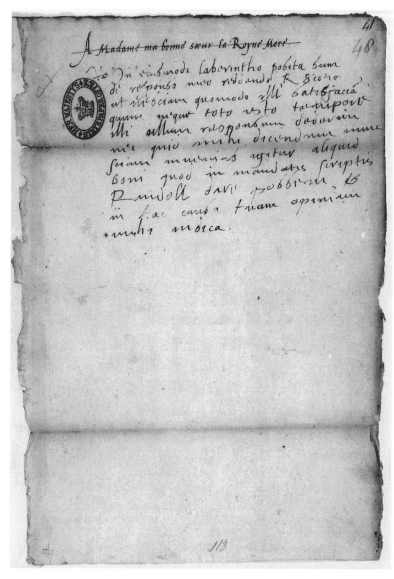

A Madame ma bonne sœur la Royne Mere

In eiusmode Laberintho posita sum
de responso nunc reddendo R Scoto
ut nesciam quomodo illi satisfaciá
quum neque toto isto tempore
illi ullum responsum dederim
nec quid nunc dicendum sum
sciam muneriis igitur aliquid
boni quod in mandatis scriptis
Randolf dari possunt. &
in hac causa tuam opinionem
mihi mora.

FIGURE 5   Letter 26, to William Cecil, September 23, 1564; PRO, State Papers Scotland,
Elizabeth, 1564, 52/9/65, fol. 113r. Reproduced by permission of the Public Record Office,
the National Archives, England.

than you mencioned
    haue bine thoght of perchanche for your good as muche and for
                    conveniently   executed
my surty no les. / wiche if presently coulde   haue bine ~~finisshed~~ had
                in quiet
not bine differd. but I hope I shal die   with nunc dimittis wiche can
not be without I se some chanses of your folowing surty after my
grave[d][3] bones

LETTER 26 ?? QUEEN ELIZABETH TO WILLIAM CECIL,
PRINCIPAL MINISTER, SEPTEMBER 23, 1564[1]

~~A Madame ma bonne soeur la Royne Mere.~~

~~Ve~~ In eiusmodi Laberintho posita sum de responso meo reddendo
Reginae Scotiae ut nesciam quomodo illi satisfaciam quum neque toto
esto[2] tempore illi nullum responsum dederim nec quid mihi dicendum
nunc sciam inuenias igitur aliquid boni quod in mandatis scriptis
Randoll dare possvm et in hac causa tuam opinionum mihi indica.

POEM 4 ?? NO CROOKED LEG, CIRCA 1565[1]

No croked legge no blered
eye no part deformed out
of kinde nor yet so ouglye
halfe can be as is the inward
suspicious minde.
       Your Lovinge
       maistres.
       Elizabeth R

3. "d" supplied conjecturally because of worn page edge.
1. *Source:* PRO, State Papers Scotland, Elizabeth, 1564, 52/9/48, fol. 113r. A Latin note in Elizabeth's hand, using a sheet on which she had started a letter to Catherine de Médicis, queen
mother of France, in her best italic. William Cecil's endorsement reads "23 September, 1564,
at Saint James'. The Queen wryting to me being sick. Scotland."
2. **esto** isto.
1. *Source:* Windsor Castle, Royal Library; reproduced with the gracious permission of
Queen Elizabeth II. Elizabeth I entered these lines on the last leaf of her French psalter, a

SPEECH 9, VERSION 1 ᘒᕯ QUEEN ELIZABETH'S SPEECH TO A JOINT
DELEGATION OF LORDS AND COMMONS, NOVEMBER 5, 1566[1]

If the order of your causes had mached the waight of your matter the
one might wel ^haue^ craued reward and the other muche the soner
satisfied but Whan I call to mynd how ~~far of frome a princely hart~~ far
from dutiful care ~~and~~ yea rather ^how^ ny a traiterous trik this tumbling
cast ~~b~~ did springe ^I muse^ how ~~muche~~ ^men^ of Wit can so hardly use that
gift the hold ~~To be~~ I maruel not ~~at~~ muche that brideles colts do not
knowe ther ridars hand Whome bit of kingely raine did neuer snafle
yet /[2] Whither it was fit that so great a cause as this shuld haue had his
beginning in suche a publik place ~~as wher~~ as that let ^it^ be well waighed
~~if all of~~ must all iuel bodings that might be recited ~~was~~ ^be^ founde litel
inough to hap to my share ~~let~~ Was it wel ment think you that those that
knewe not how fit this mattere was to be graunted by the Prince wold
preiudicat ther Prince in agrauating the matter so all ther arguments
tended to my careles care of this my dere realme

SPEECH 9, ADDITIONAL DOCUMENT C ᘒᕯ QUEEN ELIZABETH'S
DIRECTIONS TO CECIL FOR LIFTING HER PREVIOUS ORDER
FORBIDDING THE HOUSE OF COMMONS TO DEBATE MATTERS
CONCERNING THE SUCCESSION, NOVEMBER 24, 1566[1]

The Queens Maiesty hath commanded me to lett you vnderstand, that
wheras shortly after she had gyven hir answer to certen of the Lords
and ~~of~~ certen of this howse, in the matters intended to have bene

---

duodecimo, black-letter volume that cannot be readily identified because it has lost its front
leaves. This may be the "obscure sentence" referred to by Burghley as written by the queen
in "a book at Windsor" when she was "much offended with the earl of Leicester" in August 1565; hence our dating.

   1. *Source:* PRO, State Papers Domestic, Elizabeth 12/41/5. William Cecil's endorsement
reads "a part of the begynning of the Queen's Majesty's spech to 30 lords and 30 commons
on Tuesday the vth of November 1566. Anno regni 8. The Queens own hand."

   2. The MS mark here is a curved slash (virgule) that closely resembles a long *s*, possibly
with a looped ending.

   1. *Source:* PRO, State Papers Domestic, Elizabeth, 12/41/30, fol. 61. Text, heading, and endorsement in William Cecil's hand, with corrections in Elizabeth's hand indicated by the
underlined insertions and their accompanying deletion marks. The heading reads "24
Nouember. To be declared to the Comen hows by the spekar." The endorsement reads "24.

required of hir Maiesty, as the ~~tyme~~ necessite of the tyme and other weighty considerations presently moved hir, vppon ~~information gyven to hir that~~ the sight of certain ~~mater~~ matters Wiche some persons intended ~~to propov~~ vnder pretence of dealyng in the former svte, to propovnd ~~certen speciall matters~~ in this hows touchyng the Crowne of this realme, very vnmete for the tyme and place, and ~~very~~ certenly danngeroos to the comen quietnes of hir subiectes now assembled, did by ~~send~~ hir Maiesties Commandment will ~~that~~ yow all to stay your procedyng any furder in the sayd matter ~~in~~ at this tyme, and now being informed by such of this howss as she hath cause[2] to creditt, that ther ~~nether was nor~~ is not now any determination of this howse, to receave or allow any such danngeroos matter as she befor did dout, is therefor pleased to ~~remove~~ delyver yow ~~herewith~~ at this time hir formar Commandmentes, not dowtyng but yow will be answerable in your whole doynges, to the good opinion which hir Maiesty is induced to conceave of yow in this behalf. and thynketh it good that yow have regard ~~in~~ to the expedition of the matters ~~of~~ of most moment remaynyng amongst yow, consideryng the expence of the tyme past, and the shortnes of that which is now to come, the term endyng also so shortly as it shall

SPEECH 9, ADDITIONAL DOCUMENT D ❧ PART OF A SUBSIDY BILL SENT BY PARLIAMENT TO QUEEN ELIZABETH, WITH HER ANGRY ANNOTATIONS, NOVEMBER 29, 1566[1]

[The bill's third section is followed by two half-lines of marks like letters, ending in "*Anno.* 1566." This is the mock-up of the signed writ that the Commons wants from the queen in return for the subsidy they will grant her. The lower four inches

---

November 1566 anno 9. The report of the Queen Maiesties messadg to the Comon hows. for delyveryng of the same from a tumult. ~~anno 8º 9º Elizabeth.~~"

2. **cause** *CW,* p. 101, mistakenly reads "come."

1. *Source:* BL, MS Lansdowne 1236, art. 27, fol. 42. Elizabeth began with emphasis marks, dark carets inserted in the text addressed to her, and turned to commentary at the foot of the sheet, continuing onto the back. For a photographic reproduction, see Joel Hurstfield, *The Elizabethan Nation* (London: BBC, 1964), p. 53. Endorsements in three different hands read "1566."; "Touching the declaration of a Successor to the Crown."; and "Queen Elizabeth's running hand." The last is a reference to the near-illegibility of her hasty italic at points here.

of the page had been left blank. In this space and continuing on the back, Elizabeth scrawls roughly:]

set thes two ~~writ~~ concernings into one mening and my counsell is all
giuen let not other regard them selues so holy as I haue no corner left
for me let them knowe that I knewe thogh I folowed ~~nottt~~ not that some
of them wold my ~~poure~~ conscience bettar served me thatt ther lewde
practises could auaille with me / I knowe no reason whi ony my privat
answers to the realme shuld be made for ~~preamble~~ prologe to a
subsides bote nether not do I vnderstand why suche audacitie shuld be
vsed to make without my licence an acte of my wordes ar my wordes
like lawiers bokes wiche ~~d~~ now a dayes go to the wiar drawers to make
subtall doings more plain is ther no hold of my speche ~~on~~ without a
acte compel me to confirme shall my princely consent be turned to
strenghen my wordes that be not of them selues substantiues ~~Ther is~~ I
say[2] no more at this time but if thes felowes wer wel answered and
payed with lawfull coyne ther wold be fewer counterfaits amonge
them /

SPEECH 10, VERSION 1 ❧ QUEEN ELIZABETH'S SPEECH
DISSOLVING PARLIAMENT, JANUARY 2, 1567[1]

I loue so iuelL[2] counterfaitting and hate so muche dissemulation that I
may not suffer you depart without that my admonitions may shewe
your harmes and cause you[3] shun vnseen perilL. / Two ~~clokes~~ visars
haue blinded the yees of the lokers one in this present session so far
furthe as vnder pretence of safing all the haue done none good. And
thes the be / Succession and liberties. As to the first the princes opinion
and good WylL ought in good ordar haue bine felt in other sort than in
so publik a place ~~ons to~~ be vttered it had bine convenient that so

2. **I say** "I" mistakenly omitted in *CW*, p. 103.

1. *Source:* BL, MS Cotton Charter IV.38 (2), formerly Cotton Titus F.I, fol. 92. For a photographic reproduction, see *CW*, p. 104. The heading contains an evident dating error, "1563
5th Elizabeth" (instead of "1567 9th Elizabeth"), and a memorandum in the same hand at the
bottom of the verso page reads "All this Letter was the Queens owne hand and the draft she
framed her selfe."

2. **iuelL** alternatively, "welL" (what would be the *i* is undotted).

3. **you** addition inserted in left margin.

Waighty a cause had had his originalL, from a ^zelous^ princes
considerations not ^from^ ~~of a~~ so ^lippe^ labored orations out of suche
~~iangling~~ subiectz mouthes Wiche What the be time may teache you
Knowe and ther demerites wyl make them acknowlege / hoW the haue
done ther leWde indeVour to make alL my realme suppose that ther
care Was muche Whan myne was none at alL. ther handeling of this
dothe ^welL^ shewe the being ^holy^ ignorant hoW fit my graunt ~~Was~~ ^at^
^this time^ shuld be to suche a demaund in ^this^ one thinge ~~the~~ ^ ther
imperfaict dealings ar to be excused for I think this be the first time
that so Waighty a cause passed from so simple ^mens^ mouthes ^as began
this cause /^ ^as^ to liberties Who is so simple that doutes Whither A
prince that ~~his~~ hed of alL the body may not command the fete not to
stray Whan the wold slip God forbid that your liberty shuld make my
bondage ^ or that your laWfuL liberties shuld any Wais haue bine
infringed ^no no^ ^ my commandement ~~brake~~ tended no Whit ~~therof~~ to
^that ende^ you Wer sore seduced ~~and~~ you haue met With a gentiL prince
els your nideles scruple ~~had~~ ^might^ perchaunce haue brede your caused
blame ^

[At this point Elizabeth keys in with carets two successive additions to her main
text, both written sideways in the left margin.]

^ ~~as~~ if I had not more pitied you than blamed ^you^ ^ the laWfullnis of
wiche commandement ^might easely by good right be shewed you
perchanse to ther shame that brede ^you^ that colored ^dout^

[Main text resumes:]

   And albeit the southing of suche be reproVable in alL yet I Wold not
you should thingke my simplicitie suche as I can not make distinctions
amonge ^you^ as of some ^that ~~p~~broched the Vessel not wel fined and
began thes attemps not forseeinge Wel the ~~e~~ ende ^others[4]^ that respected
the necessary factes of the matters and no whit Vnderstode
circumstanssis expedient not to haue bine forgotten therin, others
Whos eares wer deluded by pleasing perswations of comen good Whan
the very yelding to ther owne inVentions might haue bred alL your
Woes others Whos capacities I suppose yelded ther iugement to ther

---

4. **others** addition inserted in left margin.

frindes WiL some other that serued an Ecchoes place WelL amonge
alL thes sondry affects I assure you ther be none the beginnars only
except Whom I ether condemne for iuelL mynded to me or do suspect
not to be my most loyalL subiects therfor I conclud with this oppinion
Wiche I WylL you to think Vnfainedly tru that as I haue tried that you
may be deceaV[5] so am I perswaded you WilL not begile the assured ioy
that euer I toke to se my subiects loVe to me more staunche than ever I
felt the care in my self for my selfe to be great wiche alone hathe made
my heuy burden light and a kingedomes care but easy cariagge for me
~~wiche yf I kept not more for conscience than for glory I could Willingly
Wische a wisar my rome~~[6]

 Let this my displang stand you in stede of sorar strokes neVer to
tempt to far a princes ~~poW~~ paciens and let my comfort pluk up your
dismayed sprites and cause you think that ∧ in hope that your
foloWing ~~d~~ behauors shall make amends for part of this you retorne
With your princes graces. ~~and~~ ~~of~~ ~~w~~ Whose care for you doubt you not
to be suche as she shalL not nide a remembrancer for your Wele/

LETTER 33 ❧ QUEEN ELIZABETH TO WILLIAM CECIL, LORD
BURGHLEY, APRIL 11, 1572[1]

My Lord me thinkes that I am more beholdinge to the hindar part of
my hed than wel dare trust the forewards side of the same, and therfor
sent to the Leuetenant and the Serjeant as you knowe best the ordar to
defar this execution till the here furdar and that this may be done I
doute nothinge without curiocitie of my further warrant for that ther
rasche determination upon a very unfit day was countermaunded by
your considerat admonition the causes that moue me to this ar not now

---

5. **deceaV** final letters of the word may be hidden under the binding.

6. The sentiment cancelled here will first find public utterance in Elizabeth's speech responding to the first Parliamentary petitions for executing Mary, Queen of Scots, November 12, 1586; see Speech 17, p. 69, below.

1. *Source:* Bodleian Library, University of Oxford, MS Ashmole 1729, art. 7, fol. 13. Burghley's endorsement reads "11 April 1572. The Queen's Majesty with her own hand for staying of the execution of the D. O. [N.] Received at 2 in the morning." We supply the "N" from an eighteenth-century copy, Bodleian, MS Smith 68, art. 54, fol. 54.

to be expressed lest an irreuocable dede be in mene while committed. If the wyl nides a Warrant let this suffice all writen with my none hand.

Your most lovinge soveraine

Elizabeth R[2]

LETTER 36, POSTSCRIPT ❧ QUEEN ELIZABETH TO GEORGE TALBOT, EARL OF SHREWSBURY, OCTOBER 22, 1572[1]

My faithfuLL ShreWesbury Let no grief touche your harte for feare of my disease for I Assure you if my creadit Wer not greatar than my ~~my~~ shewe, ther is no beholdar Wold beleve that ever I had bin touched With suche a maladye/

Your faithefuL Lovinge Soveraine Elizabeth R

LETTER 41, SUPERSCRIPTION ❧ QUEEN ELIZABETH TO GEORGE AND ELIZABETH TALBOT, EARL AND COUNTESS OF SHREWSBURY, JUNE 25, 1577[1]

Your most Assured Lovinge Cousin and Soverayne/

Elizabeth R

2. **R** mistakenly omitted in *CW,* p. 131. We thank Katherine Duncan-Jones for this correction.

1. *Source:* Lambeth Palace Library MS 3197, fol. 41r; remnants of a seal attached. Reproduced with the permission of the Archbishop of Canterbury. For a photographic reproduction, see *CW,* p. 213.

1. *Source:* Lambeth Palace Library, MS 3206, fol. 819; remnants of a seal attached and slits for ribbon. Reproduced with the permission of the Archbishop of Canterbury. For a photographic reproduction, see *CW,* p. 228.

PRAYERS 30–35
Queen Elizabeth's Prayer Book, circa 1579–82[1]

PRAYER 30 𝄞 THE FIRST ENGLISH PRAYER [SIGS. 3R–8R]

O moste Glorious **K**inge, and **C**reator of the whole worlde, to whome all thinges be subiect, both in heauen and earth, and all best **P**rinces most gladlie obaie. **H**eare the most humble voice of thie handmaide, in this onelie happie, to be so accepted. **H**ow excedinge is thie goodnes, and how great myne offences? **O**f nothing hast thow made me not a worme, but a **C**reature according to thine owne image, [inverts Psalm 22:6] heaping all the blessinges vpon me that men on earth holde most

1. *Source:* BL, MS Facsimile 218, sigs. 3r–36r, a tiny volume measuring 2 by 3 inches in what has consistently been regarded as Elizabeth's formal italic hand; photocopy of original, which was lost at the beginning of the twentieth century. See our source note in *CW,* pp. 311–12. Sig. 1v has a portrait miniature of Monsieur (reproduced in *CW,* p. 312), and sig. 38r has a portrait miniature of Elizabeth (reproduced in *CW,* p. 320). To avoid what would otherwise be a plethora of footnotes, square brackets at the end of a clause or versicle enclose references for biblical citations and, where applicable, a statement of the adaptation performed.

Portions of this text display a system of embellishment that became popular in italic handwriting between the mid-sixteenth and the mid-seventeenth century. It is known as "testigiatta" (headed), after the curved, club-like onsets for such letters as *b, c, d, f, h, k, l,* and long *s;* see the elegant illustration in Anthony G. Petti, *English Literary Hands from Chaucer to Dryden* (Cambridge, Mass.: Harvard University Press, 1977), p. 19, fig. 25. Among styles of formal italic, Petti groups beside testigiatta what he calls the "hybrid form of *cancellaresca . . .* practised by Queen Elizabeth from her early youth" (ibid., p. 19). Heavily traced letters added after the text was written—some of them with testigiatta embellishments—are signaled by boldface in our transcription below.

In a yet unpublished conference presentation ("The Queen's Own Hand," July 2001), H. R. Woudhuysen has disputed the identification of the prayer book hand as Elizabeth's. He inclines, instead, to identify the hand as that of John Palmer, who matriculated at Trinity College, Cambridge, in 1575, and became a fellow in 1582; he died in 1614. There are no known connections between Palmer and Elizabeth. While the prayer book hand and Palmer's hand show some strikingly similar features (especially the forming of *E, D,* and *P,* and of terminal *e* and *s*) as well as similarities shared jointly with Elizabeth's Shrewsbury inscriptions (the forming of *A* and *C*), there are also certain clear dissimilarities between the prayer book text and Palmer (especially the prayer book's *g, ss, st,* and *-L,* which tally with Elizabeth's characteristic inscriptional forms in other writings). The evidence presented thus far, therefore, is somewhat equivocal.

The issue of ascription is further complicated by the lack of any temporally close instances of Elizabeth's formal italic hand from the period of the prayer book (1579–82), beyond the two short Shrewsbury inscriptions of 1577. At present, Marcus aligns with Woudhuysen, while Mueller finds insufficient reason to exclude the girdle prayer book from the category of Elizabeth's autograph compositions.

happie. Drawing my blood from Kinges and my bringing vp in vertue:
giuing me that more is, euen in my youth knowledge of thie truthe: and
in times of most danger, most gracious deliuerance: pulling me from
the prison to the pallace: and placing me a Soueraigne Princesse ouer
thie people of England. And aboue all this, making me (though a
weake woman) yet thy instrument, to set forth the glorious Gospell of
thy deare Sonne Christ Ihesus. Thus in theis last and worst daies of the
world, when warres and seditions with grieuous persecutions haue
vexed almost all Kinges and Contries, round about me, my raigne hath
been peaceable, and my Realme a receptacle to thie afflicted churche.
The loue of my people hath appeared firme, and the deuises of myne
enemies frustrate. Now for theis and other thy benefites (ô Lord of all
goodnes) what haue I rendred to the? [Psalm 116:12] Forgetfulnes,
vnthankfulnes, and greate disobedience. I should haue magnified the
I haue neglected the. I should haue praied vnto the, I haue forgotton
the. I shoulde haue serued the, I haue sinned against the. This is my
case. Then where is my hope? If thow Lorde wilt be extreame, to marke
what is doon amisse, who may abide it? [echoes Nahum 1:6] But thou
art gracious and mercifull, [Psalm 103:8] longe suffering, and of greate
goodnes, not delighting in the death of a Sinner. Thou seest whereof
I came, of corrupt seede: what I am, a most frail substance: where I
liue in the worlde full of wickednes: where delightes be snares, where
dangers be imminent, where sinne raigneth, and death abideth. This
is my state. Now whear is my comforte? In the depth of my miserie I
knowe no helpe (ô Lorde) but the height of thy mercie, who hast sent
thine onelie Sonne into the worlde, to saue sinners. [echoes 1 John 4:9,
10] This God of my life, and life of my soule, the King of all comfort, is
my onelie refuge. For his sake therefore, to whome thou hast giuen all
powre, and wilt denie no petition, heare my praiers. Turne thie face
from my sinnes (ô Lorde) [echoes Psalm 51:9] and thine eies to thy
handyworke. Create a cleane heart, and renew a right spirite within me.
[Psalm 51:10] Order my steppes in thie worde, that no wickednes haue
dominion ouer me, make me obedient to thie will, and delite in thy law.
[echoes Psalm 119:16] Graunt me grace to liue godlie and to gouerne
iustlie: that so liuing to please the, and raigning to serue the I maie euer
glorifie the the Father of all goodnes and mercie. To whome with thy
dear sonne, my onely Sauiour, and the Holie Ghost my Sanctifier, thre
persons and one God: be all prais dominion and powre, world without
end. AMEN

PRAYER 31 ❧ THE FRENCH PRAYER [SIGS. 8v–14v]

Mon Dieu et mon pere puie qu'il ta pleu desployer les tresore[2] de ta
grande miserecorde enuers moy ta tres humble seruante m'ayant de
Bon matin retiree des profons abismes de l'ignorance naturelle et des
supperstitions damnables pour me fair iouïr de ce grand soleil de
Iustice qui apporte en ses rayons Vie et Salut. Or ce pendant laissez
encores tant de Rois, Princes et Princesses en l'ignorance soubz la
puissance de Satan, dont ie te loueray en magnifiant ton nom, o mon
Pere: et chanteray Psaulmes auec ceulx qui craignent ta Maiesté, et
aussi long temps que i'auray vie. Car tu es mon seigneur et mon Roy,
ie raconteray a la posterité, auec liesse les effectz de ta singuliere bonté.
C'est toy qui m'as esleué et exalté par ta prouidence au Trosne, et m'as
Souronnée[3] de pais, a celle fin que ie gouuerne mon peuple et nourisse
ton Esglise. Ie te remercie mon bon dieu de l'honneur que tu m'as
faict, et ie te suplie me faire la grace: que ie m'acquiste de mon deuoir
gouuernant bien l'estat et administrant fidelement la iustice: sans auoir
exception des personnes, et ainsi ie sentiray auec mes subiects ta tres
saincte benediction de laquelle ie cognoy estre venieu la Paix
accompagnée de beaucoux des biens, de laquelle iusqu'a maintenant,
a ton honneur et soulagement de ton esglise, i'ay iouy ce pendant mes
plus proches Voisins ont senti les maulx de la guerre sanglante et les
poures enfans persecutez ont trouvé auec repos aseuree demeure
donc mon Dieu et Pere ie te rend graces immortelles de m'auoir fait
l'honneur d'estre Mere et nourice de tes chers enfans. Certes c'est toy
ô mon Sauueur qui m'as donné auec la puissance la volonte de faire
les choses par lesquelles tu as verifie tes   aintes[4] promesses et as faict
sentir les effectz de tes singulieres Bontez a les Seruiteurs et a ton peuple.
Poursui doncq Seigneur de te seruir de moy me rendant volontaire à
auancer ton regne. Et pour ce que ie cognoy a la verité que ie ne me suis
entierement acquitée de ma charge, ne faict valoir les dons desquelz tu
m'as ornée, faisant tout effort a te seruir et honnorer selon ta sainte
Parolle, ie confesse sans hipocrisie, que ie ne merite pas, d'estre seruië et

2. **tresore** tresors.

3. **Souronnée** Couronnée.

4. **tes aintes** tes saintes. A large space intervenes between these two words, which suggests
a plan to insert a majuscule S in a separate operation (as a medieval scribe would have done);
however, the insertion was not made. The S intended here may have been inserted in the
place of the C needed above (see n. 3).

honnorée ainsi a iammais couuerte d'ignominië, et de tous
abandonnée: Neanatmoins tu cognois que i'en suis marrië, et bien
dollente, s'a esté innfirmité humaine. Helas mon Dieu ne me iuge pas,
selon mes oeuures, car elles sont comtaminées. ainsi me regarde des
ieulx de ta Paternelle clemence, ie cognoy et confesse comme la verité
est, que ie t'ay offencé en plusieurs sortes, ayez donc mercy de moy et
me pardonne selon tes promesses. Car tu es mon pere, ie cognoy mes
transgressions et mes pechez noirs et sanglants, sont coustumierement
deuant moy pour m'epouanter mais tu m'asseures par ta parole et
vertu de ton Esprit. Cest contre toy, c'est contre toy seul que i'ay péché,
[echoes Psalm 51:4] faisant et permettant par negligence faire mal contre
tes lois, de sorte que si tu me punissois auec tout mon peuple bien
asprement, ie confesse l auoir bien merité Certes ie confesse l auoir bien
merité, ce seroit a bon droit tes iugemens seroyent trouué iustes,
neantmoins, qu'il te souuiénne de tes anciennes bontez, et me fais grace
selon ta clemence, et grandes compassions. poursui donc mon bon
Dieu, pour l amour de toy, et de ton cher filz de me faire sentir tes
benedictions, me gouuernant et defendant moy et mon peuple de tous
mes ennemis, qui sont aduersaires de ta verité et qui se leuent contre
ton christ, machinans tousiours trahison comme ouuriers d'iniquité.
Conserue donc la mere et les enfans que luy as donné, ainsi nous te
seruirons encore mieulx, au bien de ta poure Eglise. Monstre ô mon
Seigneur et pere, aulx ennemis de ta verité; ta force et leurs fais
cognoistre que toy seul regnez vestu de magnificence qui enuironnes
ton Eglise comme de haultes montagnes de la vertu de laquelle tu es
ceinct. Vueille donc par ta misericorde rendre ferme et stable le Throne
auquel tu m'as esleuee, le soutenant par ta grande puissance et donne
bons aduis et conseils a mes conseilliers et fidelite a tous mes seruiteurs
et a moy Souci amour constance et Discretion, a receuoir les conseilz de
mes fideles seruiteurs. Et pource faire donnez nous plus abondamment
des graces de ton Esprit, a fin ô mon roy Roy[5] que nous nous iections
entre tes bras nous laissant conduire de toy et viuans sans crainte de noz
ennemis / te seruions tous les iours de nostre vie renonçant au monde et
a toutes les vanitez d'ycelluy, tendans au but de la supernelle vocation
Exauce moy mon Dieu et Pere par Iesus Christ ton cher   ilz[6] **Amen.**

---

5. **roy Roy** repetition in the body of the text, across a page break. Since the text is format-
ted with catchwords also, "roy" occurs a total of three times.

6. **ilz** filz. Another large space suggests another omitted majuscule—here, *F.*

PRAYER 32 ॐ THE ITALIAN PRAYER [SIGS. 15R–20V]

Riconoscendo veramente sinceramente io confesso hauer date solo o sommo Imperador e clementissimo mio Padre riceuuto il settro e la corona, epercio, hora quanto pui[7] humilmente posso mi presento dauanti al trono sacro della tua altissima Maesta, nella cui presentia. Lasu[8] alto in cielo, pregando qui in terra le ginocchia spando il mio humile e contrito Cuore qual mi sento trafitto da vn vero sentimento di tanti mei e si fatti errori e peccati quali confesso rendermi indigna della vita eterna, non die della reale dignità. Ma perche io misento e conosco chiamata ueramente alla certa cognitione del tuo diletto figliuolo e da te fonte de vita prendo ardire ne suoi soli meriti appoggiata di consecrarti il mio scettro, e supplicarti come mio benignissimo Padre, di non voler venire meco in guidicio. Hoime chi potrà mai consistere nella tua presentia se suoi delitti non gli saranno gratuitamente perdonati e la perfetta eintiera giustitia del tuo Christo imputata. Degnati donque aprire gli ampli tesori della tua misericordia accio che io sia liberata da tanta miseria e ensieme scoprimi i viui fonte laode[9] io sia purgata e fatta netta da tutte le mie macchie di pecato per la vertù delle aque pure e munde che sono nele[10] tuoi sacri fonti e cosi fatta netta sarò finalmente riceuuta ne tuoi eterni padiglioni ne quali habitando teco ô mio dolce Signore perpetuamente con i santi Re contemplaro la tua serena faccia godendomi felicissima e contenta la vita sempiterna. E mentre tipiacera ô mio sommo Imperadore lasciarmi uiua in terra ti supplico tenermi sotolombra delle ali della tua diuina potentia: [echoes Psalm 61:4] come tu ai fatto con man potente dopoi la mia fanciulza[11] liberandomi de mille mortali pericoli, gouernandomi sempre con il tuo santo spirito auenga che colui solo e[12] securo che habita nel secreto de laltissimo e loggia nel ombra del omnipotente, [echoes Psalm 91:1] e ha per scudo la verita santa. Hor tu sei laltissimo e omnipotente Dio pero à te solo ho posta la speranca mia. [Psalm 31:1] Fa Signor chio non sia confusa io sento hauere bisogno in questa mia vocatione essendo io debole e sogetta all

7. **pui** piú.
8. **Lasu** La sú.
9. **fonte laode** fonti laonde.
10. **nele** nei.
11. **fanciulza** fanciuleza.
12. **e** è.

humana ingnorantia: di buoni auisi, di consigli saui e pronti soccorsi in
ogni tempo massima quando venissi ad essere combattuta d'impetuosi
venti e fiere tempeste ache soglion essere sogetti i Re Christiani
hauendo per inimico il mondo assogettito a quel fiero lion rogente che
circondando sempre cerca preda. [echoes 1 Peter 5:8, 9] E bench[13] mi
goda ancora la pace che tu mi hai donata come clementissimo mio
Padre nondimeno so soprastarmi graui e mortali pericoli hauendo di
molti nimici che sono aduersarij della tua verita qual ho in questo mio
regno riceuuta. Però mio sommo pastore difendimi: tu sei il fortissimo
dio degli exerciti talche tu mi puoi defendere solo: come altresi
consigliarmi in ogni mea difficultà, essendo sapientissimo. Tu fai quelo
che tu voi in cielo e interra e tuoi consigli sono fermi estabili
erendonvani gl' humani fallaci. Donque Signiore mio fammi sentire
pui che mai la tua gratia, ei diuini fauori: accio che io aspettando il
giorno della mia partita seruendoti, glorifichi il tuo santo nome. E cosi
finalmente riceua la corona incorrutibile esaudiscimi mio soauissimo e
potentissimo Padre per il tuo diletto figliuolo mio Saluatore Amen.

PRAYER 33 ☙ THE LATIN PRAYER [SIGS. 21R–26V]

Domine Deus, aeterne Pater, cuius est potentia imperium et gloria:
[adapts Matthew 6:13] qui es super omnia, per omnia et in omnibus:
per quem reges regnant et principes dominantur in terris: [echoes
Proverbs 8:15] qui omnia imperio et potestati hominis subiecisti vt se
totum homo sub potestatem verbi et voluntatis tuae subijciat: iudicia
tua da mihi **Regina**[14] vt iudicem populum tuum in iustitia et pauperes
tuos in iudicio. [echoes Psalm 72:1, 2] Fragile corpus animum opprimit
et terrenum domicilium tardat mentem multa cogitantem, nec inter
homines natos quisquam tuum consilium nouit aut mentem tuam
intelligit, nisi tu prius dederis sapientiam et diuino spiritu tuo illum
afflaueris. **D**a mihi ancillae tuae cor docile, vt sciam quid acceptum sit
coram te: mitte de celo spiritum sapientiae tuae et illius ductu cor
meum rege. [echoes Psalm 19:14] **O** beatum illum quem tu instruis
Domine, et in voluntate tua doctum facis: sine qua nec bene mihi velle,

13. **bench** benche.
14. **mihi Regina** mihi Reginae

nec alijs benefacere, nec parere tibi pro officio, nec imperare populo
cum aequitate valeo. Quamobrem potentissime Rex, et Pater
clementissime, accedo suplex ad thronum gratiae tuae, coram scabello
pedum tuorum flecto genua, manus attollo, intendo oculos, fundo
verba, pectus tundo, corpus animumque prosterno, ex animo quàm
possum demisissimè petens vt spiritus tuus doceat me et erudiat me
in omnibus viis tuis: vt magis mihi placeat sapientia tua quàm millia
auri et argenti. [echoes Psalm 119:33, 72] Imperti domine spiritum
tuum sanctum, qui mihi semper et ubique adsit, me gubernet et ad ea
sola meditanda, tractanda, constituenda decernenda dirigat et impellat
quae ad nominis tui laudem, ecclesiae commodum reique publicae
vtilitatem spectent. Sic sapientiae tuae opibus instructum[15] alijs adsim,
vt mihi non desim, sic alios sceptro regam vt mihi tuo verbo imperem:
in republica moderanda sic dominetur carni anima animae ratio,
rationi fides, fidei gratia tua, vt mihi nihil placeat quod tibi displiceat:
nihil mihi sapiat quod verbo tuo non arrideat. Verbum tuum Domine
sit oculis meis lux, lucerna pedibus, mel ori, auribus melos, cordi
iubilus: sit lumbis meis cingulum veritatis, pectori lorica iustitiae,
capiti galea salutis, manui dextrae gladius spiritus, sinistrae scutum
fidei, toti denique corpori armatura dei.[16] Sit animae salus; vitae
praesidium, spes in metu, in amore delitia, in cibo pastus, quies in
somno, in vigilia cogitatio, pax in conscientia in consilio prudentia,
in seueritate moderatio, in clementia aequitas, in vtroque aequabilitas:
regula in iudicio, in consultatione oraculum, in bello fortitudo, gloria
in pace, in certamine victoria, in victoria triumphus. Sit in manu mea
sceptrum, in capite diadema, in solio maiestas et in toto meo imperio
mea gloria mea beatitas. Tui solius prae caeteris omnibus amore, bone
Iesu, cor meum ardeat, memoria vigeat, ratio intelligat, mens sapiat,
totus animus gestiat, et gaudio exiliat spiritus, vt te sequar, in lege tua
vt ducem, in verbo audiam vt praeceptorem, amem in promissis
vt patrem, in beneficijs honorem vt regem, in operibus colam vt
creatorem, timeam in minis vt dominum, in meritis amplectar vt
seruatorem, in dictis, factis, cogitatis omnibus glorificem vt deum:
cui cum Patre et Spiritu sancto sit omnis honos gloria et maiestas in
omnem aeternitatem. Amen.

15. **instructum** should read "instructam" as self-reference.
16. This catalogue of images draws on Psalm 119:105, 103; Psalm 40:6, 8; and Ephesians 6:14, 16, 17.

PRAYER 34 ☙ THE GREEK PRAYER [SIGS. 27R–30R]

ῚΟΤΑΝ μὲν πρὸς τὰ κακὰ τοῦ κόσμου τούτου ἀναβλέψω καὶ τὰς
πράξεις φαύλων μῖσος ἐχθρῶν τοὺς ἀσεβῶν κινδύνους καὶ
τεχνάσματα, δόλερα κατίδω¹⁷ ἐν οἷς διαγόντες ἡμεῖς οἱ δοῦλοι
σοῦ συνεχῶς κινδυνεύομεν· ἔτι δὲ καὶ μᾶλλον ὅταν ἀναμνήσκομαι
τῆς ἰδίας ζωῆς τά πταίσματά και πλημμηλήματα ὅσα ἐκ νεότητος
παρακεῖται μοὶ, φοβοῦμαι, αἰσχύνομαι καὶ ἀθυμίας πληροῦμαι.
Ὅταν δὲ πάλιν τὴν μεγάλην χεῖρά σου, τὸ μέγεθος καὶ τὸ συνεχὲς
τῆς σῆς εἲς ἐμε βοηθίας ἐννοήσω, ἀναλαμβάνω πάλιν τοὺς
λογισμοὺς κὶ¹⁸ κουφοτέρη γίνομαι ταῖς ἐλπίσιν. Διὰ τοῦτο
προσηλθοῦσα¹⁹ νῦν σοι ἐν ψυχῇ συντετριμένη πρῶτόν μεν
εὐχαριστῶ σοι κύριε Ἰησοῦ Χριστέ ὦ σῶτηρ μου ἐπὶ πᾶσιν οἷς
παρέσχου μοι ἀγαθοῖς ὅς ἐκ τοσούτων κινδύνων διασωζομένην ἐπὶ
βασιλικὸν τὸν θρόνον τῆς δυναστείας ταύτης ὑψώσας ἐμὲ μηδὲ ἐν
αὐτῷ παύεις συντερῶν²⁰ με. Ἔπειτα δὲ ἱκετεύω κὶ ὁμολογῶ σοι
Χριστέ μου. Οἶδα γὰρ τὰ παραπτώματα μοῦ κὶ τὰς πράξεις, ἀς ἐγὼ
κατειργηϲάμην ἀλλὰ τοῦτο πάλιν οἶδα ὡς οὐ μέγεθος ἁμαρτημάτων
ὑπερβαίνει τοῦ σωτῆρος μου τὴν πολλὴν μακροθυμίαν. Οὐ γὰρ
γυναῖκα ἁμαρτολὸν προσηλθοῦσαν σοι μετὰ δακρύων ἀπέφυγες
οὐδὲ τελώνην ἀνάβαλου μετανοήσαντα οὐδὲ λῃστὴν ἐπιγνόντα τὴν
βασιλείαν σοῦ ἀποδίωξας²¹ μηδὲ διώκτην μετανοήσαντα κατέλιπες
ὁ μην·²² ἀλλὰ τοὺς ἀπὸ τῆς μετανοίας ἅπαντας ἐν τῷ χωρῷ τῶν σῶν
φίλων μετέταξας. Διὸ ὡς θαροῶν²³ τῇ ἀφάτῳ σου ἀγαθότητι
προσέρχομαι κὶ δέομαί σου Χριστὲ κύριέ μου, δέσποτά μου,
λυτροτά²⁴ μου, βασιλεῦ τῶν αἰώνων ἄνες ἄφες, ἱλάσθητι κὶ

17. **κατίδω** second aorist of καθοράω, to look down upon, behold.
18. **κι** καὶ, here and below.
19. **προσηλθοῦσα** προσελτηοῦσα.
20. **συντερῶν** συντηρῶν.
21. **ἀποδίωξας** ἀπεδίωξας.
22. **ὁ μην** The phrase is ungrammatical—"he not"—and it is fragmentary. We have left it
untranslated in *CW*, p. 319. The preceding biblical allusions are to Luke 7:37–38, 48; 19:2–11;
23:42–43; and Acts 9:4–5; 22:7–15; 26:14–18. During the later Middle Ages and continuing for
some while in the Renaissance, the raised dot observable after this word had a punctuation
value that fluctuated between that of a modern colon and that of a modern period—which
is to say, it could mark the end of a clause or the end of a sentence. See M. B. Parkes, *Pause
and Effect: An Introduction to the History of Punctuation in the West* (Berkeley and Los An-
geles: University of California Press, 1993), pp. 45–46, 52, 82, 210–11.
23. **θαροῶν** θαρρῶν.
24. **λυτροτα** λυπρόητα?

συγχώρησόν μοι ἁμαρτολῇ κὶ ἀναξίῳ τῇ δούλῃ σοῦ ὅσα σοὶ ἐκ
νεότητος ἥμαρτον εἴτε ἐν γνώσει κὶ ἀγνοίᾳ εἴτε ἐν λόγοις κὶ ἔργοις
ὃς μόνος ὢν ἅγιος τῶν ἁγίων ἁγίασόν μου τὴν ψυχὴν κὶ τὸ σῶμα,
τὸν νοῦν καὶ τὴν καρδίαν, καὶ ὅλην με ἀνακαίνισον. Καὶ γένου μοι
βοηθὸς κὶ ἀντιλήπτωρ κυβερνῶν ἐν εἰρήνῃ τὴν ζωήν κὶ τὸν λαὸν
μοῦ ὃς μόνος ὑπάρχων εὐλογημένος πάντοτε, νῦν κὶ εἰς ἀπεράντους
αἰώνας. Ἀμήν.

PRAYER 35 ❧ THE SECOND ENGLISH PRAYER [SIGS. 31R–36R]

O lorde God Father euerlasting, which raignest ouer the Kingdomes of
men, and giuest them at thy pleasure: which of thy great mercie, hast
chosen me thy seruant and handmaid to feede thy people and thyne
enheritance: so teache me, I humblie beseach the, thy worde, and so
strengthen me with thy grace, that I maie feede thy people with a
faithfull and a true hart: and rule them prudentlie with powre. Oh
Lorde, thou haste set me on highe, my fleshe is fraile and weake. If I
therefore at anie time forget the, touche my harte ô Lorde that I maie
againe remember the If I swell against the, pluck me down in my owne
conceipt, that thou maist raise me in thy sight. Graunt me ô Lorde a
listning eare to heare the, and a hungrie soule to long after thy worde.
Endew me with thy heauenlie spirite. Geue me thy spirite of wisdome
that I maie vnderstand the. Geue me thy spirite of truth, that I maie
knowe the: thy feeling spirit that I maie feare the: thy spirit of grace that
I maie loue the: thy spirit of zeale that I maie hunger and thirst after the:
thy perseuering spirit that I maie liue and dwell and raigne with the. I
acknowledg oh my King without the my throne is vnstable, my seat
vnsure, my Kingdome tottering, my life vncertaine. I se all thinges in
this life subiect to mutabilitie nothing to continue still at one staie, but
feare and trembling, hunger and thirst, coulde and heate, weaknes and
faintnes, sorow and sicknes, doth euermore oppres mankinde. I heare
how oft times vntimelie death doth carie awaie the mightiest and
greatest personages. I haue learned out of thy holie worde that horrible
iudgment is nighe, vnto them which walke not after thy will, and the
mightie swaruinge from thy law, shall be mightely tormented. Therefore
sith all thinges in this worlde, both heauen and earth shall passe and
perish and thy worde alone endureth for euer: engraft ô moste gracious

Lorde Christe this thy woord of grace and life so in my harte, that from
henceforth I neither follow after fained comfortes, in worldelie power,
neither distract my mind to transitorie pleasures, nor occupie my
thoughtes in vaine delightes, but that carefullie seking the where thow
shewest thy self in thy worde, I maie surely finde the to my comforte,
and euerlastinglie enioy the to my saluation. Create therefore in me ô
Lorde a new harte and so renew my spirite within me [echoes Psalm
51:10] that ^thy^ lawe maie be my study, thy truthe my delight; thy church
my care: thy people my crowne: thy righteousnes, my pleasure: thy
seruice my gouernment; thy feare my honor: thy grace my strength: thy
fauor my life: thy gospell my kingdome: and thy saluation my blisse: and
my glory. So shall this my kingdome through the be established with
peace: so shall thie church be edified with power: so shal thy gospell be
published with zeale: so shall my raigne be continued with prosperitie:
so shall my life be prolonged with happines: and so shall my self at thy
good pleasure be translated into immortalitie. Which ô mercifull Father
graunt for the merit of thy Sonne Iesus Christ: to whome with the Holie
Ghoste be rendred all prais and glorie for euer. Amen

LETTER 45 ☙ QUEEN ELIZABETH TO MONSIEUR (FRANÇOIS
HERCULE DE VALOIS), DECEMBER 19, 1579[1]

[Addressed] A mon trescher Mounsieur Duc D'Anjou

Mon trescher Si la chose longuement attendue euct ^este^ bonne quant
elle arriVa l'eusse este mieulx satisfaicte de la longue attente qu'il a pleu
a Stafford me prester Mais Voyant que la Paix semble que ademy faicte
Ie ne Voy trop de rayson qui faicte sa demeure Sinon qu'il me faict a
croyre que se fuct par Vostre commandement a qui l'ay toute Volunte
qu'iL Obaye / Et ayant tout astour receu lettres de france que Le Roy
prolonge ceste paix soubs quelques difficultes qui ne se pourront trop
tost concluire Ie serois tresayse qu'on laissatt s'esbahir de son longue
arreste m'assurant que quelcuns s'en font leur ieue Et pour la cause du
Roy de Nauarre et sa partie Cesei Ie prendray la hardiesse de Vous dire
qu'il uous touchera bien preus[2] en reputation que ~ne~ le laissates en pire

1. *Source:* Hatfield House, Cecil Papers, 135/23, fol. 40, with remnants of two seals.
2. **preus** près.

estat qu'ilz furent au commencement de ces nouueaulx troubles Car si
leur plus grandes seurtes leur fussent arraches commant se fieroient y
du Roy adioustant que le Roy mesme me manda dire par son
Embassadeur qu'il ne leur nieroit la primiere pacification et ne
demanderoit sinon les Villes et lieux, nouVellement prises Vous me
pardonneres la curiosite qui me tient ~~au~~ de Vos actions A qui Ie souhait
tout l'honneur et louange qui peut arriuer a la perpetuelle renommee
de Prince, Ie m'asoure que desir de grandeur apres ceste paix ne vous
aueuglera les yeuLx pour Vous fayre omettre ce qui sera pour la salut de
ceulx qui se fient en Vostre bonte / Quant aux commissaires Ie croy
qu'ilz resembleront aux motz qui trop de fois se recitant font la langue
chopper hors d'ordre Ie Voy que le temps coule et moy auec pour me
rendre mal idoine ~~pour~~ de contenter Comme Ie souhaite Et suis quasi
d'acord auec l'opinion de ceulx qui ne laissient a uous souVenir de mes
defaultz Mais dieu i'espere gouuerneray le tout pour vostre bien, Ne
uous desplaise Mounsieur que Ie demande quelque responce de Semier
pour lequel Ie souhaite queLque fin de son malheur Ou qu'il soit
condamne iustement et uous purge d'un crime qui souuient[3] on
impose aux princes, desquelz les faueurs se disent tener par filetz bien
tendres Ou qu'iL soit employe en vostre siruise pour estouper les
bouches de maldisantz qui ne laissent a passer leur temps es affayres
pour en fayre leur expositions, Mon trescher Ie uous baille ores un bel
miroir pour y Voir bien clair l'imbecilite de mon entendement que ay
trouVe un temps si propre pour en esperer une bonne Conclusion
poisant le lieu ou demoures auec la Compagnie qui y est Nous poVres
habitans de L'Isle barbare ~~n~~ nous deVons garder de comparoistre en
iugement[4] ou si ingenieux iuges de nostre scauoir tiennent leur Siege en
si hault lieu de uostre faVeur Mais m'apelant a Mounsieur Seul non
diuise Ie ne laisseray tomber mon proces / Et si me feries donner Le
St^(r)apado Ie ne mettray glose a ce texte M'assurant que l'entendes que
trop /. EN fin ma seule requeste consiste en ce que tousiours me tenes
pour la mesme que m'aues oblige de uous estre dedie et que ne puis
estre que icelle qui uous ay ~~eo~~ loge au primier rencq de ce qui m'est plus
cher, Comme Dieu le peult mieulx tesmoingner A qui Ie ne Cesseray
mes suplications de uous octroier Cent ans de Vie. Auec mes bien

---

3. **souuient** souvent.
4. **comparoistre en iugement** to appear to receive sentencing. The phrase is a legal idiom
in Scots ("compear in judgment") as well as French ("comparaître en jugement").

humbles souuenances de m'estre recommande a mon trescher / De
Westmester ce 19 de December

> Vostre tresassuree comme y estant obligee
> Elizabeth R

LETTER 49 ಶ QUEEN ELIZABETH TO MONSIEUR, MARCH 17, 1581[1]

[Addressed] A Monsieur D'Anjov
Mon trescher Cousin

Mon trescher L'honneur qui[2] me faictes est bien grand me mandant
souuant de Vos lettres mais l'ayse que I'en concoive l'excede de
beaucoup Ne souhaittant rien tant que la continuation de Vostre bonne
Opinion en mon endroict Vouz marciant tres humblement des doulces
fleurs cuillis par la main qui retient les petitz doibtz qui[3] Ie benois Vne
million de fois Et Vous prometz qu'il ny auoit iamais ^present^ mieulx
porte car la Verdure y demeura aussy frais que sy s'euct est[4] cuilly en
mesme instant Et me representant tout Vivement Vostre uerdoyanct
affection en mon endroict Et espere de me donner oncquies iuste
~~occation~~ ^cause^ qu'elle flestrie a mon occation Monsieur Ie n'eay garde
a en perdre Vn fuillet ny fleur pour tout les aultres ioyaulx qui[5] I'ay
Ie Vous suplie croyir que Ie ne peuLx exprimer le contentement que
ce porteur m'apporte Et me pardonnes si plustot il ne fust de retour
en attendant mon Courrier par lequel I'ay receu Vne lettre de Vous,
en laquelle uous m'obliges infiniment neantmoins par tant
~~que Ie m'assure Ie n'eusse receu si Simie euct bien entendue ma lettre~~
~~Mais peuLt estre qu on ne la Vouldroist entendre bien~~
d'honorables offertes toutes plaines d'affection qui combein que du
tout ne y puis Ie du tout satisfayre si est ce qui ne manqueray a le
ricognoistre par tout les moyens qui seront en ma puissance[6]

1. *Source:* Hatfield House, Cecil Papers, 135/21, fol. 36, with remnants of two seals.
2. **qui** que.
3. **qui** que.
4. **est** été.
5. **qui** que.
6. **en laquelle . . . en ma puissance** These revisions are inserted above or below lines of scored-through phrasing.

Ie me Contente Monsieur que Vous uous assures de moy comme de la plus fidelle amie que oncques Prince euct Et si Vous espuiras[7] a tel Rochir toutes les tempestes de la Mer n'auront garde a le remuer ny queLques orage sur la terre ly detournera a ~~de~~ Vous honorer et aymer / Il ny a eu un mot escript en intention de me separer de Vo~~us~~otre bonne affection mais a ce que n'en fussies ignorant de tout qui se fist icy Mais que Ie dois pencer: Ie ne scay Sinon que Vous me rendes Vostre obligee a Iamais Et ne penceray Iamais aultre de uous que le mesme honneur et monceaul tout plain de Vertue / Comme scait le Createur a qui auec mes trescordielles recommandations Ie prie de Vous octroier tout L'honneur et contentement du monde Vous supliant de me tenir tousiours en Vos bonnes Graces. De Westmester ce 17 de Mars /

Vostre tresobligee a Iamais
Elizabeth R

LETTER 56 ༄ QUEEN ELIZABETH TO CATHERINE DE MÉDICIS, QUEEN MOTHER OF FRANCE, ON MONSIEUR'S DEATH, CIRCA JULY 1584[1]

[Addressed] A Madame ma bonne Soeur La Royne Mere

Madame Si l'exstremite de mon malheur n'euct egale mon doleur a sa cause et ne m'euct rendue insuffisante a toucher par plume la playe que mon Coeur soufrit Se ne me seroit possible que Ie me fusse tant oublie a ne Vous Visiter par la Compagnie de regret que Ie Vous faye qui Ie m'assure ne peult surmonter le[2] mien Car Combien que l'y[3] estres mere Si est ce qu'il Vous reste quelques aultre enfants mais a moy Ie ne trouVe de Consolation sinon la mort qui l'espere nous fera bien tost rencontrer / Madame si Vous pourries Voyre la figure de mon Coeur Vous la Verries le pourtraict d'un Corps sans asme Mais Ie ne Vous fascheray plus de mes plaintz en ayant trop de Vostres Il reste astour

7. **espuiras** espéreras?

1. *Source:* BL, MS Cotton Galba, E.VI, fol. 255. Script very loosely formed and scratchy; paper also badly worn. Brackets enclose conjectural restoration of letters wholly worn off the paper surface.

2. The *e* of *le* is heavily retraced over an *a*.

3. **l'y** lui.

que Ie Vous aduoue et Iure que tourne^{ray} une bonne part de son amour
au Roy mon bon Frere et Vous uous assu~rant que me trouueres la plus
fidelle fille et Soeur que iamais ^{princes} eurent Et ce pour principalle
Cause qu'il Vous appart~enait de si pres a qui Ie m'estois du tout
dedie. Ce qui S'il euct eu la faueur diuine de plus longue ^{Vie} uous
l'enferies[4] plus seqours / Madame Ie uous prie donner ferme Credit a
Ce Gentilhomme qui Vous dira de ma part plus amplement de [me]s
pencees en Vostre endroit / Et Croyes que Ie les accompliray fidelement
comme Si Vous fuisse fille naturelle /
Comme Dieu Scait,[5]

à qui Ie prie Vous donne   Vostre tres affectionnee Soeur et Cousine
Longue Vie et toute   Elizabeth R
Consolation

LETTER 57 ᒃ QUEEN ELIZABETH TO KING JAMES VI OF
SCOTLAND, CIRCA JUNE OR JULY 1585[1]

[Addressed] A mon bon frere Le Roy d'Escose

Right deare brother Your gladsome acceptance of my offred Amitie
togither with the desiar you seem[2] to haue ingraven in your mynde to
make merites Correspondant makes me in fuL opinion that some
ennemis to our good wyL shalL loose muche traveL with making
frustrat thar baiting stratagemes wiche I knowe to be many and by
sondry meanes to be explored / I can not halt with you so muche, as to
denye that I haue seen suche euident shewes of your contrarieus
dealings that if I mad not my rekening the bettar of the moneths I
might condemne ^{you} as unWorthy of suche as I mynd to shewe my
selfe toward you, and therfor I am wel pleased to take any Coulor to
defend your honor and hope that you wyl remember that who seaketh
tWo[3] stringes to one bowe the may shute strong but neuer strait and if

---

4. **enferies** enverries (spelled according to sound).

5. Wear to this area of the page has almost obliterated this favorite epistolary formula.

1. *Source*: BL, MS Additional 23240, art. 5, fols. 15r–16v; MS volume entitled *Autograph Correspondence of Q. Elizabeth with James VI. of Scotland, 1582–1596*.

2. **seem** written in left margin.

3. **tWo** *W* is written over an *o*.

you suppose that princes Causes be Vailed so couVertly that no
intelligence may bewraye them deceave not your selfe we old foxes can
find shiftes to saue our selves by others malice and come by knowelege
of greattest secreat spetiallye if it touche our freholde It becometh
therfor alL of our rencq to deale sincerely lest if we use it not Whan we
do it We be hardly beleaved I write not this My deare brother for dout
but for remembrances / My ambassador writes so muche of your
honorable traitment of him and of Alexandar that I belive the be
Convertid scotes You oblige me for them for wiche I rendar you a
milion of most intire thankes as she that meaneth to desarue many a
good thoght in your brest throWe goᵒd ∮ desart / And for that your
request is so honorable retaining so muche reason I wer Out of sences
if I shuld not suspend of any hiresay til the answer of your oWne action
wiche the actor ought best to knowe and So assure your selfe I meane
and Vowe to do with this request that you wyl affourd me the the⁴
reciproque And thus with my many petitions to the Almighty for your
long life and preservation I ende thes skribled lines /

Your Verey Assured LoVinge
Sistar and Cousin
Elizabeth R

LETTER 58 ❧ ELIZABETH TO JAMES, AUGUST 1585[1]

[Addressed] A mon bon Frere et Cousin Le Roy d'Escoze.

Right deare brother I find to true the frenche adage Qu'un maL ne vint
Iamais seul for as the horrible and soudain murdar of my most faithfuL
subiect and most Vaillant baron was unto me a hartsore and Grivous
tidinges, So was it ten fold redoubled with knowelege that a skot shuLd
dare Violate his handes on any of our noble bloude in a peasable
Concord whan Our frendship shuld haue sent out his hotest beames to
the kindeling of the entier affection of bothe realmes that any of that
nation shuld ons dare haue had a thoght to maculate[2] suche a Contract
of Amitie I perceaue by my Ambassador that your Grief is litel les than

---

4. Repetition in the MS.
1. *Source:* BL, MS Additional 23240, art. 6, fol. 19r–20v.
2. **maculate** spot, stain—from Latin *maculatus.*

suche a hap deserveth and do perceaue that you haue not spared your
Wel fauored to cause him answer ᵈ suche a suspicion I thinke my selfe
therfor greatly obliged unto Your Care for my satisfaction and therin I
thanke you for being so considerast[3] of your oWne honor Wiche I
assure ʸᵒᵘ lieth a bleding in the boWelz of many an IngLas man VntiL
ful rayson be made for suche a treacherye God send us bettar luck after
our League be finisched than this bloudy beginninge may geue
Calandes[4] of elz many a red side wil folowe suche demerites

but I hope you wyl spare no man that may be douted of suche a
meaning I meane not only of the murdar but of the breaking out vpon
our borderars wiche comminly ar the beginnings of our quarelz I dout
nothinge of your curieus Care in this behalfe and for ᵗʰᵃᵗ the warden of
that marche hathe bine the Open and commen fosterar and
Compagnion of the traitor Westmarland and his complices in france
and Scotland I hope you wiL agrie easely to send him to my handes
wher he shal neuer receaVe iniurie nor iVel measure And thus desiring
to Credit my Ambassador in certain particularites that he shal impart
unto you as ~~my~~ to my Selfe I recommend you to Gods safe tuition who
Graunt you many gladsome Yeres /

Your most Affectionat Sistar and Cousin
Elizabeth R

LETTER 59 ❧ ELIZABETH TO JAMES, NOVEMBER 1585[1]

[Addressed] A mon trescher frere Le Roy d'Escoze

Right deare brother the strangenes of harde accidens that ar arrived
here of unLoked for or unsuspected attemps in SkotLand iven by some
suche as Lately issued out of our Lande Constraineth ᵐᵉ as weL for the
Care we haue of your person as of the discharge of our oWne honnor
and Consciense to send you immediatly this Gentleman one that
appartaineth to us in bloud bothe to offer you alL assistance of helpe as
aL good indeuor of CounceiL and to make hit plaine that we delt
plainLy thes Lordes makeng great outCryes that I wold not or coulde

---

3. **considerast** considerate—from Latin *considerare.*
4. **Calandes** Latin *calendae,* the first day of the Roman month; also, foretaste, prelude.
1. *Source:* BL, MS Additional 23240, art. 7, fol. 23.

helpe them to be restored I by ther great importunitie yelded that if I
might be fried of my assurance given Unto you for ther safe Kiping I
Wold Consent unto ther departure and so after your answer as my
thoght most honorable that the might take ther way to Germany with
your Gracieus Graunt of som livehode after a wekes space I gaue them
my pasport and so dismissed them without I swere unto you ons the
sight of any one of them, Now whan I way how suddenly beyond ꝯ my
expectation this suddan stur ariseth and fering lest some iVeL and
Wicked person might surmise that this Was not without my forsight I
beseche you trust my actions accordinge the measure of my formar
dealings for your safety and ansuerable to the rule of reason and you
shal find that few princes wyl agrye to Constraint of ther equalz muche
les with compulsion of ther subiectz Iuge of me therfor as of a kinge
that Caries no abiect nature and thinke this of ᵐᵉ that rather than your
daungier I wyl Ventur myne and albeit I must Confesse that it is
dangerous for a prince to irritast[2] to muche through iuel aduise the
generalitie of great subiectz so might you or noW haue folowed my
aduise that wold neuer betray you with unsound CounceiL And noW
to Conclude making hast I pray you be plain With this bearar that I
may knoWe What you wold that I shuld ᵈᵒ without excuse hireafter
that constrained you did hit for I dare assure ʸᵒᵘ of his Secresye and
therof be you bold. For the lord russelz dethe and other thinges I
referre me to this gentLman Who I dare promis is Of no faction beside
my wyL God blesse you in al safety as I wysche myself
Feare not for your life must be
thers or elz the Shal smart weL   Your tru assured Cousin and Sistar
every mothers son of them /[3]   Elizabeth R

Right deare brother I am not a liteL satisfaict of many a carefulL thoght
that my mynde tossed up and downe with doutes what Care might do

---

2. **irritast** irritate, provoke anger—from Latin *irritare*.
3. Postscript squeezed into bottom left corner of verso sheet.
1. *Source:* BL, MS Additional 23240, art. 10, fols 30r–31v, with remnants of seal attached. Addressed in another hand: "To my dearest brother and Cousin the king of Scotts."

to a kings brest inVirunned of a seubdain with so vnlooked for an
accident my thankes therfor may scarse be contained in this paper for
your most acceptable messanger whom it pleased you to Commaund[2]
my satisfaction of your good estat togither with your good Liking of
the Lordes and ther action whom I beseche God no Longar preserue in
Life than the be ready for your preservation to spend aL thers So far
wer euer my intentz from any trechery toWarde you And wher as your
desiar seameth great that the League in hand myght come to ende I am
addressing a GentiLman vnto you for the same purpose and wyL deLay
no time for so good a intent trusting than that no whispering treason
shaL haue credit in your eare to retarde or Cut of so nidefuL an action
suppose ~~huke~~ Suche ~~a~~ I pray you to resemble a golden ʰᵒᵘᵏᵉ that oft
deceaues the vnwary fische and makes him receaue his worst in Lieu of
bettar hope Amidz aL thes kind dealings of yours Let me not forget
hoW Litel care the Worlde shaL thinke you prise me at if in middest of
greattest frindship my Los of honor be no whit repaired for the
shamfuL murther of the baron RusselL, pondar it depeLy I beseche ʸᵒᵘ
for hit striketh nere me So publik an iniurye to haue no redres without
we shewe the thoght wiche God alone reserves his part the like answer
was never yet Giuen and hope for bettar paiment /
        for your Churche matters I do bothe admire and ʳeioise[3] to see your
wise paraφrase[4] wiche far excedeth ther texte Since God hathe made
kinges Let them not unmake ther authorite and Let brokes and smaL
riVers acknowLege ther springes and flowe no furdar than ther
bankes / I praise God that you vphold euer a regaL rule / for alL other
matters wiche this Gentilman hathe toLd me I wiL hope stiL that your
faithfuL profession of Constantie in my behalfe shaL far Surmount the
devellishe practises and sutteL iniquitie of those wiche undar pretence
of your aduancement wiL ~~skanted~~ your best fortune and albeit I am
aduertised iven from amonge themselves that your assurance to them
doth shewe that aL my faire offers from you be ad Eφesios[5] and
ridiculus meaning whoLy to foLow them and temporise with me Yet I
mynd to peccare in meliorem if I must nides be begiled and mynd not

2. **Commaund** commend?

3. **ʳeioise** Elizabeth writes an enormous miniscule "r" at the beginning of this word.

4. **paraφrase** paraphrase, with Greek phi as shown.

5. **ad Eφesios** to Ephesians, companions in merrymaking (Latin phrase with, again, Greek phi).

to trust them til I see you faille me and than deceptis ad decipientem
digne vertitur til than I wyL trust your worde and dare assure you shal
neuer on my behalfe haue Cause to repent your Voues[6] meaning you no
les good than I pray God euer to afourde me prayinge him Longe to
Conserue you and to ende this Lettar Let me not forget to recommend
this Gentilmans good behavor in this his charge hauing used it to your
honor and his great pra^{i}se thus I finische to troble you but do rest

> Your most Assuredz Louing Sistar and Cousin
> Elizabeth R

LETTER 63 ❧ ELIZABETH TO JAMES, MARCH 1586[1]

The expertist Seamen My deare brother makes Vant of ther best
shippes whan the pas the highest bellowes without yelding and broke
nimlest the roughest stormes the Like profe I suppose may best be
made and surest boste of frindes whan greattest persuasions and
mightiest ennemis Oppose them selVes for parties if than a Constant
irremouable good wylL appere thar is best trialL made and for that I
knowe ther is no worse Orator for truthe than malice nor shwredar
in Vahar than en Vye and that I am sure you haue wanted nether to
assaile your mynde to win it from Our frindeship if not auailing alL
thes minars[2] you kipe the hold of your promised in Ward affection as
Randol at lenghe haue told me and your oWne lettars assure me I dare
thus boldLy affirme that you shall ^haue^ the bettar part in this bargain
for Whan you Way in equaL balance with no palsey hande the Very
ground of ther desires that wold withdrawe you it is but roote of
mischif to peril your selfe with ~~out Who to~~ hope to harme her who euer
hathe preserved you and sins you may be sure that skotland nor your
selfe be so potent as for your greatnis the seake you nor neVer did but
to iniure a thirde and if you rede the histories ther is no great cause of
bost for many conquist thogh your Contry saruid ther malice this you
see the beginning why euer skot^Land^ hathe bine sought Now to come
to my ground worke only naturaL affection ab incunabulis sturrid me

6. **Voues** The first letter could be a V or a W.
1. *Source:* BL, MS Additional 23240, art. 12, fols. 38r–39v.
2. **minars** underminers.

to saue you from the murderars of your father and the periL that ther
Complices migt brede you. Thus as in no Counterfait miroir you may
behold without maske the faces of bothe beginnars it is for you to Iuge
what ar like to be the best Euent of bothe and therafter I pray God you
may use your best choise to your surest good no semblant false to
begiLe, And as I reioyse to haue had euen in this hammering worLde
suche presant profe of your sinceritie So shal you be sure to imploye it
upon no gileful person nor suche as wil not take as muche regard of
your good as Of her owne / tochinge an instrument as your Secretarye
termes ^it that you desiar to haue me signe I assure ^you thogh I can ^play
of some and haue bine broght up to knoWe musike yet this di^sscord
wold be So grose as wer not fit for so wel tuned musike Must so great
dout be made of fre good wyL and gift be so mistrusted that our Signne
EmanueL must assure No my deare brother teache your neW raWe
Counselars bettar manner than to aduis you suche a paringe of ample
meninge who shuld doute performance of a kinges offer what
deshonor may that be demed folowe next your owne nature for this
neVer came owt of your shoppe / but for your fuL satisfaction and to
plucke from the wicked the Weapon the wold use to brede your doubt
of my meanings Thes the be / fi^rst I wil as longe as you with iueL desart
alter not your Course take Care for your Safety helpe your nide and
shun aL actes that may damnifie you³ in any sort ether in present or
future time and for the portion of relife I mind never to lessen thogh as
I see Cause I wiL ^rather augment / and this I hope may stand you in as
muche assuranse as my name in parchement and no les for bothe our
honors / I Can ^not omit also to request ^you of alL Amitie betwin vs to
haue good regard of the Longe waiting expectation that alL our
subiectz lokes after that some persons be deliuered in to my handes for
some repaire of my honur thogh no redres for his dethe according as
my Ambassador RandoL shal signifie and that ther be no more delais
Wiche haue bine ouer many already And thus I end my trobling you
comittinge you to the tuition of the LiVing God Who graunt you many
yeres of prosperous raigne /

> Your most assured Louinge Sistar and Cousin
> Elizabeth R

---

3. **you** written in right margin.

LETTER 66 🙖 ELIZABETH TO JAMES, LATE MAY 1586[1]

I muse muche right deare brother how possiblie my wel ment Lettar
prociding from so fauteLes a hart could be ether misliked or
misconstred and first for my promis made of reciproke vsage in alL
amicable maner I trust I nether haue nor never shall make fraction of
in the lest scruple and as for doute of your perfourmance of your VoWe
made me I assure you if I did not trust your wordes I shuld estime but
at smale Valew your Writings and if you please to reade againe my last
lettar you shaL perceaue hoW muche I prise your tried Constancy for
all the many assaultes that I am sure your eares haue bin assailled with
and therfor I am far from dout whan suche profe is made me You might
Worthely forthinke you to haue bestowed so muche faithful dealinge
upon one that ether had smal iugement or muche ingratitude and
therof I may clerely purge me from suche crime for I haue more iust
cause to acknowelege thankefulnis manifold than in ~~one~~ any part to
ouerrun my owne wit to leue it behind me And for the some that you
suppose my many affaires made me forget togither with the maner of
the instrument or Lettar quocumque nomine datur for the first I asure
you I neuer gaue commission for more some other might mistake as
RandoL wil tel you and for the lettar some wordes and fourme Was
suche as fitted not our two frindeshipes as Randol also can ~~tel~~ shewe
you but I haue sent you a lettar that I am sure Containes alL you desired
in spetialL wordes wiche I trust shaL content you althogh I must say for
my selfe this muche that the pithe and effect of alL you receued afore
And beseche you thinke that I finde it my greatest fault that I remember
but to WelL Yea many times more than I WoLde but neuer aught that
may be for your beholfe ether in honor or contenta[tion][2] shal euer slip
out of my mind but wil take so good regarde into it as ~~yet~~ it that euer
shal nerely touche my selfe / As knoweth God Who euer preserue you
from deceit[ful] counseiL and Graunt you true knolege of your assured
With Longe and many yeres to raigne /

> Your most affectionate and assured Louinge Sistar and Cousin
> Elizabeth R

---

1. *Source:* BL, MS Additional 23240, art. 15, fol. 45, with remnants of seal attached. Addressed in another hand: "A mon bon frere et Cousin. Le Roy d'Escosse."
2. Here and below, missing letters, enclosed in square brackets, are supplied from the later transcription that follows on p. 47 of the same MS collection.

LETTER 70 ❧ ELIZABETH TO JAMES, OCTOBER 4, 1586[1]

[Addressed] A Mounsieur mon bon frere et Cousin Le Roy D'Escose

I hope My deare brother that my manye Waighty affayres in present may
make my laWful excuse for the retardance of the answer to your
Ambassaduurs charge but I doute not but you shaLbe honorably
satisfaict in alL the pointz of his Commission and next after my oWne
errand done I must rendar you my innumerable thankes for suche
amicable offers as hit hathe pleased you make making you Assured that
with Gods grace you shal neuer haue cause to regret your good thoghtz
of my meaninge to dese^{r}ue as muche good wiL and affection as Euer
One prince ~~owen~~ owed an other Wisching alL meanes that may
maintaine your faithful trust in me that neuer wyL seake aught but the
incr^{e}ase of y^{our} honor and safty I Was in mynd to haue sent you suche
accidentz as this late monethe broght furthe but the sufficientie of
mastar ArchebaL made me retaine him and do rendar you many loVing
thankes for the Ioy you toke of my naroW escape from the Chawes[2] of
Dethe to Wiche I might easely haue fallen but that the hand of the hiest
saued me from that snare and for that the Curse of that desaing rose vp
from the wicked sucgestion of the Iesuites Wiche make hit an axceptable
Sacrifice to God and meritorieus to themselfe that a kinge not of ther
profession shuld be murthered therfor I could kipe my pen no longar
from discharging my care of your person that you suffer not suche
Vipars to inhabite your lande the Say you Gaue ~~them~~ Leue undar your
hand that the might safely Come and Go for Gods Loue regard your
surety aboue all perswations / and account him ~~to~~ no subiect that
intertaines them make not Edictz for skorne but to be obserued Let
them be rebelles and so pronunsed that preserue them / for my part I
am sorier that the Cast away so many Goodly GentiLmen than that the
soght my Ruine I thanke God I haue taken more dolor for some that ar
giLty of this murther than beare them malice that the soght my dethe I
protest hit before God but suche iniquitie wolL not be hide be hit neuer
so craftely handelid and Yet whan you shal here alL you Wyl Wondar
thatt one accoWnted Wise Wyl use suche matter so fondly but no
marveL for whan the ar giuen to a reprobat sence the offen make suche

---

1. *Source:* BL, MS Additional 23240, art. 16, fol. 49, with remnants of seal attached. Its endorsement reads "Of the 4 of october 1586."

2. **Chawes** *C* is heavily written over an *S.*

slip I haue bine so tedieus that I take pitie of your paine and so wyL ende
this skribling Praying you beliue that you could neuer haue chosen a
more sure trust that wiL neuer begile than my selfe

Who dayly prayes to
God for your longe   Your most assured Louing Sistar and Cousin
prosperitie[3]   Elizabeth R

LETTER 73 ࣣ❧ ELIZABETH TO JAMES, OCTOBER 15, 1586[1]

[Addressed] A mon bon frere et Cousin Le Roy D'Escose

My deare brother hit hathe sufficiently infourmed me of your singular
Care of my Estat and brething that you haue Sent one in suche diligence
to understand the Circumstancis of the treasons wiche lately wer
lewdly[2] attempted and miraculously vttred Of wiche I had made
participant Your Ambassador afor your Lettars Came / and now am I to
shewe you that as I haue receaved manye writings from you of great
kindnis Yet this Last Was fraughted[3] with so Careful passion and so
effectualL utterance of alL best Wisches for my Safety and offer of as
muche as I could haue desired that I Confes if I shuld not seake to
decerue it and by meritis tye you to Continuance I wer iuelL wordy
Suche a frind And As the thankes my hart yeldes my pen May skant
rendar you So shaL the oWnar euer decerue to shewe hit not iveL
imploied but on suche a Prince as shall requite Your good wyL and kipe
a WachefuL yee to alL doings that may Conserne yow / And wheras you
offer to Send me any traitor of myne residing in your land I shal not
faille but expect th'accomplischement of the same in Case any suche
shal be and require you in the mene time that Spidy deliuerye may be
maid of the Cars wiche toucheth bothe my Conscience and honor / I
thanke God that you beWare so sone of Iesuites that haue bine the
Source of al thes trecheries in this realme and wyl Sprede like an iuel
Wide if at the first the be not Wided out I Wold I had had prometheus
for companion for Epimetheus had like haue bine myne to Sone / What
religion is this that the pay the way to Saluation is to kil the Prince for a

---

3. Postscript squeezed into bottom left corner of verso sheet.
1. *Source:* BL, MS Additional 23240, art. 17, fol. 53. Its endorsement reads "Of the 15 of october 1586/."
2. **lewdly** basely; word written in margin.
3. **fraughted** "freighted" or "fraught."

merit meritorieus this is that the haue alL Confessed without tortur or
manace I swere hit on my Worde far be hit from Skotland to harbor any
Suche and therfor I wische your Good proVidence may be duly
executed for elz Lawes resemble Cobwebbes Whens great bees get out by
breaking and small flies stiks fast for Wekenis / As Concerning the
retarding of your ansWers to aL pointz of your Ambassadors charge You
had receved them or noW but that Matters of that waight that I am sure
you Wold willing^{ly} knoWe Can not as yet receaue an Conclusion and til
than Mastar Douglas doth tarye and with his retourne I hope you shal
receaue honorable requital of his amicable Embassade So as you shal
haue no Cause to regret his arriVaL As knoweth the Lord whom euer I
beseche to bringe you many Ioiful dayes of Raigne and life /

I must giue you many thankes   Your most Assured Louing and faithful
for this poore subject of myne for   Sistar and Cousin
Whom I wil ^{not[4]} stik to do al   Elizabeth R
pleasvre for your request and Wold
wische him undar the grond if
he shuld not serue you with greatest faithe
that any seruant may I haue wylled
him tel you some thinges from me I
beseche you heare them fauorablie /[5]

SPEECH 17, VERSION 2 ⁋ QUEEN ELIZABETH'S FIRST REPLY TO
THE PARLIAMENTARY PETITIONS URGING THE EXECUTION OF
MARY, QUEEN OF SCOTS, NOVEMBER 12, 1586[1]

[Headed, with corrections in Burghley's hand] ~~A Copy~~ *of her Maiesties
most gracious Answer deliuered* by hir self ~~personally~~ *verbally to the
Petition*^{er}s *of the Lords and Commons* being the estates *of* ~~hir~~ *Parliament.
~~the 12th of novembre. 1586.~~ /*

[The] bottomles graces and immeasurable benefitts bestowed vpon
mee by the Almightie ~~God~~ [are] and haue bin such, as I must not only
acknowledg them, but ~~also~~ admire them, accompting them as well

---

4. **not** inserted in the margin.
5. Postscript squeezed into bottom left corner of verso sheet.
1. *Source:* BL, MS Lansdowne 94, art. 35A, fols. 84r–85r; copy in a formal (or "set") italic
hand, probably that of Sir Robert Cecil, with a heading corrected in the hand of Sir Robert's

miracles, as benefitts, not so much in respect of his diuine Maiestie with whome nothing is more common then to do thinges rare and singuler, as in regard of oure weaknes, who cannot sufficiently set forth his wonderfull woorkes and ~~graces~~ ~~benefitz~~ graces which to mee ~~ward~~ haue bene so many, so diuerslie folded and imbrodered[2] one ~~within~~ vppon another, as in no sort ~~I~~ am I able to expresse them.

And although there liueth not any that may more iustly acknowledg themselues infinitely bounde vnto God then I ~~may,~~ whose life he hath ~~wonderfully~~ miraculously preserued, at sondrie tymes (beyond my merit) frome a multitude of perills and daungers, yet is not that the ~~thing~~ cawse for which I ~~account~~ my self the deepliest bound to giue him ~~the most hartie him~~ my humblest thanckes, or to yeld ~~him the~~ greatest recognition, but this which I shall [te]ll you hereafter, which will deserue the name of wonder. If rare things and [sel]dome seene be worthie ~~so to be accounted,~~ of account euen this it is ~~namely~~ that as I came to the Crowne with the willing hartes ~~of my~~ of subiects so do I now after (xxviij yeres raigne) perceaue in you ~~all~~ no deminution of ~~youre~~ goodwilles, which if happelie[3] I should wante, well mowght I breath, but ~~not~~ never thincke I liued, ~~if that were diminished.~~

AND now ~~notwithstanding, if~~ albeit I finde ~~apparantlie~~ my life hath bin ~~most~~ ful daungerouslie sought, and ~~my~~ death ~~by her~~ contriued by suche as no desurt procured it yet am I ~~in respect~~ thereof so cleare frome malice, which hath the propertie to make menne gladde, ~~and reioycefull~~ at the falls and faultes of theire ~~enemies,~~ Foes and make

---

father, Lord Burghley, and with revisions in Elizabeth's cursive italic, indicated here by un-derscoring. The endorsement reads "1586. The former Copy of her Maiesties first speach. the 12th of Nouember." Fire damage and tears along the upper half of the left margin of the recto leaf and the upper half of the right margin of the verso leaf have been supplied by readings from a closely according text, London, Inner Temple Library, MS Petyt 538, vol. 10, fols. 6v–7r; these readings are enclosed in square brackets. Speech 17 largely as revised by Elizabeth was printed as R[obert] C[ecil], *The copie of a letter to the earle of Leycester. With a report of petitions made to the queenes maiestie from the lordes and commons in Parliament. And her answeres.* (London: C. Barker, 1586), sigs. Ci r–Civ v (*STC* 6052).

2. Elizabeth praises God's handiwork with an image of her own handiwork. As in her girl-hood, so too as an adult she continued to embroider book covers—for example, the em-blematic one with Latin mottos that she made for her copy of a New Testament in English (*STC* 2881.5; London: Laurence Tomson, 1578?), preserved as Bodleian Library, University of Oxford, MS e Mus. 242.

3. **happelie** haply.

them seeme to do ~~things~~ for other cawses, when ~~as with~~ rancor <u>is the ground</u> ~~they are stirred to pursue theire intention, as I protest it is to mee, and hath bene a thing most greiuous, to thincke~~ <u>yet protest it is and hath bene my grevous thoght</u> that one not different in sex, of like estate and my neare kinne, shold be ~~so uoide of grace, or false in faith as now to seeke my death, by whome so long her life hath bene preserued, with th'Intollerable perill of my owne.~~ <u>fallen into so great a Crime.</u> Yea I had so litle purpose to pursue her with any colour of malice, that as it is not vnknowne to some of my Lords here (for now I will play the blabb) I secretlie wrote her a lettre vpon the discouerie of ~~her~~ <u>sondry</u> treasons, that if she ~~wolde repent her thoroughlie of her euill course,~~ <u>wold</u> confesse ~~it~~ <u>them</u> and priuatlie acknowledge ~~it~~ <u>them</u> by her lettres vnto ~~mee,~~ <u>my selfe</u> shee neuer should <u>nede</u> be called for ~~it~~ <u>them</u> into <u>so</u> publike ~~a~~ question. Neither did I it of ~~any~~ minde to circumuent her, for then I knew as much as shee cold confesse, and so did I write.

And if ~~at this present,~~ <u>euen yet</u> now the matter is made <u>but</u> to apparant, I thought shee trulie ~~were~~ <u>wold</u> repent~~ant~~ (as perhapps she wolde easely appeare in out~~er~~<u>ward</u> sheowe <u>to do</u>) and that for her none other wolde take the matter uppon them, or that we were but as two milke maides, with pailes ~~under~~ <u>vpon</u> oure armes, or that there were no more dependency vpon us, ~~and~~ <u>but</u> myne owne life were onlie in ~~perill,~~ <u>danger</u> and not the whole estate of youre religion and well doings, I protest (wherein you may beleeue mee, for ~~although,~~ I may haue many vices, I hope I haue not accustomed my tongue to be an Instrument of vntruthe~~s~~) I wolde most willinglie pardon and remitt ~~her~~ <u>this</u> offence.

Or if by my death other nations and kingdomes mig[ht truely saie this Realme had] attained a <u>euer</u> prosperouse and florishing estate, I wold [I assure you not desire to] liue, but gladlie giue my life to th'end my death mig[ht procure you a better prince.]

And for youre sakes it is that I desire ~~most~~ to liue, to kepe [you from a worse] as for mee, I assure you, I finde no great cause I sholde be [fond of lief, I take] no such pleasure in it, that I sholde much wishe it, nor [conceve suche terror] in death, that I shold greatlie feare it, and yet I say that [if the stroake were] comming <u>perchanche</u> fleshe and blood wolde be moued with it and seeke [to shonne it.]

I haue had good experience and triall of this ~~life,~~ <u>world</u> I know [what it is to be a subiect:] what ~~it is~~ to be a Soueraigne, what ~~it is~~ to haue good n[eighboures, and evell.] I haue found treason in trust;

seene great benefitts lit[tle regarded, in stede of] gratefulnes, ~~contrary~~
courses of purpose to crosse. thei[se former remembraunces,] present
feeling, and future expectacion of euills, I [saie haue moued me to
thinke] An iveL is muche the bettar the les while hit ~~endureth as~~ and so
them[4] ~~them~~ happiest that are hence, and taught mee to be[are with a
better minde these] treasons, then is common to my sexe, yea with a
better hart perhaps then is in some menn. Which I hope you will not
merely impute to my simplicitie, or want of vnderstanding, but rather
that I thus conceiued, that had theire purposes taken effect, I sholde not
haue founde the blow, before I had felt it, nor though my perill shold
haue bene great, my paine shold haue bene but small and shorte,
wherein as I wold be loth to dye, so bloodie a death, so dowbt I not but
God ~~will~~ wold haue geue_n me grace to be prepared for such an euent
chanche whan hit shal which I referre to his good pleasure.

   And now as towching theire treasons, and conspiracies together
with ~~her that was~~ the contriuer of them, I will not so preiudicate my
selfe, and this my Realme, as to say or thincke that I might not without
the last statute by th'auncient lawes of this land, haue proceeded against
her, which was not made particulerly to preiudice her, though perhaps
~~she and her practises~~ hit might then be suspected in ~~respect of ther
inclination, and the~~ respect of the disposition of ~~those, that depended
on her~~ suche as depended that way

   It was ~~also~~ so farre frome being intended to intrapp her, that it was
rather, an admonition, ~~a~~ to warn~~ing, and diswasion vnto her, frome
incurring~~ the daunger thereof. but sith it is made, and in the force of a
lawe, I thought good, in that which might concerne her, to proceede
according therunto, rather then by course of common lawe, wherein if
yow the Judges haue not deceaued mee, or that the bookes you brought
mee were not false, which God forbidd I mowght as Justly haue tried
her, by th'auncient lawes of the lande.

   But yow Lawiers are so nice and so precise in sifting and scanning
euery word and letter, that many times yow stand more vpon forme,
then matter, vppon syllabs, then the sense of the lawe. For in this
strictnes, and exact following of common forme she must haue bene
indited in Staffordshire, ~~haue~~ and[5] haue bene arraigned at the barre,

4. **An ivel . . . them** inserted in the left margin.
5. **and** inserted in the left margin.

holden vp her hand, ~~and~~ bene tried by a Jurye, a proper course forsoth
to deale in that maner with one of her estate. I thought it better
therefore (for avoiding ~~of all~~ thes and more absurdities), ~~and more~~
~~honorable~~ ~~to~~ to comit the cause to the inquisicion of a good nomber of
the greatest and most noble personages of this Realme, of the Judges
and others of good accownt, whose sentence I must approue.

And all litle inowgh for wee Princes, I tell you are set on stages, in
the sight and veiw, of all the worlde duly obserued, th'eyes of many
behold our actions, a spott is sone spied in our garments, a blemish
quickly noted in our doinges. It behoueth vs therefore to be carefull
that our proceedings be Just and honorable.

But I must tell you one thing ~~further that~~ more that in this late Acte
of Parliament you haue laied an hard hand on mee, that I must giue
direction for her death, which cannot be ~~to mee~~ but most greiuous ~~and~~
~~displeasaunt.~~ and an yrksom burdon to me And ~~to th'intent you do not~~
lest you might mistake mine absence frome this Parliament (which I
had almost forgotten) although there be no cawse why I should
willinglie come amongst multitudes, for that amongest many, some
may be euill, yet hath it not bin the dowte of any ~~thing, a~~ suche danger
or occasion that kept mee ~~away~~ from thence but only the great greif to
heare this cawse spoken of, especiallie ~~that this~~ that such a one of state
and kin should nide so open a declaration as a nation sholde be so
spotted with blotts of disloyaltie, Wherein the lesse is my greife for that
I hope the better part is myne, and those of the worse not much to be
accounted of, for that in seeking my destruction, they mighte haue
spoiled theire owne sowles.

And euen now cold I tell you that which wold make you sorie, It is a
secrett, and yet I will tell it you (although it be knowen I haue the
propertie to keepe Counsaile but to well, ~~often~~ times to mine owne
perill) It is not long since mine eyes did see it written that an othe was
taken within ~~14~~ few daies, either to kill mee or to be hanged themselues,
and that to be performed ere one moneth were ended.

[Comment written in left margin facing the preceding paragraph:]

Her Maiestie referred the further knoledg hereof to some of the Lords
there present wherof the Lord Thresurer seemed to be one for that he
stood vpp to verefy it.

[Main text resumes:]

Hereby I see youre daunger in mee, and neither can or will be so vnthanckfull or carelesse of your consciences, as to take no care for youre safetie.

I am not vnmindfull of youre othe ~~of~~ made in the association, manifesting ~~to mee,~~ your great goodwilles and affections taken and entered into vpon good conscience ~~and true knowledge of the guilt~~[6] for safe~~gard~~ty of my person, donn (I protest to God) before I euer heard ~~of~~ it, or ~~litle~~ euer thought of such a matter, till ~~3~~ a thowsand ~~of~~ hands Obligacions were shewed mee at Hampton Court, signed and subscribed with ~~th'andes~~ the names and seales of the ~~best~~ greatest of ~~my Realme.~~ this land Which ~~neuerthelesse~~ as I ~~do~~ acknowledge ~~as an~~ the greatest argument of youre ~~loyall~~ hartes, to me and ~~trew~~ great zeale to my safetie, ~~for which I thincke my selfe bounde carefully to consider of it, and respect you therein.~~ so shal my bonde be strongar tied to greater care for all good.

But for ~~asmuch as~~ that this matter ~~is verie~~ is rare, weightie, and of great consequence, and ~~that I haue not yet perused youre petition,~~ I thincke you do not looke for any present resolution, the rather for that as it is not my maner in matters of farre lesse moment, to giue speedie awnswere without due consideration, So in this of such importaunce, I thincke it verie requisite with earnest praier to beseech his diuine Maiestie, so to illuminate myne vnderstanding and inspire me with his grace, as I may do and determine that which shall serue to the Establishment of his Church, Preseruacion of youre Estates and prosperitie of this Common wealth vnder my Charge. Wherein for that I know delay is daungerous, you shall haue with all conueniency our Resolution deliuered by our message ~~to you all.~~ And what euer any Prince may meritt of theire subiects, for theire approued testimony of theire vnfained synceritie, either by gouerning iustly, voide of all partiality, or suffrance of any ~~Iurisdi~~ Iniuries donn euen to the poorest, that do I assuredly promis Inuiolablie to performe for requitall of youre ~~good~~ so many desertes.[7]

---

6. The phrase "true knowledge of the guilt" is too heavily canceled to be read with certainty.

7. The Petyt MS lacks this final paragraph.

SPEECH 18, VERSION 2 ❧ QUEEN ELIZABETH'S SECOND REPLY TO
THE PARLIAMENTARY PETITIONS URGING THE EXECUTION OF
MARY, QUEEN OF SCOTS, NOVEMBER 24, 1586[1]

Full greuous is the way whose goeing ~~in~~ on and ~~out findes~~ ende bredes
comber for the hier of a laborious Iourney.[2]

I haue striued more this day then euer in my life whither I shold
speake or ~~hold my peace.~~ use silence If I speake and not complaine I
shall dissemble, If ~~contrariewise~~ I hold my peace your labor taken
weare ~~in~~ ful vaine. / For me to make my mone weare strange and rare,
for I suppose youe shall find few that for theire owne perticuler will
comber youe with such a care. Yet such I ~~doe~~ protest hath bene my
greedie desire and hungry will, that of your consultation might haue
falne out some other meanes to work my saftie ioyned with youre
assurance (then that for which youe are become so ernest suitors) as I
protest I must needes vse complaint, though not of youe but vnto youe,
and of the cause; for that I doe perceaue by youre advises, praiers, and
desires, there falleth out this accident, that onelie ~~the bane of my Iniurer~~
my Iniurars baine must be ~~the suretie of my life.~~ my lifes suretie

But ~~if there liueth anie creature so vile or wicked of concept, as once~~
~~to carrie that thought of me,~~ if any ther liue so Wicked of nature to
suppose that I prolonged this tyme only, pro forma, to the intent to
make a shewe of clemencie, thereby to set my praises to the
wyerdrawers, to lenken them the more they doe me so great a wrong as
they can ~~neuer~~ hardly recompence. Or if anie ~~peruerse~~ person ~~doe~~ ther
be that thinkes or imagine that the least vaineglorious thought hath
drawne me furder herein, ~~thereby to be glorified,~~ they doe me as open
iniurie as euer was done to anie liueinge, creatur as he that is the maker
of all thoughts knoweth best ~~to be true.~~ to be tru. Or if there be anie that
think that the ~~doers are~~ Lordes[3] appointed in comission durst doe no
other as fearinge therebie to displease, or to be suspected to be of a

---

1. *Source:* BL, MS Lansdowne 94, art. 35B, fols. 86r–88r. Again, a copy probably in Robert
Cecil's formal italic, with revisions in Elizabeth's cursive italic, indicated here by underscoring. A marginal heading of twenty-two words at the beginning of the text has been so heavily overwritten that nothing can be read. The endorsement reads "The 2 copy of her
Maiestys second speach 24 Novembre. Before her Maiestie corrected it." Like Speech 17, Version 2, Speech 18, Version 2, was published in R[obert] C[ecil], *The copie of a letter to the earle
of Leycester,* largely as revised by Elizabeth, except for its final two paragraphs.

2. The maxim is set off as though it were the scriptural text for a sermon.

3. ~~doers are~~ Lordes Robert Cecil's correction.

contrarie opinion to my safety, they doe but heape vpon me Iniurious
conceipts. For either those put in trust bie me ~~for this action~~ to supplie
my place, haue not performed theire dutie towards me ~~in that I gaue
them in chardg,~~ or els they haue signified vnto youe all, that my desire
was, that euerie one shold doe according to his conscience, and in ~~that~~
the course of theise proceedings, shold enioy both freedome of voice,
and libertie of opinion and ~~t~~what they Wold not openly the might
privatly ~~tell~~ to my self declare.[4] It was of ~~an honorable~~ willing minde
and greate desire I had, that some other meanes might be found out
wherin I shold haue taken more comfort then in anie other thinge vnder
the sonne. And ~~seeinge~~ sins now it is resolued, that my suretie cannot
be established, without a Princess head, I haue iust cause to complaine
that I who haue in my tyme pardoned so manie rebells, winked at so
manie treasons, and either not produced them, or altogether slipt them
ouer with silence, shold now be forced to this proceeding against such
a person. I haue besids during my reigne seene and hard manie
opprobrious bookes and pamphlets against me, my realme, and state,
accusinge me to be a tyrant I thank them for theire almes, I beleue
therein theire meaning was to tell me newes, and newes ~~to me~~ it is in
deede to me, I wold it weare as ~~great news~~ strange to heare of theire
impietie. What will theie not now say, when it shall be spread, that for
the safetie of her life a maiden Quene could be content, to spill the blood
euen of her owne kinswoman. I maie therefore full well complaine, that
anie man~~s~~[5] shold thinke me giuen to creweltie, whereof I am so guiltless
and Innocent, as I shold slander God, if I shold saie he gaue me ~~such~~ so
Vile a mynd: Yea I protest ~~vnto youe~~ I am so farre from it, that for myne
owne life, I wold not touche her, neither hath my care bene so much
bent, how to prolong myne, as how to preserue both, which I am right
sorie is made so hard, yea so impossible./[6]   I am not so void of
iudgment as not to see myne owne perill, nor yet so ignorant as not to
know it weare in nature a foolishe course, to cherish a sword to cut
myne owne throat, nor so careless as not to waigh, that my life daielie is
in hazard, but this I do consider that manie a man wold put his life in
danger, for the safegard of a kinge, I doe not say that ~~I meane to doe so,
so wil I~~ but I praie youe thinke that I haue thought vpon it.[7]   But

4. **to my self declare** insertion runs over into the left margin.
5. **man̄** Robert Cecil's correction.
6. A twelve-letter space occurs mid-line, at this point in the text.
7. A six-letter space occurs here.

sith so manie hath both writen and spoken against me I praie youe giue
me leaue to say somewhat for my self, and before youe retorne to your
contries lett youe knowe, ~~youe haue travayled for me~~ for what a one yow
haue passed so carefull thoghts that will neuer be forgetfull of youre
exceding cares for my safetie. And as I thinke my self ~~greatelie~~ infinitely
beholdinge vnto youe, all that ~~youe~~ seeke to preserue my life by all the
meanes youe ~~cann,~~ may so I protest that there ~~is liuing no~~ liueth no
Prince ~~that euer hath bin or can be more thankfull vnto youe for it.~~ nor
euer shalbe more mindfuL to requite so good desartz wherein as I
perceaue youe haue kept your old wont in a generall seeking ~~of~~ the
~~safetie of~~ lengtning of my ~~life,~~ dayes so ~~doe I conceaue that I am~~ am I
sure that neuer ~~hable to~~ shal I requite it, vnles I had as many liues as youe
all, but for euer I will acknowledge it while there is ~~in me anie life~~ any my
brethe left me . /

    Althogh I may not iustefie but may iustly condemne my ~~selfe~~ sondry
~~Next I will make~~ you ~~my confession to him that made me, and say~~
faultes and sins to God Yet for my care in this gouuerment let me ~~acqu~~
~~before youe all, that I am a synner, full of faults, a wretch that haue bene~~
acquaint you with my intentz
~~much forgetfull of my dutie towards God,~~ for if I shold say otherwise I
~~shold offend both God and youe, and most of all forget my self. And~~
~~seeing so manie pennes haue ben vsed to discourse the actions of youer~~
~~gouernoure, I wil say somewhat for my self~~

                          sceptar my titel made me not forget the
    When ~~I~~ first I tooke the ~~crowne, I not somuch remembred, the~~
giuar and therfor began as hit became me, with such religion as bothe
~~cepter, but him that gaue it and therefore sought to establish in this~~
I was borne in ~~and~~ bread in,
~~kingdome, his church~~ and that Religion, wherein[8] and ~~wherein I hope~~
~~to~~ I trust shall die in, although *then entred I into the schole of experience*[9]
I was not so simple as not to know what danger and perill so great an
alteration *~~what fitted a king to do and theare I sawe he skant was well~~*
~~furnished if either he lacked iustice, temper, magnanimitie or iudgement~~
might procure me, how manie great princes of the contrarie ~~that terme~~
~~themselues Catholique~~ opinion wold attempt all they might against
me, and generallie what enimitie I shold therebie breede vnto my self;

---

8. **and that Religion, wherein** though marked for retention, these words are rendered su-
perfluous by Elizabeth's revision, "with such religion as bothe I was borne in and bread in."

9. This and the following italicized and stricken-through phrases appear to be in a third,
cursive italic hand, neither Elizabeth's nor Robert Cecil's.

which all I regarded not, knowing that he for whose sake I did it ~~wold safelie~~ <u>might and wold</u> defend me, ~~for which it is that euer since, I haue bene so dangerouslie prosecuted, as I~~ rather marvell that I ~~am,~~ <u>mai be</u> then ~~that I am not,~~ <u>that I shul not be</u> if it weare not Gods hollie hand that contynueth me beyond all <u>other</u> expectation.

    I was not simplie trained vp, nor in my yewth spent my tyme altogether idly, and yet when I came to the crowne, then entred I first into the scole of experience; bethinking my self of those things that best fitted a kinge, Iustice, temper, Magnanimitie, Iudgment;[10] for I found it most requisite that a Prince shold be endued with Iustice, that he shold be adorned with temperance, I conceaued magnanimite to beseeme a Royall estate possessed by whatsoeuer sex, and that it was
for the
necessarie that such a person shold be of Iudgment:[11]   ~~of which~~ two latter I wyll not boast But for the two first this may I truly say: ~~last two I will not speake, for that I am not greatlie trobled with them;~~ among my subiects I neuer knew a difference of person wheare right ~~and yet I remember well that Salomon saith, that nothinge is more~~ was one, nor neuer to my knowledg preferrd for fauor what I thought ~~requisite for a king then Iudgment: for the first, this maie I truely saye,~~ not fitt for worth nor bent myne eares to credit a tale that first was told ~~that I was neuer led to consent to anie thinge that I thought vniust, I~~ me, nor was so rashe to corrupt my iudgement with any censure er I ~~neuer preferred anie in respect of the preferrer, if I thought him not my~~ heard the cause I will not say but many reports might fortune be ~~self worthie of the preferment, nor euer in matter of Iustice, respected~~ brought me by suche as must heare the matter ~~that thire~~ <u>whose</u> ~~the person to the alteration of my censure; I neuer lent my eare to~~ partiality might marre the right for we princes cannot heare ~~bu~~ all ~~corrupt my iudgment, or changed my opinion of any, but by the iust~~ causes ourselues ~~but I dare boldly affirme~~ But this dare I boldly affirme ~~motion of those, that weare by me put in trust, to examyne the cause,~~ ~~wherein as in a thing comon to all Princes I must of force vse some for~~

10. **those things that best fitted a kinge . . . Iudgment:** Elizabeth, who as princess had read the Greek text of Plato with her tutor Roger Ascham, alludes to Book 4 of the *Republic* where justice, temperance, courage, and wisdom (or judgment) are identified as the cardinal political virtues, and attributed to the virtuous ruler (441e–442e). Another text familiar to her, Cicero's *De officiis,* Book 1, chap. 5, secs. 15, 63, is the source for equating courage in Plato's grouping with magnanimity. This passage is a rare articulation of Elizabeth's guiding political principles.

11. A six-letter space occurs at this point in the text. Revisions in the following interlineated passage are entirely in Robert Cecil's hand. Elizabeth's hand resumes with "<u>But ful welL.</u>"

~~theire aduice, yet will I this take vpon me that to my knowledg~~ my
verdict went ~~euer~~ with the truth of my knowledg.

~~As it was~~ But ful welL wished ~~by~~ Alcibiades ~~to~~ his frend that he shold
not giue anie aunswere till he had recited the letters of the Alphabet, so
haue I not vsed ouer sodaine resolutions in matters ~~of anie weight nor
determyned oft without deliberation.~~ that haue touched me ful nere
you Wyl say that With me I think And therefore as touching youre
counsels and consultations, I conceaue them to be wise, honest, and
conscionable: so prouident, and carefull for the saftie of my life, (which
I wish no longer then may be for youre good) that though I ~~can~~ neuer
can yeld youe ~~due~~ of recompence ~~your due~~ yet shall I indevoure my self
to giue youe cause to think your good will not ill bestowed, and striue
to make my self worthy for[12] such subiectes and as for your petition I
shall praie youe[13] for this present to content your selues

[Two diagonal penstrokes score the next passage from upper left to lower right
through the end of this paragraph; one stroke continues lightly into the second
line of the next paragraph.]

ansWerles   for
with an aunswere ~~without aunswere, which is,~~ if I shold say it shold not
                                          to tel you
be done, (by my faith) weare more then I ment, If I shold say it shall be
done, it weare more then I cold now assure or were conuenient here to
be declared: I therefore protest as there was neuer anie Prince more
beholding vnto her subiects ~~then~~ I ~~am vn~~to youe, so was there neuer
Prince, more willing to do youe good then I in my mynd, though I may
fayle in the means. /

Your Iudgment I condemne not, neither do I mistake your reasons,
but praie youe to accept my thankfullnes, excuse[14] my doubtfullnes,

12. **for** or, alternatively, to; Elizabeth's loosely written letterforms are ambiguous.

13. **I shall praie youe** One scratchy, discontinuous penstroke from what looks like Elizabeth's pen begins at the base of this "I" and ends at the "x" in "excuse my doubtfulnes." A second penstroke begins at the base of the "e" in "youe" and ends at the "v" in "vnto her subiects."
Elizabeth makes other, local deletions and insertions in this stretch, as indicated, but the diagonal penstrokes appear to mark a still later intention to delete the remainder of this paragraph. It is not, however, deleted in the printed copy. The light intervention here contrasts
sharply with Elizabeth's heavy, extensive cancellation of words, phrases, and passages in the
earlier portions of the MS.

14. **excuse** The longer diagonal penstroke ends at the "x" in "excuse."

and take in good part my aunswer aunswerles: wherein I attribute
not so much to my owne Iudgment, but that I think, many perticuler
persons may go before me, though by my degree I go before them,
therefore if I shold say, I wold not doe what youe request, it might
peraduenture be more then I thought, and to say I wold do it, might
perhaps breed perill of that youe labor to preserue; being more then
in youer owne wisdoms and discretions wold seeme conuenient,
circumstances of place and tyme being duely considered. /

LETTER 74 ⮑ ELIZABETH TO JAMES, JANUARY–FEBRUARY 1587[1]

[Addressed] To my verey good brother and Cousin the King of Skotz

I finde my selfe so trobled lest sinistar tales might delude you My good
brother that I haue willingly found out this messanger whom I knowe
most sincere to you and a true subiect to me to carry unto You my most
sincere meaning toWard you and to request this iust desiar that you
neuer dout my intiere good WylL in your behalfe and do protest that
if you knewe iVen sins the arriValL of your Commissionars (Wiche
if the list the may telL you) the exstreme dangier my life Was in by
an Embassadors honest Silence if not invention and suche good
Complices as haue them selves (by Godz permission[2] vnfolded the
hole Conspiratie and haue aduouched hit befor his face thogh hit be
the periL of ther oWne Lives Yet voluntaryly One of them neuer beinge
Suspected brake hit with a Councelar to make ᵐᵉ acquainted therWith
You may see whither I kipe the Serpent that poisons me Whan the
Confes to haue reWard by sauing of her Life the wold haue had mine /
do I not make my selfe troWe ye a goodly pray for euery Wretche to
deuour Transfigure your selfe into my state and Suppose What you
aught to do and therafter Way my life and reiect the Care of murdar
and shun alL baites that may untie your Amities and let alL men
KnoWe that Princes knoWe best ther oWne Lawes and misiuge not
that you knoWe not for my part I Wyl not liue to Wronge the menist
and So I Conclude you with your oWne wordes you wyl prosecute or

1. *Source:* BL, MS Additional 23240, art. 18, fols. 57v–58r, with seal and ribbon attached. The
endorsement reads "Resauit 17 february 1586 be post."
2. A closing parenthesis is lacking in the MS.

mislike as muche thos that seake my ruine as yf the sought your hart
bloud and Wold I had none in myne if I Wold not do the like As God
knoWeth to Whom I make my humble prayers to inspire you with
best desiars

I am sending you a GentiLman fourWith
the other being fallen sik who I trust shal
yeld you good reason of my Actions³

Your most
affectionated Sistar
and Cousin
Elizabeth R

LETTER 75 ⪻ ELIZABETH TO JAMES, CIRCA FEBRUARY 1, 1587¹

[Addressed] To my deare brother and Cousin the Kinge of Skotz

be not Caried aWay My deare brother with the lewd perswations of
suche as instede of infourming you of my to to nidefuL and helpeles
Cause of defending the brethe that God hathe giuen me to be bettar
spent than spilte by the bloudy invention of traitors handz May
perhaps make you beliue that ether the offense Was not so great or if
that cannot serue them for the ouer manefest trialL wiche in publik and
by the greatest and most in this land hathe bine manifestly proved Yet
the Wyl make that her life may be Saued and myne safe Wiche Wold
God wer true for whan you make VeWe of my long danger indured thes
foWre Welny fiue monethes time to make a tast of the greatest witz
amongs my oWne, and than of frenche and Last of you you wyl graunt
with me that if nide wer not mor than my malice she shuld not haue her
merite And noW for a good Conclusion of my Long taried for answer
Your Commisssionars telz me that I may trust her in the handes of
some indifferent prince, and haue alL her Cousins and allies promis she
wyL no more seake my ruine. Deare brother and Cousin Way in true
and equal balance Wither the lak not muche good ground whan suche
stuf serues for ther bilding Suppose you I am so mad to trust my life in
anothers hand and send hit oWt of my owne If ᵗʰᵉ young Master of
Gray for Curring faueur with you might fortune say hit Yet old ᵐᵃˢᵗᵉʳ

3. This postscript is squeezed into the lower lefthand corner of the sheet.
1. *Source:* BL, MS Additional 23240, art. 19, fols. 61r–62r. Bruce reports an endorsement,
"Resauit 8 Feb^rij 1586 be post," which is no longer fully legible since the MS was mounted on
stubs.

MylVin hathe yeres ynough to teache him more Wisdome than tel a
Prince of my iugement suche a Contrarieus friVolous maimed Reason
Let your Councelors for your honeur discharge ther duty so muche
to you as to declaire the absurditie of suche an Offer and for my part
I do assure my selfe to muche of your Wisdome as thogh like a most
naturalL Good Son you charged them to seake alL meanes the could
diuis with Wit or iugement to saue her life Yet I can not nor do not
allege any fault to you of thes persuations for I take hit that you Wil
remember that aduis or desiars aught euer agree ~~euer~~[2] ~~euere~~ with the
Surtye of the party sent to and honor of the sendar Wiche Whan bothe
you Way I doute not but your Wisdome wiL excuse my nide and Waite[3]
my necessitie and not accuse me ether of malice or of hate / And noW
to Conclude make Accownt I pray you of my firme frindeship, loue and
Care of wiche you may make sure Accownt as one that never mindz to
faile from my Word nor sWarue from our league but Wyl increase by
alL good meanes any action that may make true shewe of my stable
Amitie from wiche My deare brother let no sinistar Whisperars nor
busy troblars of Princis states persuade you to leaue your Surest / and
Stike to vnstable Staies, Suppose them to be but the Ecchos to suche
Whos stipendaries the be and Wyl do more for ther gaine than your
Good And So God hold you Euer in his blessed kipinge and make you
see your tru frindz Excuse my not writing sonar for pain in on of my
yees was only the cause

Your most Assured Louinge Sistar and Cousin /
Elizabeth R

LETTER 77 ᘒ᙮ ELIZABETH TO HENRY III OF FRANCE, MAY 1587[1]

[Addressed] A mon bon frere Le Roy treschrestien

Mounsieur mon bon Frere, Est il possible que moy meritant tant en
vostre endroict pour l'entiere affection et solide Amitie que de

---

2. ~~euer~~ This deleted addition had been inserted in the left margin.
3. **Waite** "wait" or "weight"; either sense is possible.
1. *Source:* Bodleian Library, University of Oxford, MS Add. C.92 (formerly, MS Arch. F.c.8),
fol. 26.

longueman vous ay tousiours porte oultre d'honneur que Ie tiens du
Rencq de Roy Ie deusse estre traicte si estrangement voyre plustot en
Vraye Ennemye que Vous ayant escript par mon Ambassadeur chose
de grande importance fort Convenable pour vostre Scene² et a moy
Ce que me touche d'aussy pres que chose en se monde qu'il ne vous a
pleu ly daigner audience Ce deux mois, c'est ~~plus~~ une chose iamais nye
a Prince de mon qualite Et aussy pour auoir arreste tous les Vaisseaux
de nos subiectz Vraye acte d'hostilite Ce que Ie me figure n'estre de
Vostre scene ny par vostre mandement et nonobstant on le ne repond
que c'est par vostre ordre Ce qui me rend bien estonne quelle en seroit
la Cause, Car pour ~~estre ce~~ estre chose si insupportable d'endurer si
mauuaise si traicteuse d'ou l'ay merite meilleur actions Que Ie Vous
suplie que par escript ou parolle l'en sois satisfaict, Car l'ay de Jour en
Jour tant de plainctes et querelles de mes affliges subiectz que sans que
Vous y remedies bien tost Ce n'est point possible que Ie leur niye Iustice
pour s'en Venger Comme Dieu scait

a qui Ie prie Vous Conceder   Vostre bien affectionee
bonne Vie et Longue me   Soeur et Cousine
recommandant bien   Elizabeth R³
fort a Vos bonnes Graces / ⁴

LETTER 78 · ELIZABETH TO JAMES, CIRCA JULY 1, 1588¹

[Addressed] To our right deere brother the King of Scotland

I am greatly satisfied My deare brother that I find by your owne graunt
that you bileue the trothe of my Actions so manifestly openly proved
and thanke you infinitely that yow profes so constant defence of your
Country ~~and~~ togither myne from alL spaniardz or strangers A matter

2. **Scene** Elizabeth apparently makes innovative use of this word here and below; Paul
Robert, *Le Grand Robert de la langue française,* 2nd ed. rev. Alain Rey (Paris: Dictionnaires
Le Robert, 1985), does not record the meaning of a wrought-up situation, a quarrel or dis-
pute, until the late seventeenth century.

3. A large tear obliterates most of the endorsement's three lines but leaves readable the date
"Mai 1587."

4. The ending of this letter is squeezed into the lefthand side of the sheet next to the signature.

1. *Source:* BL, MS Additional 23240, art. 22, fol. 71. The endorsement reads "9 July 1588."

fur otherwise giuen out by bothe our Enemies Wiche blotting your
fame with assurance of doble dealing as thogh you assured them
underhand to betake you to ther course, Wiche What a stain hit Wer in
a Princis honor you your selfe in iugement can WeL deme for my part I
wyl euer trust your word til I be to sure of the Contrary Right wel am I
persuaded that your great^tist daunger shuld chanche you by Crossing
your strait pathes for he that hathe two stringes to his bowe may shoute
strongar but neuer strait, and he that hathe no sure foundation Can not
but ruine God kipe you euer therfor in your wel bigone pathe / I haue
sent you this Gentilman as wel to declare my good agrement to send
some finischars of our leage as other matters Wiche he hathe to
communicate unto you if hit please you to heare him as my desiar of
answering your Good frindeship and amitie in as ample sort as with
honor I may as One that neuer seakes more of you than that Wiche
shalbe best for your selfe Assure your selfe of me therfor and shewe by
dides euer to mantaine hit and neuer Was ther in Christendome
betwine two princis Surar Amitie nor soundar dealing I ~~Wo~~ Vowe hit
and wil perfourme hit

And for that you speake oft of satisfaction I haue much Vrged as
noW againe I do to knowe what therby is ment Sins I bothe mynde and
also do ~~me~~ Whatsoeuer may honorably be required of Suche as I profes
my selfe and therfor I require you therin to answer me, and so trusting
that all your protestations lately made me by Cary shalbe readely
perfourmed togither with your Constant resolute Cours of late
professed I end to molest you Longar but with my thankes to God that
any your offendars be entred to your handz and not the les not hauing
bine done without some of our helpe Wiche gladz me no les than
happened to our selfe Whose forse shal neuer faile you in all leaful
Causes as KnoWeth God Who euer bles you from all malignant spiritz
and increas your happy yeres /

Your most Assurest Sistar and Cousin /
Elizabeth R

LETTER 79 ❧ ELIZABETH TO JAMES, AUGUST 1588[1]

[Addressed] To my verey good brother the Kinge of SCottz.

Now may appeare My deare brother, how malice ioigned with might
strikiest to make a shamefuL end to a Vilanous beginning for by
Godz singular fauor hauing ther flete wel beaten in Our naroW Seas
and pressing with alL Violence to atcheue some watering place to
Continue ther pretended InVation the Windz haue Caried them to
your Costes Wher I dout not the shal receaue smaL succor and les
Welcome Vnles thos Lordz that so traitors Like Wold belie ther owne
prince and promis an other King reliefe in your name be suffred to
liVe at libertye to dishonor you periL you and aduance some other
(wiche God forbid you suffar them liue to do) Therfor I send you this
Gentilman a rare younge man and a wise to declare unto <u>yov</u>[2] my
fuL Opinion in this greate Cause as One that neuer WyL abuse you
to serue my owne turne nor WyL you do aught that my selfe Wold
not perfourme If I Wer in your place / You may assure your selfe
that for my part I dout no whit but that alL this tirannicaL proWd
and brainsick attempt Wil be the beginning thogh not the end of the
ruine of that King that most unkingly Euen in midz of treating peace
begins this Wrongful War he hathe procured my greatest Glory
that ment my sorest Wrack And hathe so dimmed the Light of his
Sonshine that who hathe a wyl to obtaine shame let them kipe his
forses Companye / but for al this for your selfe sake let not the frendz
of Spain be suffred to yeld them forse for thogh I feare not in the
end the sequele Yet if by hauing them unhelped you may increase
the Englisch hartz unto you You shal not do the Worst dide for your
behalfe for if aught shuld be done Your excuse Wyl play the boiteux
If you make not sure worke with the likely men to do hit / Looke
wel vnto hit I beseche you The necessity of this matter makes my
skribling the more spidye hoping that you WyL mesure my good
Affection with the right balance of my actions Wiche to you shalbe
euer suche as I haue professed not doutinge of the reciproque of your
behalfe According as my last messangier unto you hathe ~~ha~~ at lenth

---

1. *Source:* BL, MS Additional 23240, art. 24, fol. 77, with remnants of seal and ribbon attached.
2. **yov** underlining in MS.

signefied for the Wiche I rendar you a Milion of gratefuL thankes
togither for the Last generalL prohibition to your subiectz not to fostar
nor ayde Our generall foe / Of wiche I dout not the obseruation if the
ringeleadars be safe in your[3]   handz / As knoweth God
                                                        Who euer haue you
    Your most assured   in his blessed Kiping
    Louing Sistar and   with many happy
    Cousin /   yeres of raigne.
    Elizabeth R[4]

PRAYER 36 ❧ ON THE DEFEAT OF THE SPANISH ARMADA, 1588[1]

Most powrefuL and Largist Giving God whos eares hit hathe pleasyd
So beningLy to Grace the petitions of Vs thy deuoted Saruent ~~that~~ not
With euen measure ~~cannot~~ to our desiars but with ∧far amplar fauor
hathe not only protected Our Army from foez pray, and from Seas
danger but hast detained malisiciVs desonurs[2] iVen hauing fors to
resist Vs from hauing poWer to attemmpt Vs or assaile ~~theim~~ them[3]
Let humble acknowLegement and most reuerend thankes sacrifice
suppLy ~~the~~ Our Want of SkiL to Comprehend suche endLes Goodnis
and Vnspeakable Liberalitie Euen Suche / Good Lord as Our Simple
tounges may not Include suche Wordz as merites suche Laudes / but
this VoWe Except[4] most deare God in Lieu of bettar merite that
Our brithes We hope to ther Last Gaspes shaL neuer Cease ~~to~~ the

---

3. A ten-letter space intervenes between "your" and "handz" in the MS.

4. Atypically, the subscription is found on the left in this letter and the closing phrase on
the right.

1. *Source:* Hatfield House, Cecil Papers, 147, fol. 213r; draft, bound immediately following
the French stanzaic verses (Poem 14), but an independent composition on different, smaller
paper. For a photographic reproduction, see *CW*, p. 422, facing Prayer 36. Dating is conjectural, based on the prayer's subject and the characteristic looseness of the letterforms. The
possibility cannot be excluded that the prayer was composed even later to record the queen's
thanks for delivery from one of the several threatened invasions by a reconstituted Spanish
Armada during the 1590s.

2. **desonurs** dishonorers.

3. **them** i.e., the English army.

4. **Except** accept.

memorialL of Suche fLoWing Grace as thy bounty filLs Vs with but
with suche thoghts shaL end the World and Liue to the
Al thes with thy ~~hel~~ good Grace
We trust performe
we shaL

POEM 15 ᆇ TWENTY-SEVEN STANZAS IN FRENCH, COMPOSED
CIRCA 1590[1]

Avecq l'aueugler si estrange
  Si au rebours de mon Nom
bien che tout Le mal me deçoit
de ce part que fus homme
Me recogneu que beste   5
Cest estre en que fus nay
  tant de tout se perda~~ict~~
Que' alors en moy se Vist
  rien ~~de moy si Long que moy~~ que fust ~~en~~ a moy
Si Loing ~~que~~ le fus de moy ~~mesme~~   10

  Combien que au mal Ie me resiste
estant un peu en resueiL
Ie Vis mes deux ~~ombres~~ hommes en Un
  Et au bout l'estois Le plus sure
En voyant qu'il ny ~~eust~~ fust Vn   15
  de moymesme Ie prins enVie
Alors de ~~m'espreuuer~~ m'esprouVer
  Mais de honte que Ie senty

---

1. *Source:* Hatfield House, Cecil Papers 147, fols. 207r–212r. Although written on different
paper, of a different size, Elizabeth's Prayer 36, which we have taken to refer to the Armada
victory, is bound immediately following this poem; hence our conjectural date. Throughout
this text, which we interpret as a working (i.e., non-final) draft, Elizabeth's hand is rapid,
sprawling, and so loosely formed that, in particular, it becomes impossible to distinguish reliably between the letterforms *e* and *i*. At these repeated junctures, orthography and grammar determine our construals—thus, *Ie* (not *Ii*), *de* (not *di*), and *que* (not *qui*, as object pronoun with a non-human antecedent).

Ne me trouVant pour regner
  En mon Royaulme Ie me garde   20

Quant me trouvay tant perdu
  Dv ~~il~~ mal me pensay partir
Mais quant m'esforse faire la change
  Ie me tro^{u}Ve si stropie
Qu'il ne fust possible muer   25
ALors me donna tant tristesse
  Voyant Le mal ~~que~~ tant s'efforse
Que tel estant son Viguer
  Voulant esprouver mes forses
fust esprouVe ma faiblesse   30

  Secours ne me manqua
Me leuer seul l'esprouVe
Mais Celuy qui m'aida
Au Commancer me ~~soustenait~~ soustenait
  Au demy me delaissa   35
Son doleur ne Laissa
  Iamais pour me soustenir
Sans ~~pour son aide~~ donner aultrement son aide
  par ou a ma fo^{i}blesse
me pouvois aider   40

  Comme L'enfant qui non Va
Mais s'acLine[2] pour plus aler
S'il soit Sage qui Le mene
  Et tient garde Ou il Ua
Peu a peu il s'en despeche   45
  Ainsi Celuy qui me mena
Comme Vn enfant me tir~~e~~^{a}it
Les princip~~l~~es m'enseigna
  Le surplus que n'~~a~~ aprendy
Le guardoit pour Le Capable   50

2. **acLine** encline (obsolete form).

Ie m'arriue au primier degre
 de La grace qui Commençe
  d'ou CeLuy qui est bien lie
S'iL ne perde La teste
  Se tient pour bien liVre   55
La La Lumiere s'esclaira
  Les tenebres s'esuanuirent
Combien que Le SoleiL n'aparuct[3]
  ou Le Ciel ~~ne se~~ S'ouurist, Le CLair Iour ~~appa ru~~
    se monstra[4]   60

 ~~Ie Viens au primier degre~~
~~de La Grace qui se Commance~~
 ~~d'ou celuy qui est deja arriVe~~
~~S'il ne perde La teste~~
 ~~Se tient pour bien Livre~~

Moy Voyant qui a l'aube
 Ie Commence a m'entendre
Lors fust temps de me partir
 Mais non de telle Sorte
Que ne scaUois bien gouVerner   65
 ~~ppeu a ppeu~~ me souuenna
Car l'estois tant triste
 que Le Songe qui me fascha
du Songe ~~passe me tormenta~~ qui fust passe
 Sembla me tormenter   70

 Comme Vn pasteur qui a dormy
A La nuict en ~~son~~d Cabine
 Qui Venant Le matin
Se Leue moyty endormy
 Et Va a La Mountaine   75
Et Sufflant aux mains
 S' esbranle et resueille

---

3. **aparuct** historical past tense of "aparer," an obsolete form of "(ap)paraître."
 4. Elizabeth squeezed the line numbered 60 into the bottom right of the page next to line 59, as indicated.

Ansy L'ame qui fust morte
    En desirs que trop Vaines
Se trouva que fust Veillant   80

Iusques a l'abisme du CieL
    Ie Vi l'ayr Seren
Et me souVenant de La baptesme
    Ie Cognu que si Loing
I'estois tousiours de moymesme   85
    Ie Vi Le Soleil en son semblance
Si beau et si Luisant /   tant de Lumiere
    que Come que se fust en Orient ^   en un instant /
                                       Se monstra en
                                       Occident[5]   90

Or Le Second Secours
    Commença me Soustenir
de que me sceu prevaloir
    de maulx de ce monde
Sans periL de me ruiner   95
    De mon mal me pense Sain
Mais non tant sans paine
    Que Se fut tant en ma puissance
Chiminer autant par Le tortu
    Comme par Le plain   100

Me souuenant bien[6] ╪ En Songe
    reguardant en hault
Ie me trovy si auançe
    que en moy Seul La Coustume
~~resta du peche~~ me demoura du peche   105
    Et a pecher me detourna
Et prest a fuir fust mon Ame
    Le mal Ie aprehendois
Mais Si tost fust tue
    Que tantot Le mal Se Vist   110

---

5. Elizabeth used a caret to key the lines numbered 89 and 90 into the lower right corner of the page, next to lines 87 and 88, as indicated.

6. Elizabeth's handwriting is perfectly ambiguous between "bien" and "dieu" here. Either reading makes sense: "Remembering well in dream" or "Remembering God in dream."

ALors nouvellement faict
    Ie Vi L'estat de mon Coeur
Qu'estoit tant ruine
    Que La raison se tenant en l'ame
Ly fist Le plus despit   115
    ~~Ie Vi~~ Cree comme de rien
Ie Vi mon homme au dedans
    Si reduict de La en son Centre
Que La Vie passee
    L'osta d'un mal encountre   120

Laissant d'estre estrangier
    Ie ~~fuist~~ refaict en un moment
Auecque tout bien ConIoinct
    Sur Ce qui est Le mieulx
l'enhaussas[7] Le Countrepoint   125
Car Celuy qui me Crea
    Qui en tout se contente
En diuers sortes me fourna
    ~~D~~ Au Commancer me fist
Et puis me Convertist   130

Estant si hault avance
    Comme l'ay dict et tranfourmé
En mon ordre ~~d~~ ordonné
    Ie Vi mon regne bien gouverne
Par raison et non par degre   135
    Ie Vi trois Ames ressamblans
Mis en exercise
    Chascun en son office
L'une pour Commander
    Et Les deux pour seruir   140

Ie Vi ~~tout~~ tantost La fantasie
    Comme Enfant respirant

---

7. **enhaussas** historical past tense of "enhausser"; the implied metaphor is either that Elizabeth has raised God's sword or that she, as God's deputy, is that sword. We thank Constance Jordan for this reading and gloss.

Mais La Raison ne Le ~~suffra~~ permis

    pour Le bien de l'aultre part

Qui passast La Querelle   145

    Vi ~~mes mon~~ mes Lourds Sentimentz

~~Combi~~ Sans en auoir L'enuie

Et TrouVa que Selon ~~ces~~ Leur mires

    ~~Ils ne Cherchoient~~

    Seuls ilz Chersoient

Leur primier mouVementz   150

Ie vis ~~au~~ le plus haut SΦere[8]

    De l'ame qui gouuerna

Et comme me Sembla

    Au dedans brusLa

Et ~~d~~ dehors adumbrant[9]   155

La Ie Vi L'entendement

    ~~Auec~~ Ayant La Verite pour Obiect

Et Vi tout Le Gouuerment

    Si ~~tout~~ pres d'estre parfaict

Que me rendes Content[10]   160

Ie Vi La Volunte donner charge

    Absolu et Ordinaire

Qui par accroistre Sa Suite

    Iusques a l'extraordinair

Elle alla tout bellement   165

Ie Vi La part qui est l'esperon

    Du Salut et La bride

Ie Vi Amour qui haulsa voile

de desir qui pour Quardon

    Se va bien ~~bie~~ paye de la toile   170

---

8. **SΦere** Sphere. Elizabeth's use of Greek phi to render an "f" sound is an occasional idiosyncrasy of her spelling. Compare the two instances in Letter 60, written to James—a similarly learned regal correspondent.

9. **adumbra** the coined intransitive verb derives from transitive Latin *adumbrare*, "to shadow, to obscure."

10. **Content** a noun.

Ie Vi plus l'haulte memoire
   tresor de~~e~~ l'humain b^(i)en
Ou Ie trouue La Large histoire
   De mon estre qui fust si Vain
Que n'estoit pour donner Gloire   175
   Se fust bien pour me Souuenir
De mon inique mal absent[11]
   Depuis mon Ame a Consenty
Que me SouVenant du passe
   Se Corrigea[12] Le present   180

Le passe et que Viendra
   Tout Le[13] mis deuant
Et ~~pour~~ d'auoir este Inconstant
   Ie Viens a ly reciter
      fit
Que ne ~~rendict~~ estre Constant   185
   Retourne a ma Conscience
Ce qui est et Ce qui fust
   Le tout mis en~~e~~ ma presence
Sur moy qui retins le manement
   Se mi^(s)t en sa demeure   190

   Le regret de ma faulte
du peche me liVra
   Car tant m'affligea
Que seul mon Soing se fust
   de n'en auoir de Soing asses   195
   scachant que
Mire[14] ~~estant~~ en Ioye
   Ie duis patir
   tournois
Me ~~mettoit~~ a tant depleurer

11. **absent** in the sense of Latin *absentare*, "to send away."
12. **Corrigea** historical past tense in place of a conditional.
13. **Le** lui.
14. **Mire** mieux.

Que mille fois mon Aise
Renouvella me[15] paines   200

Pour accroistre le doleur
de ~~d~~ ma passee follie
    Contemplant mon Creatur
Il me souuena du fabrique
    De moy triste pecheur   205
Ie Vi que Dieu me rachepta
    Contre de Luy estant crueL
Et reguardant bien qui iL fust
    Ie Vi ~~bien~~ comme il se fist moy
    A si que Ie me fis Luy   210

Ie Vis que quant il me forma
    Nul estat me donna
Mais metta en ma main
    Que moymesmes pre~~m~~ⁿast
Ce que plus me Contenta   215
    Qui pourroit estre bistial
     aultrement
Ou ~~pour~~   humain
    Ou qui fust AngelicaL
Et que se fust en mes mains
    Prendre Le ~~deuin~~ diuinaL[16]   220

Ie Vi son haulte providence
    Ou tout est faict qui se passe
Que Iamais me donna aduis
    Qui ne fust pour le bien
De ma propre Cognoissance   225
    Ie Vi La Cause pourquoy il Vouloit
Auoir faict Le feu EuerneL,[17]
    Et fust pour m'enhorter
Pour me garder de L'enfer
    Que Ie gaignas Le Paradis   230

---

15. **me** mes.
16. **diuinaL** coinage analogous to "bistial" (bestial).
17. **EuerneL** éternel.

Ie Vi que quant ~~ma~~ La Iustice
    Alla forze et de discord
Que a forse de ma malice
    Cherchant misecorde[18]
~~Ie~~ Ly fais demander Iustice   235
    Voyant cecy l'apperceu tel dessaing
En moy de penitence
      vn moment de ceste paine
    Que ~~pour aligerer telle paine~~
Aligeroit L'eternal tourment

Ie fuis si hault pour ConVertir   240
    E~~t~~ de dieu tant aide
Que tost au plus hault degre
      a
    ~~Auec~~ mon deliberer firme
Me Vis que fus Enhaulse
    Tant au dedans La porte me ~~re~~ trouve   245
Tant en paix et si hault
    La guerre Si Loing Ceda
Que La Chair tomba morte
    pour se tenir Viue l'ame

      graces
La~~e~~ derniere de ~~faueurs~~   250
    Est La mesme qui tous Confirme
Apres La Seconde et primiere
    Et y mettant tost son Cachet
Me Laissa a ceste mode
    Me Laissa en tel Salut   255
Et un tel estat me metta
      ~~Un~~ d'
    Et fist dedans moy ~~tel~~ accord
~~Auecq La Auecq la nature La Vertu~~
La vertu ~~auecq~~ auec La nature
    ~~E~~ La Coustume auec La Vertu

---

18. **misecorde** miséricorde.

Comme l'aueugle de tout qui se presente   260
    tinnt telle egualite
Et tellement se Comporte
    Et son estre Si EgaL
Ne s'esmeult ne fasche
    Annsy l'ame en substance   265
Metta ces temperemantz[19]
    Auec si eguaL accord
Que en elle ni a ne pouVoit
    Auoir habit l'inconstance /

LETTER 82 ꝯ QUEEN ELIZABETH TO HENRY IV OF FRANCE,
CIRCA 1590[1]

*[Addressed in another hand] A mon trescher bon Frere et Cousin Le
Roy treschrestien /*

Si d'auenture en Vne Vision M. de beauuois Vous estonne mon
treschir frere, Ne Vous desplaise Que Le desir qu'iL tient de uivre et
mourir a Vos pies Ly a Contrainct de Vous offenser n'en ayant
l'authoritie Et m'a prie de grande Instance que Ie entremele mon
Credit pour l'absolution de Ce peche, IL auroit honte de demourir[2]
a son ayse quant son Cher Maistre habite si pres de ses ennemis,
Ce qui Ie trouue si raisonable que plustot Ie prens enuie de son heur
en cest endroict que pour faillir a Vn si fidel Seruiteur Voyre pour
Vous mesmes a qui Ie souhaite Le nombre redouble de teLz qu'il
uous est et pour La fidelite, experience, et Valeur Pourtant Ie
m'assure tant de Uostre bonte que ne me nyeras si honorable
requeste Et aussy pour ly auoir impose quelque charge de ma part
sans laquelle il n'euct eu son Conge, C'est pour Vous pencer auec
Vn memoriall de moy quant Vous vous monstreras auoir plus de
besoing d'une bride que eperonne, En L'honneur de dieu

---

19. **temperemantz** "temperings," from French *tempérer*, "to moderate by mixing together."
1. *Source*: Folger Shakespeare Library, MS V.b.131, with remnants of Elizabeth's seals. Dating of this letter is conjectural, based on apparent references to the English expedition of 1589. See Letter 80, *CW*, pp. 360–61. Again, in this letter Elizabeth's hand is so rapid and loosely formed that *e*'s and *i*'s are difficult to distinguish.
2. **demourir** demeurer.

Consideres Combien il importe a toute La Cause La Conseruation
de uostre persone Vous me pardonneres a Vous dire que se[3] qui
se nommeroit Valeur en un aultre a Vous on l'imputera a temerite
et fablte[4] de tel Iugement qui soiet le plus a un grand Prince, Sy a
ceste seuLe heure On feroit preuue de Vostre Courage Ie Vous
souhaiterois plus tot mille dangiers que telle doubte, Car a mon filz
si i'en eusse Ie le Verrois mort plustot que Couard, Mais auec trop de
experience en[5] ayant faict exemplaire assurance de Vostre inVincible
magnanimitie Ie Vous ConIure par tout ce qu'aimes Le mieulx
que Vous Vous respectes non Comme priVe Souldait ais[6] Comme
Grand Prince, Peult estre que Vous mespriseres Ce ConseiL comme
Sortant d'un Coeur paoureusx de femme mais[7] Quant il Vous
SouViendra par combien de fois Ie n'ay monstre trop de Craincte a
mon sien[8] de Pistols et Espees qui m'ont este prepare ceste pancee
passera estant faulte de que ne me recognois Coulpable, Attribues
Le pourtant a mon seule affection en Vostre endroict Et Croyes que
n'en pourres recevoir du mal que Ie n'en ay ma part. Cest escript
ne peult passer mes mains sans Vous impartir La grande diligence
et estresme Soing de Ce Gentilhomme qui ne saisse[9] a Soliciter Vos
Causes comme un tresfideL Seruiteur Que dieu vous enVoye
de Ces semblables Ly priant aussy de Vous donner bonsaduis et
Vous Conceder La Grace de prendre

tousiours Le meilleur Chemin en tous   Vostre tresassuree fidelle
Vos entreprises et uous Conseruer   bonne Soeur et Cousine
Comme La prunelle de son OeuL[10]   Elizabeth R

En l'honneur de dieu rasembles ces faubousiers a quoy sert paris et Le
Roy perir, O que Ie suis en Cholere comme Ce Gentilhomme uous dira
de ma parte

---

3. **se** ce.

4. **fablte** faibleté.

5. **en** added in left margin.

6. **ais** either "mais" or "ains," both conjunctions meaning "but" (the former simply contrastive, the latter emphatic).

7. **mais** added in left margin.

8. **sien** sein.

9. **saisse** cesse.

10. **Comme . . . OeuL** as the pupil of his eye; idiomatic for a most cherished person or thing. The last phrases of the letter are crowded into the left side of the sheet next to the closing salutation, as shown. A postscript follows across a still lower part of the sheet.

LETTER 83 ℰ➤ ELIZABETH TO JAMES, JULY 6, 1590[1]

[Addressed] To my deere brother the king of Scotland

Greatar promises, more Affection ~~and~~ and grauntz of more
acknoWeLegings of receued good Turnes My deare brother, none can
bettar remember than this Gentilman by your charge hathe made me
understand Wherby I thinke all my endeuors Wel recompensed that See
them so weL acKnoWeLeged And do trust that my Counselz if the so
muche Content you Wil serue for memorialz to turne your actions to
serue the turne of your safe Gouernement and make the Lookars on
honor your Worthe and reuerence suche a rular, And Lest fayre
Semblance that easely may begile do not bride your Ignorance of Suche
persons as ether pretend religion or dissemble deuotion Let me Warne
you that ther is risen bothe in your realme and myne a secte of perilous
Consequence suche as Wold haue no kings but a Presbitrye and take our
place While the inioy our Priuilige With a shade of Gods word wiche
none is Iuged to folow right Without by ther Censure the be so demed
Yea Looke We WeL unto them whan the haue made in our peoples hartz
a doubt of our religion and that We erre if the say so What perilous issue
this may make I rather thinke than mynd to write, Sapienti pauca I pray
you stop the mouthes or make Shortar the toungz of suche ministars as
dare presume to make Oraison in ther pulpitz for the persecuted in
Ingland for the GospeL Suppose you my deare brother that I can tollerat
suche scandalz of my sincere Gouuernement no I hope hoWsoeuer you
be pleased to beare with ther audacitie toWards your selfe ʸᵉᵗ ʸᵒᵘ ~~I~~ wiL
not suffar a Strange King receaue that indignitie at suche Caterpilars
hand that instede of fruit I am affraid WiL stuf your realme with
Venom / Of this I haue particuLarisd more to this bearar togither With
other answers to his charge besiching ʸᵒʷ to heare them and not to giue
more harborrome to Vacabond traitors and Seditious ~~vagrants~~
inVentors but to returne them to me or banische them your Land And
thus With my many thankes for your honorable intertainmentz of my
late Embassade I commit you to God Who euer preserue you from aL
iueL CounseL and send you Grace to foloW the best /

> Your most assured Louing Sistar and Cousin
> Elizabeth R

1. *Source:* BL, MS Additional 23240, art. 28, fol. 94, with seals and ribbon attached.

LETTER 84 🙖 ELIZABETH TO JAMES, JANUARY 1593[1]

My most deare brother /

Wondars and marVeilles do so assailL my Conceatz as that the long
expecting of your nidefuL answer to matters of suche waight as my Late
Lettars Caried nides not seame strange thogh I knoWe the aught be
more regardid and spidely perfourmed Yet suche I see the Eminent
danger and welnye ready approche of your states ruin, your Liues peril
and naighbors wrong as I may not (to kipe you Company) negLect
What I shuld thogh you forget that you Aught / I am sory I am driuen
from Warninge to heede and from to muche trust to seake a tru Way
hoW your dides not your Wordz may make me assurance that you be no
Way gilty of your oWne decay and other danger / Receue therfor in
short What Cours I mynd to hold and how you may make bold of my
vnfained Loue and euer Constant regard, You knowe my deare brother
that sins you first brethed I regarded alWais to Conserue hit as my none
hit had bine you bare Yea I Withstode the handz and helps of a mighty
king to make you safe, Iven gained by the bloud of many my deare
Subiectz Lives, I made my self the bulwarke bitwixt you and your
harmes, whan many a wyle was inVented to stele you from your Land
and making other posses your soiLe / Whan your best holdz wer in my
handz, did I retaine them nay I bothe ConserVed them and rendred
them to you / Could I indure (thogh to my great expense) that forennars
shuld haue foteting[2] in your Kingdome, albeit ther was than some
LawfulL semblance to make other Suppose (that Cared not as I did) that
ther was no danger ment No I neuer Left tiL all the frenche that kept
ther Life parted from your soile, and so hit pleased the hiest to bles me
in that Action as you haue euer sins raigned Void of other nation than
your oWne / Now to preserue this you haue oversLipt so many Soundry
and dangerous attemps in nether uniting with them whan you kneWe
them nor Cutting them of whan you had them that if you hast no bettar
noW than hiretofor hit wyl be to Late to helpe Whan none shal aVale
you / Let me remember you how weL I was thanked or he reWarded that
ons broght alL the Lettars of alL thos wicked Conspirators of the
spanische faction Even the selfe same that yet stiL you haue to your

1. *Source:* BL, MS Additional 23240, art. 32, fols. 108r–109r. Addressed in another hand: "For
our deare Brother the king of Scotland." The endorsement reads "deliuerd be Mr Bowes Ambassador xxi Januari. 1593."

2. **foteting** footing.

Eminent periL conserued in ther estates / Was I not so much douted as
hit was thoght an Italian invention to make you holde me dirar and
Contrived of malice not don by Cause And in that respect the poore
man that kneWe no other of his taking but as if thiues had assailled him,
he most Cruelly soufert so Giltles a marterdome as his tormentors
douted his Life, So sore had he the bootes Whan the Wer ivel Worthy
Life that bade hit / See what good inCouragement I receved for many
wacheful Cares for your best safty / WeL did this So discomfort my good
wylL as for al this did I not euer Serue for your true EspialL iven whan
you Left your Land and yours ready welny to receaue suche foraine
forsis as the required and Wer promised Wiche if you had pleased to
Knowe was and is to eVident to be proVed / but What of al this if he who
most aught did naught to assure him or to requite them / Now of late by
a fortunate good hap a Lewd felowe hathe bine apprehendid with
Lettars and instructions I pray God he be so wel handled as he may
Confes all his Knowelege in the Spanische Conspiracie and that you vse
not this man as sLightly as you haue don the RingeLeadars of this
treason / I Vowe if you do not rake hit to the botome you wyl verefie
What many a Wise man hathe (Vewing your procidings[3] Iuged of your
gilttenis of your oWne Wrack With a Wining that the wyl you no harme
in inabling you with so riche a protector that wyl prove in the ende a
destroiar / I haue beheld of Late a strange dishonorable and dangerous
pardon Wiche if hit be true, you haue not only neglected yourselfe but
Wronged me that haue to muche procured your good to be so ivel
guerdoned with suche a wrong as to haue a fre forgiuenes of aught
conspired against my person and estat / Suppose you my deare brother
that thes be not rather enseignes of an ennemy than the tact of a frinde /
I require therfor to al this a resolute answer Wiche I chalenge of right
that may be dides bothe by spidy apprehension with hidy regard and
not in sort as publik rumor may precede present action, but rather that
the be intrapped or the do Looke therfor for I may make dome you wold
not haue taken and What Wyl folowe than you shal see Whan Lest you
Looke / Think me I pray you not ignorant What becometh a King to do
and that Wyl I neVer omit praying you to trust boWes in the rest as my
selfe I am ashamed that so disordard Coursis makes my pen excide a
Lettar and so driVes me to moLest your Yees with my to Long skribling

---

3. MS lacks a closing parenthesis.

and therfor end with my ernest prayers to God that he WyL inspire you
to do in best time al for your best /

Your Loving affectionat Sistar /
Elizabeth R

LETTER 85 ᓚᕬᕘ ELIZABETH TO JAMES, MARCH 1593[1]

[Addressed] To our deare Brother the Kyng of Scotts.

/ My deare brother /
The Care of your estate with feare of your neglect so afflictz my mynd
as I may not ouerslip the sending you a noble man to sarue you for a
memorialL of my readinis and desiar of your spide, The slidik[2] dame
Who Whan she is turned Leuis no after step to witnis her arriVaL ~~but~~
saue repentance that beareth to soWer a recorde of her short abode
may make you so fur awake ~~you~~ that you haue neUer Cause throuwe
to Long discoursing, to Loose the bettar knoweLege of hideust[3] treson
One hoWre bredes a dayes gain to gilefulL spiritz and gilty Conscience
skiLs more to shift than ten Wisar hedz ~~to~~ knoWes how to Win Let
the Anfild[4] be striken While hit is warme for if hit groWe Colde the
Goldsmithe marz his Worke and the oWnar his IuelL hit Vexeth me to
Se that thos of Whom the Very filds of SkotLand Could if the mighte
sp~~a~~eke truly tel hoW ther banners wer Displaid again your person Who
diuers nights did senteneL their actz thos selfe same be but noW bid to
a Ward Who Long ago God wot, aught so haue smarted as you nide not
noW examen ther treachery AL this I say not for my Gaping for any
mans bloud God is Witnis but Wische you saVid W ∧hereuer the rest
Go, and this I must tel you that if the Lands of them that do decerue no
brethe Wer made but yours (as ther oWne ~~actz~~ actz haue Caused) you

---

1. *Source:* Folger Shakespeare Library, MS X.d.397, fol. 1v; half-sheet in Elizabeth's hand.
The partially legible endorsement reads "delivered by the Lord Borto . . . gh xvj merche
1592[3]." The second half of this letter is reproduced in facsimile in Jean F. Preston and Laetitia Yeandle, *English Handwriting, 1400–1650* (Binghamton, N. Y.: Medieval and Renaissance
Texts and Studies, 1992), p. 65.
2. **slidik** sliding, slippery.
3. **hideust** hideousest, or, reading "n" instead of "u," hidenst—hiddenest.
4. **Anfild** anvil.

shuld be a richer prince ∧and than abler of your oWne to defend a
kings honor and your oWne Life

Me thinks I frame this Lettar Like to a Lamentation Wiche you Wyl
pardon Whan the matter bidz hit so / I can not but beWaile that any
LeWd unaduised ~~Varlet of~~ hedsik felowe a subiect of myne shuld make
his Soueregn be supposed of Les Gouuernement than mistres of her
Word I haue neuer yet dishonored my tonge with a Leasing not to a
menar person than a king and Wold be aschamed to desarue so foWLe
an infamy I VoWe I neuer kneWe but did forbid that euer he shuld enter
my territory that so boLdLy atteinted your dores you knoWe best What
I Writ for that and he as I heare ~~as~~ hathe hard hit so muche as hardLy he
WyL trust my handz to be his safe refuge Yet you ∧Knowe best What
Was offerd and Why he Was not made more desperat If your Long
exspectd and neuer had as yet answer had not Lingard I think he WoLd
haue gone fur Ynough or noW, Let this suffice be youre doinges as
sounde as my profession stanche and I Warrant no spaniard nor ther
king shal haue euer footing so nire to you or me / trust I pray you neuer
a Conquerar With trust of his kindnis nor neuer raigne precario more[5]
Whan you may ruLe regis regula[6] / Now do I remember your Cumbar
to rede suche skribled Lines and pray the almighty   Your most LoVing
to Couer you safely undar his bleased Wings /[7]   Sistar
                                                                    Elizabeth R

LETTER 90 ❧ ELIZABETH TO JAMES, MAY 1594[1]

Thogh by the effectz I seld See, My good brother, that euer my aduisis be
folowed, Yet you haue Whitsafed to giue them the reding I wel
understand haVing made some of them the theme of your Last thogh
God knowes applied fur aWry from ther true sence or right desart, for if
I sin in abuse I claime you the author of my deceat in beliVing more

---

5. **precario more** by way of entreaty.

6. **regis regula** in the manner of a king.

7. This sentence is an evident addition, crowded into the left lower corner of the sheet opposite Elizabeth's subscription and signature.

1. *Source:* BL, MS Additional 23240, fol. 132. Addressed in another hand: "To our good brother the king of Scotts." The endorsement reads "maij 1594 /." Atypically, an autograph draft copy of this letter also survives; it is reproduced as Letter 90 (draft) below.

good than sequele hathe told me, for I haue great Wronge if you Suppose
that any persWation from Whomsoeuer can make me haue One iueL
opinion of your actions if them selues be not the Cause I Confes that
diuers be the affections of many men some to one some to an other, but
my rule of trust shal neuer faile me whan it is groundid not on the
sandes of euery mans humor but on the stedy Rock of approued fact I
shuld Condemne my Wicked disposition to founde any Amytie
promised vpon so tickiL ground that ~~that~~ others Hate ~~s~~ might breake the
boundz of my Loue and upon others Iugementz to bild my Confidence /
for bodwelz bold and unruly entrance into my bordars I am so fur from
gilt of suche a faulte as I protest if I had receaued an answer in seuentene
Wikes space^2 of my Lettar that Contained his offer to reVeale vnto you
the treason of the Lordz with forennars I Could sone haue banisshed
him from thens and next he Came with your oWne hand to warant that
no offence was imputid Wiche made the borderars readiar to receaue
him, but after I had not Left unpunist some of his receatars I could not
haue beliued the durst haue procurid^3 the pane due for suche desart.
and mind to make them affraid to ventur suche a Crime agane / and if ~~w~~
ordar giuen noW to alL the wardens do not suffice I VoWe ther bodies
and pursis shaL weL suffar therfor I Wil not troble you with recitaL of
What this Gentilman hathe hard in alL the other pointz but this
toucheth me so nere as I must answer that my desartz to you haue bene
so Sincere as shal neuer nide a threte of heL to her that hathe euer
procurid your blis And that you may knoWe I am that prince that neuer
Can indure a menace at my Ennemys hand muche Les of one so diarLy^4
traictid I WyL giue you this bond that affection and kind traictement
shal euer preVaile, but feare or doute shal neuer procure aught from me
and do adVoWe that if you do aught by forainers, Wiche I knowe in ende
Worst for your selfe and Country hit shalbe the Worst ~~shift~~ aide that
euer king had, And I feare may make me do more than you Wyl cal back
in hast, deare brother Vse suche a frinde therfor as she is worthe and
giue her euer Cause to remaine suche a One as her affection hathe euer
merited Whos raschenis is no suche as neglect ther oWne so nere if the
Wil not forgo ther best and shun ther oWne mishaps Whom none Can

2. **in . . . space** insertion written partly in the left margin.
3. **procurid** insertion written partly in the left margin.
4. **diarLy** Elizabeth's spelling opens up an ambiguity: is this "dearly" or "direly"—affection or threat? There is no ambiguity in the draft letter immediately following below; it reads "dearly."

at my hand procure but your oWne factz Thus hoping that this bearar
WyL tel you my faithfuL mening and sincere professions with aL the rest
that I haue Comitted to him I Leue this Skribling besiching God euer
more to Preserue you.

Your most affectionate Sistar and Cousin /
Elizabeth R

LETTER 90, DRAFT ꝶ ELIZABETH TO JAMES, MAY 1594[1]

Thogh by the effectz I seld see, My good brother that euer my aduisis be
folowed, Yet that you haue Witsafed to giue them the reading I Wy͡el
understand as hauing made Some of them the theme of your Last
thogh God knowes applied fur a Way from ther true Sence or right
desart for if I Sin in abuse I Claim you the author of my deceapt in
hauing belieuid more good thatn Sequele hathe told me for I haue great
wronge if you Suppose any persuations from Whomsoeuer can make
me haue One iueL Opinion of your actions if themselues be not the
Cause I admit that diuers be the affections of many men some to one
part some to another but my rule of trust shal neuer faile me Whan hit
is groundid not on the slipery Sandes of eache mans humor but On the
Stidy rock of Undenied fact I should Condemne my Wicked
disposition to founde my frindship promised Vpon So tickiL ground
as that the rage of others[2] Hate might breake the bandz of ᵐʸ Love and
Vpon others iugementz to bild my Confiance / for bodwelz unruly
entry to my bordars I am so fur from gilt of suche a fault as I protest
that if in seuentene Wikes I had receaued your answer to my Lettar that
Contained his offer to Uttar to you al the treasons that the northern
Lordz had With forenars I Could sone haue banisshed ~~the~~ him
therfrom and next he Came With your OWne hand to Warant your
fauor toWard him Wiche made the borderars readiar to receaue ~~the~~

1. *Source:* Hatfield House, Cecil Papers,133/80, fol. 120. As with several of Elizabeth's
speeches, so too with this letter: the draft is blunter than the sent version concerning dealings with the Earl of Bothwell and the prospect of James's seeking aid elsewhere than from
Elizabeth. This draft also contains underscoring not found in the sent version. The endorsement in a modern hand reads "An Original Letter from Queen Elizabeth to the King of
Scots. 1597 [for 1594]."
  2. **others** addition in left margin.

him but after I had not Left unpunisshed some of his <u>receattars</u> I Could
not haue beliued the durst aduentur the paine due for suche desart And
mynd to make them affraid to Commit suche Crime again; If ordar
noW giuen to alL the Wardens do not suffice I VoWe ther bodies and
pursis shal WeL pay therfor I Wyl not trobeL you with recitaL of What
this Gentilman hathe hard in alL the other pointz but this touchith me
so nere as I must ansWer that my desartz to you haue bine so sincer as
shaL neuer nide a threte of heL to her that hath euer procurid your blis
and that you may knoWe I am that prince that neuer Can <u>indure</u> a
Manace at an Enimies hand muche Les of One so dearly traictid I WyL
giue this bond that affection and kind traittement shal euer preuaile
but feare or doute shaL neuer procure aught from me and do aduoWe
that if you do aught by foraners helpe hit shaLbe the worst ayde that
Euer king had and Shal make me do more than you shal euer ondoe.
Use suche a frind therfor as she is Worthe and giue her euer Cause to
remain suche One as her Louing affection hathe euer merited So shaL
you Work your oWne best and Shun your oWne mishaps Whom none
Can at my hand procure but your oWne actes /

LETTER 93 ❧ ELIZABETH TO HENRY IV OF FRANCE,
SEPTEMBER 13, 1596[1]

[Addressed] A mon bon frere le Roy treschrestien.

Mounsieur mon bon frere
Ayant paracheve de ma part La finale conclusion de nostre Ligue auec
Les Ceremonies convenables a teL acte Ayant prevenu avec ma
precedence La SequeLe qui peut ~~me~~ convenir a telle haste Ie ne doute
nullement que daignerez Seconder Ce faict auec Vostre foy donnee a Ce
Conte qui I'ay ordonne La ReceVoir comme donne a moy Et par Ce
moyen Ombrageres Si non Couvrir mon Erreur Si tel Le puis nommer
qui fus La primier a Vous presenter La mienne Vous assurant que Si
toutz s pactes fussent aussi inVioLes que Cestuy Sera de mon Coste tout

1. *Source:* BL, MS Additional 24023, fol. 1, with two seals and remnants of ribbons attached.
Endorsed in a contemporary hand below one seal: "Lettre de la reyne dangleter apportez par
le Comte de Shrosbury." The date is taken from the endorsement on a good copy, BL, MS
Additional 48212, fol. 13.

Le monde S'estonneroit de Voir si Constante amitie en Ce Siecle,[2] Pour
Vous Ie me figure que Iamais Logiera en Vn Coeur Si genereus Vne
Seule pensee d'ingrat Ains me persuade que n'auresy Raison de me
pentir d'auoir honore, fauorise, et ayde Vn tel Prince qui non Seulement
pencera de Ce qui Ly ConVient mais tiendra Soing de Ce qui
m'appartient regardant droit au Vray but de reciprocque affection A qui
Ie Souhait toute La prosperite et Victoire qu'un Grand Roy doit desirer
Comme Dieu scait a qui Ie prie Vous Conseruer de tous ennemis
Comme Vous desire   Vostre tresaffectionnee Soeur
                                                    Elizabeth R

PRAYER 39 ᴥ ON THE SAILING OF THE AZORES EXPEDITION,
JULY 1597[1]

Ô god all-maker, keeper, and guider: Inurement[2] of thy rare-seene,
vnused[3] and seeld-heard-of goodnes, powred in so plentifull sort vpon
vs full oft; breeds now this boldnes, to craue with bowed knees, and
heartes of humilitye, thy large hande of helping power, to assist with
wonder oure iust cause, not founded on Prides-motion nor begun on
Malice-stock; But as thou best knowest, to whom nought is hid,
grounded on iust defence from wronges, hate, and bloody desire of
conquest. For scince, meanes thou hast imparted to saue that thou hast
giuen, by enioying such a people, as scornes their bloodshed, where
suretie ours is one:[4] Fortifie (deare God) such heartes in such sort, as
their best part may be worst, that to the truest part meant worst, with
least losse to such a Nation, as despise their liues for their Cuntryes
good. That all Forreine Landes may laud and admire the Omnipotency
of thy Worke: a fact alone for thee only to performe. So shall thy name

2. **Siecle** S is written over C.
1. *Source:* BL, MS Harley 6986, art. 35, fol. 58r. Elizabeth (or a capable imitator) employs the
letterforms of "set" italic, which we have called her "inscriptional hand." It is remarkably
stable through time. The letterforms here resemble those in her autograph letters from the
1550s and in her subscription and superscription added to letters from the late 1570s (see
CW, pp. 213, 228). There are, however, fewer embellished letterforms in this late text.
2. **Inurement** habituation.
3. **vnused** unusual.
4. **one** possibly with the meaning "won," which the context equally well accepts.

be spread for wonders wrought, and the faithfull encouraged, to repose
in thy Vnfellowed[5] grace: And wee that mynded nought but right,
inchained in thy bondes for perpetuall slauery,[6] and liue and dye the
sacrificers of oure soules for such obtayned fauoure. Warrant, (Deare
Lorde) all this with thy command. Amen.

5. **Vnfellowed** matchless.
6. **slauery** a literal English meaning of two classical Greek words, δουλέια and λατρέια.
When latinized in ecclesiastical usage as *dulia* and *latria*, these became the technical terms
for, respectively, the reverence to be paid to the saints and the worship to be given to God
alone.

II

NONAUTOGRAPH, FOREIGN
LANGUAGE ORIGINALS

PRAYERS 3–9
Private Prayers of Queen Elizabeth at Court, 1563[1]

PREPARATIONES AD PRECES.

PAratum Cor meum Deus, paratum cor meum: cantabo et psallam in
gloria mea. [Psalm 107:1]
In multitudine misericordiae tuae introibo in domum tuam, adorabo
ad templum sanctum tuum, in timore tuo [Psalm 5:8]
Dirigatur oratio mea, sicut incensum in conspectu tuo, eleuatio
manuum mearum, sacrificium vespertinum, [Psalm 140:2]
Apud me oratio Deo vitae meae, dicam deo susceptor meus es tu.
Quare tristis es anima mea, et quare conturbas me?

---

1. *Source: Precationes priuatae. Regiae E. R.* (London: T. Purfoot, 1563) (*STC* 7576.7), sigs.
Aii r–Fi r. To avoid what would otherwise be a plethora of footnotes, square brackets at the
end of a clause or versicle enclose the scriptural reference and, where noteworthy, a statement of the adaptation that Elizabeth has performed. Like her contemporaries, Elizabeth
often does not quote the Latin Psalms verbatim. She may substitute a synonym, alter a verb
tense or mood, or otherwise slightly modify phrasing—for example, by changing a preposition. However, her source text remains clearly identifiable throughout; it is the Septuagint
version, later known as the "Gallican Psalter." This was St. Jerome's second rendering of the
Psalms, based on Origen's *Hexapla.* Over time this version acquired supreme authority in
the Vulgate Bible and the breviary of the Catholic Church, outstripping even St. Jerome's
own direct translation of the Psalms from Hebrew. Our references conform to the Vulgate
numbering of verses and Psalms.

Spera in Deo, quoniam adhuc confitebor illi, salutare vultus mei, et
 deus meus. [adapts Psalm 41:12; 42:5]
Quemadmodum desyderat Ceruus ad fontes aquarum: ita anima mea
 ad te deus.
Sitiuit anima mea ad Deum fontem² viuum, quando veniam et
 apparebo ante faciem dei. [Psalm 41:2, 3]
Confitebor tibi in populis domine, et psallam tibi in nationibus. [Psalm
 107:4]
Vespere, mane, et meridie, narrabo et annunciabo, tu deus exaudi
 vocem meam. [adapts Psalm 54:18]
Quia magna est super Coelos misericordia tua, et vsque ad nubes
 veritas tua, [Psalm 107:5]
Sedes tua, Deus in seculum seculi: virga directionis, virga regni tui.
 [Psalm 44:7]
Exaltare super Coelos Deus et super omnem terram gloria tua, vt
 liberentur dilecti tui. [Psalm 56:6; Psalm 59:6]
Saluum³ fac dextera tua, et exaudi me. [Psalm 59:7]
Benedicam te in vita mea, et in nomine tuo leuabo manus meas. [Psalm
 62:5]
Sperabo in domino et in misericordia altissimi non commouebor.
 [Psalm 20:8, there phrased in the third person of King David]
Ecce oculi domini super metuentes eum: et in his⁴ qui sperant, super
 misericordia eius. [Psalm 32:18]
In quacunque die inuocabo te, exaudi me, multiplicabis in anima mea
 virtutem. [adapts Psalm 137:3]
Qui das salutem Regibus qui redemisti Dauid seruum tuum, de gladio
 maligno eripe me. [Psalm 143:10–11]
Qui diligis iusticiam, et odisti iniquitatem. [Psalm 44:8]
Adornasti⁵ omnes reges: omnes gentes seruiant tibi. [Psalm 71:11]
Concupiscam ipsa decorem tuum, quoniam tu Dominus Deus meus,
 et te adorabo. [adapts Psalm 44:12 to first-person reference]
Memor ero nominis tui in omni generatione in generationem,⁶ et

---

2. **fontem** Vulgate reads "fortem." Elizabeth interpolates the image of a "fountain of living
waters" (Jeremiah 2:13), from which she will drink.
3. **Saluum** Saluam
4. **in his** in eis; phrase omitted in Vulgate.
5. **Adornasti** Vulgate reads "adorabunt."
6. **in generationem** Vulgate reads "et generatione."

populi confitebuntur tibi in eternum, et in seculum seculi. [Psalm 44:18]

Ante orationes prepara animam tuam,
Et noli esse, quasi homo qui tentat deum. [Ecclesiasticus 18:23]
Turris fortissima, nomen domini.
Ad ipsam[7] currit iustusque exaltabitur. [Proverbs 18:10]
Prope est dominus omnibus inuocantibus eum.
Inuocantibus eum, in veritate. [Psalm 144:18]
Tu es ipse Rex meus, et Deus meus. [Psalm 5:3]
In te semper sperabo. [Psalm 70:14]

PRAYER 3 ☙ COLLECTA.

DOminator Domine, Deus omnipotens, Pater misericordiarum, deus omnis gratiae qui fecisti me, ad tui imaginem, vt te laudarem, me etiam (per filium tuum Iesum Christum redemisti) vt te agnoscerem. Effunde super me viscera misericordiae tuae, vt inueniat Ancilla tua cor ad orandum te, et os ad nunciandum laudes tuas, indue spiritu tuo sancto, vt meis desiderijs spretis, quae tibi placeant, ac tuae gloriae inseruire possint, supplex petam. De praeparato Habitaculo tuo respice super me Ancillam tuam, et exaudi orationem meam. Illumina vultum sanctum tuum, vt tibi seruiens cognoscam in terra viam tuam, quae deducat me ad te. Tui desiderio accende cor meum, vt te super omnia, et in omnibus queram, Diligam te qui Fortitudo mea, refugium meum, ac liberator meus es, timeam maiestatem tuam, qui solus potens es, et faciens mirabilia, firmetur sapientia tua in animo meo, quae me doceat tuam voluntatem, et legem tuam in medio cordis mei scribe, quae me dirigat in omnibus vijs tuis. Tu Rex Coeli et terrae, Rex Regum Rege me ancillam tuam, ac vniuersum populum tuum mihi commissum, gratia tua vt in omnibus parati simus, ad tuam gloriam predicandum ac agnoscendum tuum summum Imperium, per Iesum Christum. Amen

---

7. **ipsam** Vulgate reads "ipsum."

PRO PECCATORUM VENIA.

MIserere mei Deus, miserere mei, secundum magnam misericordiam
  tuam.

Et secundum multitudinem miserationum tuarum, dele iniquitatem
  meam.

Amplius laua me ab iniquitate mea, et a peccato meo munda me.
  [Psalm 50:3–4]

Vsquequo domine obliuisceris me in finem, vsquequo auertis faciem
  tuam a me. [Psalm 12:1]

Iniquitatem meam ego cognosco, et peccatum meum contra me est
  semper.

In te solum peccaui, et malum coram te feci, vt vincas cum iudicaris.

Ecce enim in iniquitatibus concepta sum, et in peccatis concepit me
  mater mea. [Psalm 50:5, 7; verse 7 adapted to feminine
  self-reference]

Recordare Domine, quoniam puluis sum, et dies mei, tanquam flos
  agri, sic efflorescent.

Misericordia tua ab aeterno vsque in aeternum super eos qui timent te.
  [adapts Psalm 102:14, 15, 17 to first-person and second-person
  singular references]

Auerte faciem tuam a peccatis meis, et omnes transgressiones meas,
  dele. [Psalm 50:11]

Delicta iuuentutis meae, ac ignorantias meas ne memineris.

Secundum misericordiam tuam memento me: propter bonitatem tuam
  domine. [Psalm 24:7]

Prauum cor hominis ab initio: nec est homo qui non peccet. [adapts
  Jeremiah 17:9; Romans 3:23]

Cor mundum crea in me Deus ac spiritum rectum innoua in visceribus
  meis.

Ne proijcias me a facie tua, et spiritum sanctum tuum ne auferas a me.

Redde mihi letitiam salutaris tuj: et spiritu principalj confirma me.
  [Psalm 50:12–14]

Reminiscere miserationum tuarum domine et misericordiarum
  tuarum quae a seculo sunt. [Psalm 24:6]

Erraui sicut ouis quae perijt, quaere Ancillam tuam Domine. [adapts
  Psalm 118:176 to feminine reference]

Sacrificium tibi spiritus contribulatus, cor contritum et humiliatum
  Deus non despicies. [Psalm 50:19]

Propter nomen tuum domine propitiaberis peccato meo, multum est
   enim. [Psalm 24:11]

Gressus meos dirige secundum eloquium tuum: et non dominetur mei
   omnis iniustitia. [adapts Psalm 118:133]

Faciem tuam illumina super Ancillam tuam, et doce me iustificationes
   tuas. [adapts Psalm 118:135 to feminine reference]

Suauis Dominus vniuersis, et miserationes eius, super omnia opera
   eius. [Psalm 144:9]

VERSICULI.

Ne intres in iudicium, cum Ancilla tua.

Quia non iustificabitur, in conspectu tuo omnis viuens. [adapts Psalm
   142:2 to feminine reference]

Si iniquitates obseruaueris domine,

Domine, quis sustinebit? [Psalm 129:3]

Ab ocultis[8] meis munda me:

Ab alienis parce Ancillae tuae [adapts Psalm 18:13–14 to feminine
   reference]

Dimissa sunt ei peccata multa.

Que diligit multum, [paraphrases Luke 7:47]

PRAYER 4 ☙ COLLECTA.

MIsericors Deus, ac clementissime pater, patiens, et multae miserationis,
ac verax, qui non vis mortem peccatoris, sed vt conuertatur, et viuat. Cor
mundum crea in me, O Deus, quod et tuam misericordiam, et meam
miseriam vere agnoscat. Tu enim Deus meus et Rex meus, Ego Ancilla
tua, et opus manuum tuarum, Ad te igitur, flecto genua cordis mei
Confiteor aduersum me impietatem meam. Peccaui, peccaui, pater, in
coelum et coram te, minor sum cunctis miserationibus tuis, [Luke 15:21]
Non custodiui foedus tuum nec ambulaui in lege tua, Derelinqui te
deum factorem meum, recessi a te saluatore meo. Aberraui a tuis consilijs. Ne facias mihi iuxta peccata mea et secundum iniquitates meas, ne
reddas mihi. Auertatur obsecro ira tua a me, et fac vt inueniam gratiam

---

8. **ocultis** Vulgate reads "occultis."

in occulis tuis secundum magnitudinem misericordiae tuae, vincat tua bonitas meam malitiam, Superet peccata mea, tua patientia.

Quoniam deus miserationum et longanimis es tu, Tibi domine iustitia, et misericordia et propitiatio, mihi autem confusio faciei meae propter iniquitates meas, remitte vniuersa dilecta mea propter nomen sanctum tuum. Da cor penitens, qui disimulas ad peccata hominum propter penitentiam.

Dic anime meae: salus tua ego sum, propicius esto (clementissime pater) tum mihi, tum populo tuo mihi commisso, qui in sola tua misericordia, ac bonitate confidimus, concede deinceps non offendere tuam maiestatem: sed tibi viuere, in sanctitate et iustitia, omnibus diebus vite nostre per misericordiam tuam in Christo Iesu. Amen.

GRATIARUM ACTIONES.

EXaltabo te, Deus meus Rex, ac benedicam nomini tuo, in saeculum, et in saeculum saeculi.

Per singulos dies benedicam tibi, et laudabo nomen tuum, in saeculum, et in saeculum saeculi.

Magnus Dominus et laudabilis nimis et magnitudinis eius, non est finis.

Generatio ac generatio laudabit opera tua, ac potentiam tuam pronunciabunt. [Psalm 144:1–4]

Confiteantur tibi Domine omnia opera tua: et sancti tui benedicant tibi.

Gloriam Regni tui dicent, et potentiam tuam loquentur. [Psalm 144:10–11]

Regnum tuum, Regnum omnium seculorum, et dominatio tua, in omni generatione, et generationem.[9] [Psalm 144:13]

In virtute tua letentur Reges, et super salutare tuum, exultent vehementer. [adapts Psalm 20:1 from singular to plural reference, and future tenses to subjunctives]

Omnes Principes adorent te Domine, et omnes gentes laudem dicant tibi. [adapts Psalm 71:11]

Confitebor tibi in toto corde meo: [Psalm 110:1] super misericordia tua et veritate tua.

Benedic anima mea Domino, et omnia quae intra me sunt, nomini sancto eius.

---

9. **generationem** Vulgate reads "generatione."

Benedic anima mea Domino: ac noli obliuisci, omnes retributiones
 eius.

Qui propitiatur omnibus iniquitatibus tuis, qui sanat omnes
 infirmitates tuas.

Qui redimit de interitu vitam tnam,[10] qui coronat te, in misericordia et
 miserationibus.

Qui replet in bonis desyderium tuum, renouabitur, vt aquilae
 inuentus[11] tua.

Faciens misericordias Dominus et iudicium omnibus iniuriam
 patientibus. [Psalm 102:1–6]

Miserator et misericors Dominus, patiens et multum misericors.

Quomodo miseretur pater filiorum: misertus est dominus, timentibus
 se. [Psalm 102:1–6, 8, 13]

Tu domine, es protector meus et susceptor meus, in quo speraui, qui
 subdis populum meum sub me. [Psalm 17:3, 48]

Deus meus et gloria mea, deus patris mei, et exaltatio mea. [Psalm 3:4;
 88:27]

Praeuenisti me, in benedictionibus dulcedinis, posuisti in capite meo
 coronam, de lapide praetioso. [adapts Psalm 20:4 to self-reference]

Propter hoc, confitebor tibi in nationibus, et nomini tuo psalmum
 dicam. [Psalm 17:50]

Cantabo Domino in vita mea, psallam Deo meo quamdiu sum. [Psalm
 103:33]

VERSICULI.

Lauda anima mea dominum.

Laudabo dominum in vita mea, [Psalm 145:1]

Dominus in coelo parauit sedem suam,

Regnum ipsius omnibus dominabitur. [Psalm 102:19]

Dextera tua Domine fecit virtutem.

Dextera tua exaltat principes. [adapts Psalm 117:16 from self- to
 third-person reference]

Timeant gentes nomen tuum Domine.

Omnes Reges terrae gloriam tuam. [Psalm 101:16]

---

10. **tnam** tuam. The typesetter has turned a letter.

11. **inuentus** Vulgate reads "iuuentus." The ostensible variant may trace to another "u"
turned as "n."

PRAYER 5 ☙ COLLECTA.

DOmine Deus misericordie, Rex meus ac populi mei, Confitebor nomini
tuo magno, quoniam adiutor et protector factus es mihi. Collaudabo te
Deum saluatorem meum, qui liberasti corpus meum a perditione, ac
eruisti me de manibus quaerentium animam meam: manus tua (Deus)
conseruauit me de tempore iniquo, tua gratia, respexit me, [echoes Luke
1:48] a iuuentute mea, et ad hoc tuum Regnum miraculose erexit.

Quae ego sum? domine deus, aut quae Domus Patris mei? vt faceres
nobiscum misericordiam hanc magnam. Tu facis pacem in diebus meis,
pugnauit pro me et meo populo, aduersus omnes inimicos nostros,
tuum Brachium cum potentia. Dedisti legem tuam sanctam vt timere-
mus te, ac a vijs erroris deduceres nos ad vias rectas. Infinita sunt tua
diuina beneficia, Imple gratia tua (benignissime pater) vt ne obliuisca-
mur retributiones has multas, sed nomen tuum sanctum magnificemus
in omnibus, laudationem tuam semper loquatur os meum, et populus
meus tibi benedicat in perpetuum, vt sciant omnes, quia tu solus Deus,
nec est alius preter te, qui vna cum Filio, et sancto spiritu, regnas, immortalis, immensus et gloriosus deus in secula. Amen.

PRECATIONES PRO REGNO.

Qvi regis Israel intende, [Psalm 79:2] qui portas in sinu tuo populum
     tuum.[adapts Numbers 11:12]
Excita potentiam tuam, et veni vt saluos facias nos.
Deus virtutum conuerte nos, et ostende faciem tuam, et salui erimns.[12]
     [Psalm 79:3–5]
Vias tuas domine demonstra mihi, et semitas tuas edoce me. [Psalm
     24:4]
In corde meo absconde[13] eloquia tua, vt non peccem tibi, [Psalm 118:11]
Da mihi intellectum scrutari legem tuam, et custodire illam in toto
     corde meo. [Psalm 118:34]
Principes terrae congregentur et conueniant in vnum: vt videant
     gloriam tuam admirabilem. [Psalm 47:5, 6]
Quis similis tui[14] in fortibus Domine? quis similis tui, magnificus in
     sanctitate terribilis, ac faciens mirabilia. [Psalm 70:19; 88:9]

---

12. **erimns** erimus.
13. **absconde** Vulgate reads "abscondi."
14. **tui** Vulgate reads "tibi."

Tu es ipse Dominus virtutum, tu Rex gloriae, [adapts Psalm 23:10 to
  second-person reference]
Confiteantur tibi omnes Reges terrae, et audiant verba oris tui, [Psalm
  137:4]
Tu es ipse rex meus et deus meus, cui psallam in omni vita mea. [Psalm
  5:3–4]
Dirige me in veritate tua, et doce me semitam mandatorum tuorum,
  [Psalm 24:4; 118:35]
Deduc populum meum in iusticia tua, propter inimicos meos, dirige in
  conspectu tuo vias meas: [Psalm 5:9]
Inueniat[15] manus tua omnibus inimicis tuis, dextera tua inueniat
  omnes qui te oderunt. [Psalm 20:9]
Esto adiutor oportuno tempore, qui saluos facis rectos corde. [Psalm
  7:11]
Domine scuto bonae voluntatis tuae, corona me. [Psalm 5:13]
Esto mihi turris fortitudinis, a facie inimici. [Psalm 60:4]
Tu dominus deus noster: nos tuus populus quem elegisti in
  haereditatem tibi. [adapts Psalm 32:12 from third-person reference]
In te letetur cor meum, et in nomine sancto tuo sperabo. [adapts Psalm
  32:21 from plural to singular reference]
Gloria mea in salutare[16] tuo: decorem tuum impones super me. [adapts
  Psalm 20:6 to first-person reference]
Qui paras in iudicio thronum tuum, et iudicas orbem terrae in
  aequitate. [Psalm 9:8–9]
Iustitiam tuam mihi da, iudicare populum tuum in iusticia, et pauperes
  tuos in iudicio.
Ego in te speraui domine, dixi deus meus es tu, in manibus tuis sortes
  meae.
Illustra faciem tuam super Ancillam tuam, non confundar, quoniam
  inuocaui te. [Psalm 30:15–18]

VERSICULI.

Domine saluam me fac Ancillam tuam,
Et populum tuum mihi commissum,
Seruiamus tibi in timore, et exultemus cum timore. [Psalm 2:11]

---

15. **Inueniat** Vulgate reads "Inveniatur."
16. **salutare** Vulgate reads "salutari."

In virtute tua letemur.

Qui preuenisti nos in benedictionibus dulcedinis, [Psalm 20:2, 4]

Sit lucerna pedibus meis verbum tuum,

Et lumen semitis meis. [Psalm 118:105]

PRAYER 6 ἓ COLLECTA.

OMnipotens, aeterne deus, Dominus dominantium, Rex regum, a quo omnis potestas, qui me tui populi principem constituisti, ac ex sola tua misericordia sedere fecisti in throno patris mei. Ego Ancilla tua sum exigui temporis, minor ad intellectum legis tuae: Da obsecro mihi cor docile, vt sciam quid acceptum sit coram te omni tempore, vt populum tunm[17] iuste iudicare possim, et discernere inter bonum et malum, Mitte de coelo spiritum sapientiae tuae qui me ducat in omnibus operibus meis. Sensu illius cor meum reple, Sapientia tua dat veram scientiam, et ex ore tuo consilium et intelligentia Assistat gratia tua (quo disponam populum tuum hunc multum, in aequitate et iusticia) ad deputandos tuos ministros, pios, probos, ac prudentes. Illis impartire ex spiritu tuo que in tui timore (nulla accepta persona) iustitiam subministrem. Consiliarios mihi fideles da, qui ex tuo consilio mihi meoquae[18] regno consulant. Pastores bonos, qui oues tuas sibi commissas ex tuo verbo diligenter pascant, omnes ministros concede qui zelo iusticiae suo tibi fungantur officio, vniuersum populum tuum, O mi Deus, (deus omnis potentiae ac misericordiae) spiritu tuo sanctissimo guberna, vt te (aelectem principem ac solum potentem[19] in sincero cultu, religiose colant mihi, eorum in terris ex tua ordinatione Regine in tua obedientia, quiete subditi sint, in mutua pace ac concordia inter se viuant. Concede (pijssime pater) propter nominis tui gloriam, omnibus ordinibus huius tui regni, abundantiam et continuationem tranquillitatis tuae, sibi inuicem per charitatem inseruiant, mutuo se ament ac beneficijs afficiant, singuli in sua vocatione ambulant,[20] pie, iuste, ac sobrie, presim ipsa ex tuo verbo singulis, in solicitudinem et diligentia,[21] infunde spiri-

17. **tunm** tuum.
18. **meoquae** meoque.
19. The expected closing parenthesis is lacking in the text.
20. **ambulant** ambulent.
21. **diligentia** diligentiam.

tum tui Amoris, quo et ipsi mihi et etiam inter se (tanquam membra vnius corporis) quam arctisime iungantur fac ita (Deus omnis charitatis) vt non seueritatis metu aut gladio, sed regio furore ac metu diuino, Regnum hoc tuum administrem. Adsis etiam summe Deus omnium principum gubernator et rector, per quem Reges Regnant, cuius omnis est fortitudo et brachium vbique extentum. Deus pacis ac concordiae, qui me ancillam tuam super populum tuum elegisti, vt tuerer in tua pace. Adsis et presis mihi spiritu tuae sapientiae, vt iuxta tuam voluntatem christianam pacem cum omnibus populis defendam, fac in Christo filio tuo (qui pax nostra est) [echoes Ephesians 2:14] omnes consentiamus, hostes tuos tua manu potentur, ac brachio excelso confunde. Ipse nobis da tuam pacem, quia non est alius qui pugnet pro nobis, nisi tu Deus noster, [Psalm 123:1, 2] qui solus fortis es, custodiens pactum et misericordiam cum ijs qui ambulant coram te in toto corde suo, inclina corda nostra ad te, vt ambulemus in vniuersis vijs tuis, ac custodiamus mandata tua: Sub tuo Imperio et principes regant, et cunctus populus pareat. Vt te summo rege ac protectore, tibi omnes seruiamus in vnitate spiritus ad tuam aeternam gloriam. Per Iesum Christum filium tuum, dominum nostrum, cui cum patre et spiritu sancto sit omnis honor et Imperium in omne aeuum.

PRAYER 7 ❧ GRATIARUM ACTIO PRO SANITATE RECUPERATA.

OPtime maxime seruator Iesu Christe Fili Dei viui. qui in terris inter mortales versatus, depulsis omnibus morbis, condonatisque tibi fidentium peccatis, te vnicum illum coelestem vereque perfectum tam animarum, quam corporum medicum esse mundo declarasti: idemque, quum tibi a vitio verteretur, quibus cum hominibus peccatoribus consuetudinem haberes, claris verbis testatus es, dicens, Non ijs qui valerent, sed qui male haberent, medico opus esse. [Matthew 9:12] En hic tibi clementissime Iesu, materiam tua potentia pariter atque clementia non indignam: en me ancillam tuam quam ab ineunte vsque aetate mea, immensis atque infinitis beneficijs cumulasti, quamque a rege genitam ad regiam dignitatem erectam, in summo inter mortales honoris gradu, nullo prorsus merito meo, tantum et gratuita tua in me bonitate atque benignitate collocasti. At eandem me nunc, vel vt ne nimis ex sententia affluens rerum mundanarum successus animum meum transuersum raperet, et mihi mej ipsius, officiique in te mei obliuionem induceret: vel que diuina tua liberalitate summis affecta beneficijs reginaque populi tui effecta, me tuae maiestatis subditam esse atque ancillam, nunquam ex animo, pro eo ac debui agnouerim, nunquam satis abvnde confessus fuerim: neque grata in te, vt beneficentissimum seruatorem, nec tibi vt clementissimo domino meo satis obsequens extiterim: vel ob alias causas diuinae tuae sapientiae optime cognitas, iam inquam, nuper an-cillam tuam, vel admonendi salabriter[22] vel iusti puniendi, atque ita eam corrigendi, emendandique gratia, periculosissimo, adeoque letali pene huic corpori morbo me affecisti: sed et animum pariter meum mul-tis angoribus grauiter perculisti: totum praeterea populum Anglicum, cuius quies atque securitas, post te proxime, in meae[23] Ancillae tuae in-columitate sita est, meo periculo vehementer preteruisti,[24] attonitumque reddidisti. Verum in iuditio tuo tamen, mitissime seruator, pro consueta tua bonitate, misericordiae tuae recordatus Ancillam tuam, super om-nem spem opemque humanam, a presente mortis discrimine liberans, vtroque paruit, et subito grauissimoque morbo meo, et repentino in-speratoque remedio mihi per tuam clementiam in re plane desperata, adhibito, diuinam tuam potentiam cum ineffabili misericordia coniunc-tam, occulis hominum ostendisti, atque declarasti.

Perfice clementissime seruator, opus salutis ancillae tuae quod miseri-corditer coepisti: absolue, o perfecte medice, quam clementer suscepisti curationem. Sana animam meam condonata mihi mea in te ingrati-tudine, mea tui obliuione, alijsque omnibus meis in tuam maiestatem criminibus atque peccatis obliteratis penitus atque deletis.

Sana mentem meam, me tua gratia coelesti formans atque instituens, vt hunc morbum mihi a te immissum patienter et aequo animo feram. vnaque sana etiam corpus meum, illudque ab omnibus prorsus morbi reliquijs, si ita tuae clementiae visum fuerit, purum redde, atque in in-tegrum omnino restitue: vt ancilla tua, facta ipsi[25] per te medicina, ex animi pariter et corporis morbis omnibus conualescat, perfectamque vtriusque sanitatem tuo vnius beneficio consequuta, ipsa, pariter atque vniuersus populus detuus[26] Anglicus, et hoc periculo edoceatur ad

---

22. **salabriter**   salubriter.
23. **meae**   mea.
24. **preteruisti**   preteristi.
25. **ipsi**   ipsum.
26. **detuus**   tuus.

Maiestati tuae reuerentiam atque obedientiam debitam exhibendam, et pro tanti periculi liberatione, perfectaque sanitatis summo beneficio, tuam clementiam, bonitatem, benignitatem, continuis laudibus perpetuaque gratiarum actione prosequatur, et celebret. Qui vna cum coelesti patre tuo, sacroque spiritu, vnus existis immortalis, immensus, et gloriosus Deus, cuius est omne imperium, potestas, atque maiestas in sempiternas atque infinitas seculorum omnium aetates. Amen.

PRAYER 8 ᙮ GRATIARUM ACTIO PRO BENEFICIIS COLLATIS.

ETerne Deus, rerum omnium conditor atque effector, atque idem tibi fidentium Pater clementissime, quum cogito quam nuper nihil omnino fuerim, sine corpore, sine anima, sine vita, sine sensu, aut intelligentia vlla, quumque adhuc essem quasi lutum in manu figuli, [Ecclesiasticus 33:13] vt pro tuo arbitratu me vel honoris vel ignominiae vas effigeres, non me misellam aliquam ex infima plebe puellam, quae in paupertate atque squalore vitam misere degerem, esse voluisti, sed regiis ortam parentibus regie enutritam atque educatam, regno destinasti: varijsque inimicorum insidijs circumuentam atque iactatam, tua assidue protectione tutatus es, et e carcere, atque vltimo discrimine liberatam, regia in terris dominatione, atque maiestate donasti: preterea vero quum consydero multos non e plebe solum, sed et ex nobilitate regioque adeo sanguine occulto, sed iusto iuditio tuo, alios corpore misere deformatos, alios miserius multo, ingenio omni atque intelligentia destitutos, alios longe miserime mente atque ratione turbatos, et tantum non insanos[27] atque furentes et fuisse, et hodie etiam esse, me vero corpore integram, forma bona, ingenio et sano et solido, prudentia etiam preter alias foeminas, eximia atque prestante, literarum praeterea atque linguarum cognitione et vsu, quum in hoc sexu esse solet, maiore, denique regijs omnibus, et regno dignis dotibus praeditam esse, atque a te gratis donatam: intelligo quantum tuae benignitati pater clementissime, prae alijs debeam, quae de te tamen nihil prae alijs premerita sim, quid enim promereri potui de te, priusquam essem, quaeque esse caepi, et talis esse, per te tuoque gratuito munere? O qui me tam multis, atque tantis beneficijs donasti, ornasti, honorasti, largire mihi diuinam spiritus tui

---

27. **non insanos** i.e., non sanos.

gratiam, vt benignitatis in me tuae immensitatem intelligam, te au-
thorem ingenue agnoscam, in te grata perpetuo siem, non de vlla dote,
quasi de meo superbiam, quae a te omnia acceperim, non quasi pro-
meruerim, quum omnia gratis supra meritum supra votum, acceperim.
Largire inquam, vt hanc tuam in me immensam munificentiam onus
esse aeque atque honorem intelligam, teque multa ab ijs, quibus multa
tribueris, exacturum esse meminerim: [Luke 12:48] vt ad populi tui rec-
tam gubernationem, regni atque reipublicae tuae salutarem administrationem, praecipue vero, atque super omnia, vt donis tuis ad tuam dono-
rum authoris gloriam illustrandam recte perpetuo vtar: cui vna cum
filio tuo Iesu Christo, seruatore nostro, et sancto spiritu, vni immortali
Deo, omnis ab omnibus debetur gratitudo honor, atque gloria, per sempiterna secula. Amen.

PRAYER 9 𐤊‍ PRECATIO PRO SAPIENTIA, AD REGNI
ADMINISTRATIONEM.

OMnipotens Deus, ac omnium regum Rex, coeli ac terrae domine, cuius
munere terreni principes mortalibus imperant, quum regum prudentis-
simus Solomon iugenue[28] fateatur, se parum idoneum fuisse qui regnum
administraret, nisi tu illi opem atque auxilium ferres, quanto minus ego
ancilla tua, sexu imbellis, natura foemina, ad administrandum haec
regna tua Angliae, et Hyberniae innumerabilemque atque bellicosam
gentem gubernandum sufficere, aut tanti oneris immensam magnitudinem sustinere queam, nisi tu clementissime pater, sicuti me immer-
entem regno liberaliter et preter multorum opinionem donasti, ita reg-
nantem tua gratia, (sine qua vel sapientissimus inter filios hominum
nihil recte cogitare potest) diuinitus imbuas, atque adiuues. Mitte ergo o
sapientiae omnis fons inexhauste, de coelis sanctis tuis, et a summa
maiestatis tuae throno sapientiam tuam, vt mecum semper sit, mecum
in gubernanda republicae excubet, atque laboret, me ancillam tuam doceat, atque instituat, vt queam discernere inter bonum et malum, ae-
quum et iniquum, vt populum tuum recte iudicare, nocentes meritis
supplicijs iuste afficere, innocentes clementer tueri, industrios et reipublicae vtiles liberaliter fouere, denique quod vni tibi acceptum esse
nouerim, id sine vllo personarum aut rerum mundanarum respectu

---

28. **iugenue** ingenue (turned letter).

suscipere, exequi, perficere velim, audeam, atque possim: vt quum tu
iustus ille iudex, qui multa magnaque ab ijs requires, quibus multa magnaque sunt credita, rationem exacta[29] reposces, male administratae
reipublicae atque regni ne rea per agar, sed si quid per humanam incog-
itantiam aut infirmitatem ancilla tua a recto aberrarim, id tua clementia
summe Rex, atque idem mitissime pater propter Iesum Christum Filium
tuum mihi condonet, simulque largire, vt post exactum mundanum
hoc regnum, tecum coelesti ac non perituro regno aeternum perfruar
per eundem Iesum Christum filium tuum et regni tui assessorem,
Dominum ac mediatorem nostrum: cui, tecum, atque cum sacro spiritu,
vni seculorum regi, immortali inuisibili, soli sapienti deo, sit omnis
honor et gloria in secula seculorum. Amen.

SPEECH 7 𝕰 QUEEN ELIZABETH'S LATIN ORATION AT CAMBRIDGE
UNIVERSITY, AUGUST 7, 1564[1]

Etsi foeminilis pudor, (subditi fidelissimi, et Academia clarissima[2])
rudem et incultum sermonem prohibet,[3] in tanta doctissimorum hominum turba narrare: tamen nobilium meorum intercessio, et beneuolentia erga academiam[4] proferre inuitant. Duobus stimulis ad hanc rem
commoueor, quorum primus est, bonarum literarum propagatio, quam
multum cupio,[5] et ardentissimis votis exopto. Secundus[6] vestra omnium

---

29. **exacta** exactam.

1. *Source:* BL, MS Sloane 401, fol. 38; "Rudolph Wilkinson's Commonplace Book" in an italic
hand of the latter half of the sixteenth century that makes heavy use of contracted forms and
preserves the anglicized, oral features of the Latin speech as Elizabeth may well have delivered it. Every known manuscript version of this speech is different; frequently the Latin is
rendered more formal and grammatically complex by the copyist. In particular, Bodleian Library, University of Oxford, MS Rawlinson Poetical 85, fols. 37v–38r, in a somewhat later hand
than the Sloane MS, contains some substantive variants noted here to illustrate how subsequent copyists smooth out the compressed, elliptical phrasing recorded in Sloane. Still more
elaborate versions are recorded in Thomas Fuller, *The History of the University of Cambridge
and of Waltham Abbey,* ed. James Nichols (London: W. Pickering, 1840), p. 195ff.; and in Fran-
cis Peck, *Desiderata Curiosa: or, A Collection of Divers Scarce and Curious Pieces Relating
Chiefly to Matters of English History,* vol. 2 (London, 1735), bk. VII, arts. 14–15, 19–20.

2. MS Rawl Po reads "clarissimi Cantabrigiensis."

3. MS Rawl Po reads "prohibeat."

4. MS Rawl Po inserts "aliquid."

5. MS Rawl Po omits "cupio."

6. MS Rawl Po inserts "est."

expectatio, Quod ad propagationem attinet, verba superiorum. (vt inquit Demostenes) pro librijs sunt inferiorum, et vim legis exemplar prin-
cipis habet. Quod si hoc verum fuit in illis Respublicis, quanto magis in
regno, Semita nulla rectior,[7] vel ad bona fortuna acquirenda, vel ad
meam gratiam conciliandam, quam vt gnauiter[8] studiis vestris (vt co-
epistis) operam adhibeatis, quod vt faciatis omnes vos oro obsecroque.
Nunc ad secundum stimulum venio. Tempore ante pomeridiano vidi[9]
aedificia vestra sumptuosa, a meis antecadentibus,[10] nobilissimis regibus extructa, et in videndo ab imo pectore suspiria ducebam, non aliter
quam Alexander,[11] qui cum legisset multa a principibus posita monu-
menta, conuersus ad familiarem, vel potius consiliarium,[12] ego (inquit)
nihil tale feci: sic[13] ego non minus, sed meum dolorem si non auferro,[14]
at minuere certò, potest vulgarij illa sententia Romam non fuisse uno die
aedificatam. Nam non est ita senilis aetas mea, nec tam longo tempore
regnaui, quia ante redditionem debitae naturae, si non citius quam spero
Atropos lineam vitae amputauerit, aliquod praeclarum et egregium
opus faciam, nec quamdiu spiritus hos[15] regit actus, vnquam a proposito
defaelcam[16] Et si contingat (quod quam cito futurum sit planè nescio,)
me mori oportere, antequam ipsum quod polliceor complere possim:
Tamen eximium[17] opus post mortem relinquam, quò et mei memoria in
posterum[18] celebris fiat, et alios excitem meo exemplo, et vos omnes
alacriores faciam ad vestra studia. Sed iam videtis quantum intersit inter
doctrinam lectam, et disciplinam[19] in animo contentam,[20] quorum
alterius sunt hûc[21] complures satis sufficientes testes, alterius autem et

7. MS Rawl Po inserts "nulla aptior."
8. MS Rawl Po omits "gnauiter."
9. MS Rawl Po inserts "ego."
10. Differing in one vowel, MS Rawl Po reads "antecedentibus."
11. MS Rawl Po inserts "magnus."
12. MS Rawl Po inserts "At."
13. MS Rawl Po inserts "et."
14. MS Rawl Po reads "Sed hunc meum dolorem non auferre."
15. MS Rawl Po reads "spiritibus hos meis."
16. MS Rawl Po reads "deflectam."
17. MS Rawl Po inserts "aliquod."
18. MS Rawl Po reads "in posteris."
19. **doctrinam . . . disciplinam** Elizabeth inverts the usual tilt of the distinction between "doctrine" and "discipline" so frequently drawn by writers of the Renaissance and Reformation era.
20. MS Rawl Po reads "retentam."
21. MS Rawl Po substitutes "tanta hic."

meipsum, et vos ipsos nimis quidem inconsideratè hodierno die testes effeci, quòd mea barbarie tam diu vestrae doctae aures detinere.[22]

POSTEAQUE HAEC

I wold to god you had all dronke this night of the riuer of Lethe, that you might forget all.[23]

SPEECH 8 ⸖ QUEEN ELIZABETH'S LATIN ORATION AT OXFORD UNIVERSITY, SEPTEMBER 5, 1566[1]

Qui male agunt oderunt lucem et idcirco quia ego conscia sum mihimet male acturae causam meam apud uos puto hoc tempus tenebrarum mihi fore aptissimum (hac tum initio vsa est quia nox erat, et omnia iam latere visa crassis occultata et circumfusa tenebris).[2] magna me verò diu tenuit dubitatio[3] taceremne an loquerer? si enim loquar, patefaciam vobis quam sim literarum rudis, quod si tacerem defectus hic videretur contemptus. quod igitur attinet ad ea quae vidi aut audiui ex quo veni in hanc Academiam fuerunt ea omnia meo sane iudicio, pereximia, quia vero tempus breue est quod superest ad dicendum duo duntaxat vobis in genere iam dicere institui quorum alterum est laudare et alterum vitu-

22. MS Rawl Po reads "detinaui."

23. MS Rawl Po concludes more conformably to the occasion by not reverting to English: "DIXI. E: REGINA."

1. *Source:* Bodleian Library, University of Oxford, MS Additional A.63, fols. 16v–17r; copy in the hand of John Bereblock, fellow of Exeter College, Oxford, who became its dean in 1566. The version printed here appears to be among the earliest, but may show some of the embellishings of the queen's Latin that later versions of her Cambridge speech do. A somewhat later version that circulated more widely than this one is Bodleian, MS Rawlinson D.273, fol. 111r; its significant variants are recorded in the notes below. Another sixteenth-century version of this speech is preserved as Bodleian, MS Rawlinson D.273, fol. 205r; its endorsement reads "ex Laurentio humfredo in libro de vita et obitu Juelle" (from Laurence Humphreys' *Life and Death of Jewel*). Anthony à Wood records Humphreys as having been present at Elizabeth's speech; see *CW*, pp. 89–90.

2. Rawl MS D273 reads "ego autem quia nihill aliud nisi male agere possum, idcirco odi lucem, et hoc est conspectum vestrum" (I, who can do nothing other than badly, on that account hate light: that is, your gaze); it omits the following remarks on night and shadows.

3. Rawl MS D273 inserts "cum singula considero quae hic aguntur, vtrum laudarem an vituperarem" (when I consider the individual things that are being done here, whether I should praise or blame).

perare. laus autem ad vos pertinet. nam non possum non laudare et vos et ea quae a vobis et dicta sunt et facta et ea probare omnia quasi pereximia ac excellentia, ceterum nonnulla quae in se imperfectiora erant, quae in prologis ipsis vestris vosmet excusastis, quatenus sum Regina probare non possum,[4] quia tamen in exordijs cautionem habuistis in suo genere tanquam perfectissime acta ac disputata non improbo. Sed alterum illud vituperare ad me proprie pertinet,[5] quia cum omnibus notum sit me aliquam operam impendisse bonis disciplinis et longius addiscendis. Pedagogi tamen mei in terram tam sterilem et infecundam operam suam posuerunt ut non possim iam cum maxime velim,[6] fructus ostendere aut dignitate mea aut illorum laboribus aut vestra expectatione dignos. Quamobrem cum vos me supra modum laudatis. ego quae mihi optime conscia sum quam sim nulla laude digna facile agnosco. finem igitur faciam huic orationi[7] meae Barbarismis plenae, si duo vota[8] prius addidero, quae in animo habeo ut me viuente sitis florentissimi, me mortua beatissimi. Dixi.

LETTER 27 ❧ QUEEN ELIZABETH TO MARY, QUEEN OF SCOTS, FEBRUARY 24, 1567[1]

Madame, mes oreilles ont esté tellement estourdiees et mon entendement si fasche et mon coeur tellement effrayé a ouir l'horrible son de

4. Rawl MS D273 elaborates this clause as follows: "neque autoritate ferre vt regina possum neque acrimonias ac iudicio probare debeo" (I as a queen neither tolerate with my authority nor ought I to approve recriminations with my judgment).

5. Rawl MS D273 adds a sizeable insertion: "Sanè fateor patrem meum diligenter curauisse vt in bonis litteris recte instituerer. atque quidem in multarum linguarum varietate enim versata sum. quarum aliquam mihi cognitionem assumo, quod etsi vere tamen verecunde dico, habui quidem multos pedagogos, qui ad me erudiendam diligenter elaboraverunt." (Indeed I confess that my father took most diligent care to have me correctly instructed in good letters. And I was engaged in the variety, truly, of many languages. Of some of these I have gained knowledge, which although true, yet I say so—modestly. I have had many teachers who have labored diligently to render me erudite.)

6. Rawl MS D273 omits the "ut" clause.

7. **orationi** oratione.

8. Rawl MS D273 substitutes "meam vnicam optationem."

1. *Source:* PRO, State Papers Scotland, Elizabeth, 52/13/17, fol. 30r. Copy. The endorsement by Cecil's clerk reads "24. februarij. 1566[7]. Copia literarum Reginae Maiestatis ad Reginam Scotiae."

l'habominable meurtre de vostre fou mary et mon tué Cousin que quasi encore nay Ie lesprit den escrire, Et combien que mon naturel me contrainct de combler sa mort m'appartenant si preez de sangue si est ce que vous dirai hardyment ce que Ien pense, Ie ne puis colore que Ie ne soys plus dolente pour vous que pour luy, O madame Ie ne ferois l'office de fidelle cousine ne daffectionée Amie si Iestudirois plustost a complaire a voz oreilles que en m'employer a conseruer vostre honneur / pourtant Ie ne vous coloray point ce qui la plus part de gens en parlent, c'est que vous regarderez entre voz doigtz sur la reuenge de ceste faite, et que n'auez garde de toucher eulx qui vous ont faict tel plaisir comme si la chose n'eust esté commise pour que les meurteurs en eussent sceu leur asseurance. de mon pensées Ie vous suplie que ne vouldroir qu'une telle pensée reste a se tour en mon coeur pour tout los du monde Ie n'auuois Iamais si mauuaise haste qui logeroit en mon cueur que d'auoire si mauuaise opinion de quelque prince que en fust, beaucoup moins lauray Ie en ceste La a qui Ie soubhaite aultant de bien que mon cueur pourra Imaginer ou que vous naguere scauuiez souhaitre. Pourtant Ie vous exhorte Ie vous conseille et vous suplie de prendre ceste chose tellement a cueur que nayez peur de toucher voyre le plus proche quayez sil le touche, et que nulle persuasion vous retire a en faire exemple au monde questez et noble Princesse et questiez loyalle femme, Ie n'escrips si vehementement pour doubt que Ien ay, mais pour laffection que Ie vous porte en particulier Car Ie ne suis ignorant que nayez de plus sages Conseillers que moy, Ce est ce que quant iL me souuient que nostre Seigneur entre douze auoit vng Judas, et que Ie masseure qung plus fidelle de moy ne y peult estre Ie vous offre mon affection en lieu de ceste prudence. Quant aux trois choses qui mont este communique par meluin, Ientendz par toutes ces Instructions que continuez en grande enuie de me satisfaire, et quil vous contentera d'octroyer la requeste que my Lord Bedford vous faict en mon nom pour la ratification de vostre traicté qui vj ou vij ans passez nestoit faict vous promettant que Ie la demandois aultant pour vostre bien que pour quelque proffit que men resouldra. Des aultres choses Ie ne vous fasheray de plus longue lettre sinon a vous remettre en rapport de ce gentilhomme et vous remercies de ce messangier et pour vos honnestes lettres lesquelles m'estoyent et sont bien agreables sortant de voz mains priant le Createur vous donner la grace de congnoistre ce traisteur et vous en garder comme de ministres de satan apres mes tres cordialles recommandacions a vous treschere soeur. de Westmester 24. de fevrier.

Elizabeth Regina.

2. PARALIPOM. 6.

*Domine Deus Iſrael, non eſt ſimilis tui Deus in cœlo & in ter-
ra, qui paſta cuſtodis & miſericordiam cum ſeruis tuis, qui
ambulant coram te in toto corde ſuo.*

FIGURE 6   Frontispiece of *Christian Prayers and Meditations* (London: John Daye, 1569)
(*STC* 6428) showing Queen Elizabeth at prayer in her private chapel. Reproduced by
permission of the Archbishop of Canterbury and the Trustees of Lambeth Palace Library.

PRAYERS 10–28, POEM 6
Queen Elizabeth's Prayers and Verses, 1569[1]

———•———

The French Prayers

UN BREF FORMULAIRE D'ORAISON.

PRAYER 10 ℰ LA PREFACE ET LA CONFESSION DES PECHEZ.

O Seigneur bon Dieu et Pere, que ton nom soit benit à iamais. Dispose mon coeur, ouure mes leures, et me conduis par ton saint Esprit, à vne vraye recognoissance de toutes mes fautes, à fin que mon Oraison soit exaucée de toy au Nom de ton filz Iesus Christ. Ainsi soit-il.

SEigneur mon Dieu, Pere eternel et tout-puissant, ie recognoy et confesse deuant ta sainte et haute Maiesté, que ie n'ay cessé depuis ma nais-

---

1. *Source: Christian Prayers and Meditations in English, French, Italian, Spanish, Greeke, and Latine* (London: J. Daye, 1569) (*STC* 6428), sigs. Hh.i r–Ll.i v. Despite references to the "queen" in various languages in this, the closing section of this volume, Elizabeth's name appears nowhere. A variety of evidence, however, points towards ascribing these prayers and verses to her. The volume has overt visual links with Elizabeth: her royal arms supply the ornaments on its first and last leaves, and the frontispiece, reproduced here as figure 6, is captioned *Elizabeth Regina*. This illustration shows her kneeling in prayer before a private altar with an opened prayer book, above which she has placed her crown. Her sword of state lies in readiness on the carpet to her right, its hilt propped against her kneeling-cushion. Given such overt visual and textual links with Elizabeth, it would have been impossible, not merely imprudent, to publish this volume without her cognizance and her authorization of its many first-person locutions as references to her. As for internal textual evidence, where grammatical agreement in French, Italian, Spanish, Latin, and Greek involves gendered self-reference, the usage is consistently feminine. Whatever the foreign language, moreover, phrase and sentence structure and even vocabulary choices show a literalistic approach to composition in which anglicisms are conspicuous. This tendency characterizes Elizabeth's non-English writings and translations from girlhood to old age (with the significant exception of the Latin she wrote under Ascham's tutelage and the partial exception of her Latin prayers here and in *Precationes priuatae. Regiae E.R.*, Prayers 3–9 above). In sum, it is highly likely that Elizabeth compiled these materials, and quite likely that she authored the prayers. The provenance of the verses is another matter; see notes 5 and 7 below. As before, square brackets at the end of a clause or versicle enclose the scriptural reference and, where applicable, a statement of the adaptation that Elizabeth has performed.

sance, et ne cesse tous les iours, estant conceuë et née en iniquité et cor-
ruption, de transgresser tes commandemens. Quoy faisant, ie ne puis
selon ton iuste iugement, euiter ruine et perdition: Toutesfois ayant des-
plaisir de t'auoir offensé, condemnant et moy, et mon peché: puis qu'il
t'a pleu de nous aymer, lors mesme que nous estions tes ennemis, en tesmoignage dequoy tu nous as donné ton filz vnique, et bien aymé, pour
mediateur et aduocat[2] entre toy et nous, nostre Seigneur Iesus Christ,
auec promesse d'obtenir en son Nom, tout ce que nous te demanderons.
[echoes John 15:16]

Vueille donc Dieu tresbenin et pere misericordieux en son Nom et en
sa faueur me faire pardon et mercy. Et en repurgeant mon coeur de toute
vanité et souillure, m'addresser et conduire par ton saint Esprit, en toutes
mes voyes, a fin que ie chemine selon tes saints et diuins commaunde-
mens tous les iours de ma vie, à la gloire de ton Nom, Par iceluy ton filz
bien-aymé. Ainsi soit-il.

PRAYER 11 ❧ L'ORAISON POUR LE MATIN.

MOn DIEV mon Pere et mon Sauueur, comme maintenant tu enuoye ton
Soleil sur la terre, pour donner la lumiere corporelle à tes créatures,
vueille aussi illuminer mon coeur et mon entendement, par la lumiere
celeste de ton saint Esprit: à fin que ie ne pense, ne dise, et ne face rien
sinon pour te seruir et complaire. Que durant tout ce iour mon but principal soit de cheminer en ta crainte, te seruir et honorer, attendant tout
heur et prosperité de ta seule benediction. Que selon mon corps et mon
ame tu sois mon protecteur, me fortifiant contre toutes les tentations du
diable, et de la chair, me preseruant des entreprinses et conspirations de
tous mes ennemis, leurs complices et adherés.

Et d'autant bon Dieu que ce n'est rien de bien commencer si on ne
perseuere, qu'il te plaise, non seulement pour ce iour me receuoir sous ta
conduite et protection, mais pour tout le cours de ma vie: continuant et
augmentant de iour en iour les dons et graces de ton saint Esprit en moy
iusques à ce qu'estant vnie et coniointe auec ton filz vnique, mon Sauueur,

---

2. **mediateur et aduocat** Exact translation of the final phrase of the prayer for the whole
state of Christ's Church in the Holy Communion service in the *Book of Common Prayer*
(Booty, p. 254).

ie puisse iouir de ceste vie bien-heureuse laquelle tu as promise à tous
tes eleuz. Par iceluy ton filz, nostre Seigneur Iesus-Christ. Ainsi soit-il.

PRAYER 12 ❧ ACTION DE GRACES.

DIeu tout bon et tout sage, Pere celeste, plein de misericorde et clemence,
reduisant en memoire les oeuures de tes mains, ie ne puis sinon admirer
ta grande sapience et bonté infinie, laquelle tu as declarée enuers toutes
tes creatures, et singulierement au regard de moy, comme de m'auoir
donné estre, mouuement, et vie: mais aussi outre les benefices infinis,
que tu distribue communément à tous hommes de la terre, tu m'as fait
tant de graces speciales, qu'il m'est impossible de les reciter, ne mesme les
pouuoir comprendre. Il t'a pleu par la lumiere de ton Euangile me deli-
urer des tenebres d'erreur et d'ignorance, voire me retirer des abismes de
de³ mort, et de la confusion horrible, ou i'estoye destinée selon la cor-
ruption de ma nature: et ainsi m'as tu transportée au royaume de ton filz
bien-aymé, lequel selon ton plaisir et decret eternel, s'est donné soy
mesme pour mes pechez.

Il y a aussi Seigneur, que m'ayant receuë en ton Eglise au nombre de
tes enfans, tu m'as eleuë et choisie par ta prouidence admirable pour me
decorer sous la Maiesté de ta grandeur d'vn estat d'honneur et d'excel-
lence, assauoir de la dignité Royale pour le gouuernement et conseruation de ton peuple.

Or maintenant selon la parole de Dauid, quelle chose rendrayie au
Seigneur pour tous ses bienfaitz enuers moy? [Psalm 116:12] Ie say que
toute ma vie deuroit estre consacrée à vne perpetuelle action de graces,
pour annoncer auec la gent sainte et le peuple acquis, les vertus de celuy
qui nous à appellez des tenebres à sa merueilleuse lumiere. Le calice de
deliurance ne deuroit bouger de mes mains, [Psalm 116:13] n'y les Can-
tiques nouueaux de ma bouche. [Psalm 40:3] Mais Seigneur, fay moy la
grace, comme iadis tu as faite à Dauid, homme selon ton coeur. [1 Samuel
13:14] Lequel traitant de ce mesme Argument, et recitant les tesmoi-
gnages de ta bonté, disoit, Ainsi est-il Seigneur, Ie suis ton seruiteur, Ie
suis ton seruiteur filz de ta chambriere, tu as rompu mes liens, [Psalm
116:16, 17] Ie te sacrificeray sacrifice d'action de graces et reclameray le

---

3. **de de** repetition across line break.

nom du Seigneur. Ainsi di-ie Seigneur de moymesme, et ce par ta grace, Ie suis ta seruante, Ie suis ta seruante. Tu as rompu mes liens, et m'as preseruée au milieu des dangers de mort, tu m'as mis au large et en sauueté. Au Roy des siecles, immortel et inuisible, à Dieu seul bon et seul sage, soit honneur et gloire és siecles des siecles par Iesus Christ son filz nostre Seigneur. Ainsi soit-il.

PRAYER 13 ❦ ORAISON POUR TOUT LE ROYAUME ET CORPS DE L'EGLISE SELON LEURS ESTAS[4] ET MEMBRES.

DIeu tout puissant, Pere celeste, tu as donné commandement à tes fideles de prier les vns pour les autres, auec promesse de les exaucer au Nom du mediateur ton filz bien-aymé.

Moy donc ton humble seruante en confiance de tes promesses, et en consideration des necessitez si grandes et si vrgentes, qui se presentent de toutes pars, Sathan faisant tous ses efforts pour mettre la terre en confusion, et sur tout pour empescher le cours de ton Euangile. Seigneur bon Dieu auquel est mon refuge et mon esperance, ie te supplie et requiers comme tu és le Pere des lumieres, [James 1:17] qu'il te plaise d'illuminer les coeurs et les entendemens de tous hommes, d'autant que tu veux toutes gens estre sauuées, et venir à la cognoissance de verité. Et comme specialement tu as ordonné qu'on prie pour les Rois et tous ceux qui sont constituez en dignité, à fin que la societé humaine viue en paix et tranquillité auec toute pieté et honnesteté.

Moy donc sachant combien les couronnes et les sceptres sont pesans, et l'administration d'iceux difficile, pour s'en bien acquitter, soit au regard de toy, mon Dieu, ou de mes subiectz, Ie te requiers de tout mon coeur, tant pour moy, que pour tous autres que tu as constituez en ce mesme degré de prééminence, de nous donner, ce que iadis t'a demandé vn Salomon, duquel tu as approuué l'Oraison, comme l'ayant mise en son coeur, [echoes 1 Kings 3:10; 2 Chronicles 1:11] et en sa bouche par ton saint Esprit, lequel nous apprend de bien prier aydant noz infirmitez.

O Seigneur bon Dieu tu m'as fait regner au milieu de ton peuple, tu donneras à ta seruante et à tes seruiteurs vn coeur entendu pour iuger ton peuple, et pour discerner le bien d'entre le mal, [1 Kings 3:9] à fin que

---

4. **Estas** Estats.

nous ne soyons point inutiles, ou mesme pernicieux en vne vocation si sainte.

Donne nous aussi des Conseillers prudens sages et vertueux, chassant loing de nous, tous ambitieux, malins, cauteleux, et hypocrites.

Donne des Iuges, hommes veritables haissans auarice, et fuyans l'acception des personnes, à fin que mon peuple soit gouuerné en toute equité et droiture, les bons soustenus en leur Iustice et innocence, les iniques punis et chastiez selon leurs demerites.

Fay aussi Seigneur que tous ceux, desquelz tu m'as commis la charge en main, me rendent le deuoir d'vne iuste obeissance, à fin qu'il y ait vne bonne et sainte vnion entre le chef et les membres, et que par ce moyen tous cognoissent que de toy seul depend l'Estat des Royaumes et le gouuernement des republiques. Et que par ainsi ie puisse à iamais chanter à ta louenge le Cantique de Dauid, ou il proteste de faire le deuoir de bon Prince.

PSEAVME. C I.[5]

Vouloir m'est pris de mettre en escriture,
Pseaume parlant de bonte et droiture,
Et si le veux a toy, mon Dieu chanter,
    Et presenter.

Tenir ie veux la voye non nuisible,
Quand viendras-tu me rendre Roy paisible?
D'vn coeur tout pur conduiray ma maison,
    Auec raison.

Rien de mauuais y voir n'auray enuie,
Car ie hay trop les meschans et leur vie:
Vn seul d'entr'eux autour de moy adioint,
    Ne sera point.

Tout coeur ayant pensée desloyale,
Deslogera hors de ma cour Royale:

---

5. The following stanzas are the work of the French Protestant poet Clément Marot (1496–1544) and were first published in his *Trente-deux Pseaulmes de David* . . . (Paris: E. Roffet, [1543]). We are grateful to Anne Lake Prescott for this identification.

Et le nuisant n'y sera bien venu.
     Non pas cognu.

Qui par mesdire à part son prochain greue
Qui à coeur gros et les sourcils esleue:
L'vn mettray bas, l'autre souffrir pour vray,
     Ie ne pourray.

Mes yeux seront fort diligens à querre.
Les habitans fidele de la terre:
Pour estre a moy. Qui droite voye ira.
     Me seruira.

Qui s'estudie à vser de fallace,
En ma maison point ne trouuera place:
De moy n'aura mensonger ne baueur.
     Bien ne faueur.

Ains du pays chasseray de bonne heure,
Tous les meschans, tant qu'vn seul n'y demeure,
Peur du Seigneur nettoyer la Cite,
     D'iniquité.

Ie te prie aussi Pere veritable et Sauueur pour tous ceux que tu as ordonnez vrays Pasteurs à tes fideles et ausquelz, tu as commis la charge des ames, et la dispensation de ton sacré Euangile que tu les conduise par ton saint Esprit, à fin qu'ilz soyent trouuez fideles et diligens en leur sainte vocation.

D'autrepart que tu chasse les faux Pasteurs, hommes corrompus d'entendement, loups pesans, ambitieux, et auarcieux, qui ne seruent qu'à destruire et perdre tes Eglises. [echoes Acts 20:29]

Et d'autant que tu requiers en tous tes enfans le zele de ta maison [John 2:16], fay moy la grace de repurger en mon peuple toutes sectes, heresies, et superstitions, à fin que tes Eglises soubz ma charge profitent et accroissent de iour en iour en la verité de ton Euangile à toute iustice et sainteté.

Que generalement il te plaise de faire vne deliuerance et restauration de tes Eglises par toute la terre, enuoyer ouuriers à ta moisson, [Matthew

9:38; Luke 10:2] hommes idoines et suffisans pour recueillir les poures brebis esgarées soubz la houlette de ce grand pasteur des ames ton filz Iesus Christ. [echoes Matthew 18:12–14; Luke 15:4–7]

Quant aux auditeurs ceux qui desia font profession de ton Nom que tu leur donne vne vraye perseuerance en foy, en charité, et en toutes bonnes oeuures pour la gloire de ton Nom, et à leur salut.

Quant aux autres qui cheminent encore en la vanité de leur sens que tu touche leurs coeurs et leur donne des yeux illuminez, à fin que tous se rengent pour te seruir et complaire.

Finalement ô Dieu de toute consolation, [Romans 15:5] ie te prie d'auoir pitié des calamitez et afflictions de toutes tes creatures en general. Des peuples que tu visite par pestes, guerres ou famines. Des personnes que tu afflige par poureté, prison, maladie, bannissement, ou autres tes verges, soit en leur corps ou en leurs esprits.

Et singulierement que tu aye pitié de tes eleuz qui souffrent et endurent pour le tesmoignage de ton saint Euangile.

Et comme il t'a pleu me faire ce bien, et cest honneur, de donner repos en ma terre, estans les autres Royaumes en horribles confusions, et que tu m'as enuoyé les entrailles de ton filz Iesus Christ, pour leur donner refuge en leurs oppressions: fay moy la grace d'estre vraye nourrissiere et tutrice des tiens selon la parolle de ton Prophete Isaye, [Isaiah 49:23] pour auoir vne vraye compassion tant de ceux qui sont icy, que de tous autres, à fin qu'en l'accomplissement de tes promesses, lors que la parolle sera dite, Venez les benits de mon Pere, possedez le Royaume qui vous a esté preparé des la fondation du monde, [Matthew 25:34] que lors tu me reçoiue. Pere celeste, au nombre de tes enfans, pour l'amour de ton filz, mon Sauueur Iesus Christ. Auquel auec toy et le saint Esprit soit honneur et gloire eternellement. Amen.

PRAYER 14 ❧ L'ORAISON POUR LE SOIR.

SEigneur mon Dieu, mon Pere, et mon Sauueur me prosternant en toute humilité deuant ta sainte Maiesté, ie te requiers bien affectueusement, comme tu m'as fait la grace d'estre paruenuë à la fin de ce iour, d'autant que tu as creé la nuit pour le repos des hommes que tu me face ce bien auec tes autres benefices infinis, de tellement reposer ceste nuit pour le soulagement de mon infirmité, que mon coeur estant tousiours esleué à toy, mon ame ait aussi bien son repos spirituel, comme le corps prend le sien.

Que mon dormir ne soit point excessif, pour complaire outré mesure à l'aise de ma chair, mais seulement pour la necessité de ma nature, à fin que demain ie soye mieux disposée à ton seruice.

Preserue moy aussi de toute souilleure de corps et d'esprit, et me garde des tentations de l'ennemy, et contre tous dangers qui me pour-royent auenir.

Et pource que ce iour n'est point passé que ie ne t'aye offensé en plusieurs sortes et manieres, comme tu enuoye maintenant les tenebres en l'absence du Soleil pour cacher toutes choses, ainsi vueille effacer toutes mes offenses par ta misericorde infinie, a fin que iamais elles ne viennent en compte deuant ton iugement.

Toutes lesquelles choses ie te requiers et demande au Nom et en faueur de ton filz vnique mon Seigneur et Sauueur Iesus Christ, comme luy-mesme nous à[6] donné la reigle de te prier.

NOstre Pere qui es és cieux. Ton Nom soit sanctifié. Ton regne aduienne. Ta volonté soit faicte, en la Terre comme au Ciel. Donne nous auiourd'huy, nostre Pain quotidien. Et nous pardonne noz offences, ainsi que nous pardonnons à ceux qui nous ont offencé. Et ne nous induy point en tentation: mais deliure-nous du mal. Car à toy est le regne, la puissance, et la gloire, és siecles des siecles. Ainsi soit il.

PRAYER 15 ❧ ORAISON POUR FAIRE DEUANT LA CONSULTATION DES AFFAIRES DU ROYAUME.

O Seigneur nostre bon Dieu qui contemple d'enhaut tout ce qui est au Ciel et en la Terre, duquel le throne est admirable et la gloire incomprehensible, deuant lequel la congregation des Anges se tient en crainte.

Nous ton humble seruante et tes seruiteurs estans icy assemblez en ta presence, pour traiter et aduiser aux affaires qui concernent la vocation sainte à laquelle tu nous as appellez par ta grace, cognoissans que tu soustiens et conserue sous la conduite de ta prouidence l'estat et gouuernement de tous les Royaumes de la terre, et que c'est à toy de presider au milieu des Princes en leur conseil.

6. à a.

D'autre part recognoissans que nous sommes enuironnez de tenebres, remplis d'erreurs et d'ignorances, et mesme indignes de ton assis-
tence si tu regardes à nos iniquitez.

Pour ces causes bon Dieu, nous te prions au nom de ton filz vnique
nostre Seigneur Iesus Christ de nous pardonner toutes nos offenses,
et pour l'amour d'iceluy nous communiquer les dons et graces de ton
saint Esprit, à fin qu'estans poulsez du vray zele de ta gloire, et d'vn
amour paternel enuers le peuple que tu nous as donné en charge. Nous
puissions auec prudence et sagesse traiter les choses qui maintenant
seront proposées.

Dispose donc Seigneur nos bouches, nos coeurs, et nos entendemens, nous faisant cognoistre les choses que tu approuue pour les em-
brasser, et discerner les mauuaises pour les decliner et chasser.

D'auantage que tu tienne tellement la main à toutes nos delibera-
tions, que tu nous en face veoir vne heureuse issuë, à la gloire de ton
Nom, au bien et profit de nostre peuple, et à la descharge de nos consciences.

Ce que te demandons humblement en la faueur de ton filz bien-aymé,
comme par luy sommes enseignez de te prier. Nostre Pere qui es. etc.

POEM 6[7] ࿐ PRIERE.

> *O Gouuerneur, de la machine ronde,*
> *Toy qui as mis, les fondemens du monde,*
> *Et le depars, ainsi que bien tu vois,*
> *A tous humains sans recueillir leur voix*
> *Tu hausses l'vn, et l'aultre tu rabaisses,*
> *Cil qui languit, en peine tu redresses,*

7. The authorship of this poem is uncertain. While its content correlates closely with the
events of Elizabeth's life, it is written in more polished language and more regular meter than
Elizabeth's other French verses (Poem 15). The verse form—rhymed pentameter cou-
plets—is identical and the poetic quality comparable to that of the French verse translation
of Katherine Parr's *Lamentation of a Sinner*, preserved in two manuscripts: BL, MS Royal
16.E.28, and Hatfield House, Cecil Papers, vol. 314. In both MSS, it is impossible to distinguish reliably between the italic scripts of Princess Elizabeth and Jean Bellemain, her French
tutor; see our preface, pp. xiv–xvii. Bellemain's death in 1552, six years before Elizabeth's ac-
cession, would have precluded his having any hand in the present text of this "Prière." It may
be the work of another, as yet unidentified French poet.

Et le fais Roy, si tel tu le veulx estre.
Ainsi m'as fait: ô mon Dieu et mon maistre,
En me tirant, hors de prison cruelle,
Prison du Corps, et de peine eternelle,
L'vne ou i'estoye, pour mes pechez commis
Des ma ieunesse, et me les as remis:
Et l'aultre estoit, pour auoir verité,
En amour prise, et mensonge quitté,
Pour suyure Christ, ainsi tu m'as tirée,
Par ta main forte, et à toy retirée,
En me donnant, ceste grand' Royaulté,
Range moy donc, à ce qu'as decreté,
Force, Conseil, auec saine doctrine,
Pour bien guider, le peuple que domine,
Ottroye moy: aussi par ta bonté,
Ne prens point garde, à mon iniquité.

FIN DES PRIERES EN FRANÇOYS.

---·•·---

The Italian Prayers

PRAYER 16 ❧ CONFESSION DE' PECCATI, AL SIGNORE.

IO T'HO FATTO Notto il mio peccato, e non ho coperto la mia iniquità: ho detto, Io confesserò le mie trasgressioni al Signore, e tu hai leuata l'iniquità del mio peccato. SALMO. 32.[8]

IDdio et Signor mio. Humilmente, et con animo pieno d'infinito dispiacere d'hauerti offeso, e d'offenderti tutto dì,[9] io humil serua tua, et peccatrice, mi presento dinanzi la tua diuina maëstà per confessare ingenuamente, e liberamente i miei peccati, et chiedertene perdon. Sono, come sai, concetta, e nata in peccato, dall'istessa massa di corruttione uenuta, onde è

---

8. The correct reference is Psalm 32:5.

9. **dì** dí. The typesetter confuses grave and acute accents elsewhere in the Italian prayers—e.g., "nè" for "né" in Prayer 17.

tolto tutto l'human lignaggio: trouomi sempre piena di cattiui affetti, e non
so mai cosa che buona sia, oue il tuo santo spirito me guidi, ma ogni hora
piego alla terra, e al male, oue mi tira il peso graue di questa carne. Le oc-
casioni d'offenderti per l'altezza del luogo oue m'hai[10] posto, per le ric-
chezze, per gli agi, et per gli honori, sono molte, e molte, Infiinitè[11] le tenta-
tioni, continue, e vrgentissime: la mia carne è fragile sí, che non fo altro che
errori, e graui peccati dinanzi à[12] te Dio mio, onde sento sopra di me l'ira
tua giusta insino allultima condennatione. Dall'altra parte hauendomi tu
piantato, per infinita tua misericordia vna viua fede nel cuore, che Christo
è la mia vera e certa salute, e che per lui è riceuuta ogni anima lauata nel
suo sangue, dalla tua pietà: ecco che vengo con sicurta, et certa fede a
trouar perdono appresso il tribunal della misericordia tua per esso Giesu
Cristo. Riceui dunque ti prego padre benigno questa tua figliuola, che viene
all'vbidienza paterna: raccogli pastore amoreuole questa pecorella errante,
che torna al tuo ouile, e guarisci medico celeste, tutte le piaghe dell'anima
mia con la medicina della tua gratia: assicurandomi prima nella consci-
entia mia, che tutti i peccati essendomi rimesi, io sia pacificata con esso te,
e appresso con lo spirito tuo rinouandomi, e sanctificandomi ogni di, meni
questa vita, che mi resta in santità, e giustitia nel tuo cospetto, e della tua
chiesa, fin che mi chiami alla gloria di vita eterna, la quale aspetto, e at-
tendo sicuramente per Giesu Cristo Signor mio, cui sia honore e gloria per-
petuamente. Amen.

PRAYER 17 ɞ ORATIONE PRIMA COME CREATURA DI DIO.

CHIVNQVE ADOra Iddio con diletto, sarà riceuuto, e la sua preghiera s'anuieinerà[13] *in fino alle nuuole. L'oratione di chi si humilia penetrerà le nuuole.* ECCLE-
SIASTICO. 32.[14]

RIconoscendo Signore, com'io sono tua creatura, creata ad imagine e
somiglianza tua, opera eccellente delle tue mani sopra tutte l'altre creature,

---

10. This letter *i* slipped out of place in its line of text, as shown.

11. **Infiinitè** Infinite.

12. **à** a. The typesetter inserts other unneeded accents throughout the Italian prayers; this example is particularly frequent.

13. **s'anuieinerà** "s'advenierà" or "s'advenirà."

14. The correct reference is Ecclesiasticus 35:20–21.

io te ne rendo gratie infinite, e ti prego humilmente, che ti piaccia far ch'io habbia continuamente cura e riguardo di non isuilire, nè imbratare questa tua santissima imagine, ristoratami per Giesu Cristo: anzi conseruandola pura e sincera d'ogni affetto carnale, riluca innanzi gli occhi di tutti lo splendore del tuo volto, c' hai sparso sopra di me, alla gloria tua, per Giesu Christo. Amen.

PRAYER 18 ࿇ ORATIONE SECONDA, COME CRISTIANA, E REGINA.

IDdio padre, et protettor mio, Grandemente mi sento debitrice alla tua clementia, hauendomi à buon' hora chiamata per la predicatione dell'Euangelio di Giesu Cristo alla vera pietà, e sincerita della tua religione, affine che con l'autorità, che m'hai dato, e co'l zelo, di che ti sono debitrice, fossi istrumento tuo di ripiantare, e stabilire in questa parte del mondo, oue t'è piaciuto ch'io à nome tuo regni, la tua pietà et santissima religione. Pregoti Dio mio, e buon padre, che si come in parte con la gratia tua ho seruito in questo alla tua santa volontà, cosi ti piaccia di torre ogni impedimento, e resistenza d'infideltà dal mio popolo, et à me di bene in meglio inspirar buona volontà, e ardente zelo, dandomi mezzi efficaci, istrumenti atti e sufficienti, accio possa, sí come desidero, spiantando ogni maluagio seme d'empietà, spargere, seminare, e radicare il tuo santo Euangelio in tutti i cuori, aggrandendo per tutto questo regno tuo terreno, quel celeste di Giesú Cristo, al quale sia sempre honore e gloria. Cosi sia.

PRAYER 19 ࿇ ORATIONE TERZA PER L'AMMINISTRATIONE DELLA GIUSTITIA.

VLtimamente Iddio supremo Re, e Signor mio: Io confesso, che molto grande fra le grandezze terrene, è l'honore, e la dignità in che tu m'hai posta, et posta, e mantenutamici miracolosamente, conseruandomi, et liberandomi da molti mali, e pericoli d'huomini cattiui. Riconosco che se fin qui con alcuna prudenza, vigilanza, giustitia equità, misericordia e in pace ho amministrato l'ufficio, che tu mi hai imposto, tutto è stato dono della tua paterna bontà con esso me. Or io ti prego caramente, che ti piaccia perseuerare, tenendomi le mani de sopra, humiliandomi sotto il tuo imperio, à cui io sono serua, e dammi che questa corona, che mi hai posto in capo, io la tenga sempe sotto i tuoi piedi: e lo scettro regale postomi nelle mani serua alla gloria tua, alla giustitia e equità del tuo popolo, alla pace, et concordia del Regno. Sia l'intelletto della tua serua chiaro e giusto, la volontà sincera, i giudici equi, e pij. Dammi Signore aiuti, consegli, e ministri abbastanti, retti, e sufficienti, pieni di pietà, e del tuo santissimo timore, sieno i popoli fideli, e disciplinabili. Perche io, e tutto il mio gregge viuendo in tranquillità, e pace, habbiamo agio, e tempo quieto di seruire alla tua maestà: pregandoti, e supplicandoti di tutto cio per Giesu Cristo Signor mio, e tuo vnigenito figliuolo, al quale con esso te, e con lo spirito santo sia honore e gloria eternamente. Cosi sia.

———•———

The Spanish Versicles and Prayers

PRAYER 20 ⮐ PRIMERA ORACION.[15]

MVCHAS SON LAS *tribulaciones de los justos, pero el Señor los libra de todas ellas.* PSALMVS 34.

DIos mio y Padre mio dulcissimo, cuya bondad es infinita, cuya misericordia nunca se puede agotar, y cuya boca siempre dize verdad: porque tu eres la mesma verdad que has prometido a los que en ti creen, à los que en ti confian y ponen su esperança libraros, amparalos y ser les Padre en todas sus necessidades assi temporales como espirituales: y esto lo has cumplido con la obra ni mas ni menos que tu lo has prometido de palabra: como lo testifican muy muchos testimonios de tu sagrada Escriptura. Assi libraste à Noe del diluuio, à Abrahan de los Chaldeos, à Lot de Sodoma, à Iacob de las sangrientas manos de su proprio hermano Esau, à Daniel del lago de los Leones y à Susanna del falso testimonio de aquellos dos malditos viejos y iniquos iuezes.[16] Yo tu humilde sierua me prostro, O Dios mio, O Padre mio

15. These versicles and prayers constitute Elizabeth's only known composition in the Spanish language, which she had learned but deliberately avoided later in her reign for political reasons. Atypically, the biblical references for the three versicles are given in Latin, not Spanish.

16. Allusion is, successively, to Genesis 7:23, 12:31, 19:16, 32:11–12, and to Daniel 6:20–22, 13:42–44.

*delante del throno de tu diuina Magestad, y te doy gracias infinitas, gracias
quan grandes yo puedo, porque me has hecho vna del numero de aquellos
que tu libraste de grandes afliciones: que me libraste de las crueles manos
de mis enemigos, los quales como lobos hambrientos me pretendian chupar
la sangre y tragar me biua. Tenian me vn tal odio, porque yo ponia en ti solo
toda mi esperança, porque yo no me auergonçaua del Euangelio de tu
amantissimo Hijo: mas antes me honraua del, como aquella que tenia por
cierto el Euangelio ser potentia tuya para dar salud à todos los que creen.
Plegate O Dios mio, dar me gracia que yo no me oluide de vn tan insigne
beneficio y merced: no permitas que la buena yerua de gratitud y agrade-
scimiento que tu Magestad ha plantado en el jardin de mi anima, la
ahoguen las espinas: las quales son la solicitud y cuydado de las cosas temporales, y el enganno de las riquezas. Haz Señor, que de tal manera yo las
possea, que yo sea señora dellas, y no ellas de mi, que yo siempre estè apare-
jada para las emplear en tu seruicio. Todo esto te demando en el nombre de
tu Hijo Iesu Christo: el qual es mi Dios, mi Señor y mi Redemptor. Amen.*

PRAYER 21 ❧ SEGUNDA ORACION.

DA A TV SIERVA vn coraçon entendido para iuzgar à tu Pueblo, y para discernir
lo bueño de lo malo: Porque quien podra iuzgar este tu pueblo el qual es tan
grande en multitud? 1. REGVM 3.

*SEñor Dios todo poderoso y Padre mio amantissimo, que por tu admirable
bondad y immensa misericordia has querido hazer à mi pobre pecadora
hija de Adan, instrumento de tu gloria, instrumento con que tu seas glori-
ficado constituyendo me por cabeça y gouernadora deste tu opulentissimo
Reyno en estos tan infelicissimos tiempos, en que tu yglesia vnica esposa
tuya es en tan gran manera oprimida de la tyrania de Satanas y de sus
ministros, ten por bien assistir me con tu sancto Espiritu, el qual es Espiritu de sabiduria y de inteligencia, Espiritu de consejo y de fortaleza, Espiritu de sciencia y de temor tuyo, para que yo tu sierua tenga coraçon entendido que pueda discernir entre lo bueno y lo malo: y desta manera sea en
este tu Reyno administrada iusticia, sea lo bueno aprouado y remunerado:
y por el contrario lo malo condenado y castigado. Pues que para esta tu has
constituido el Magistrado y le has puesto el cuchillo en la mano. Esto te
pido O Señor y Dios mio en nombre de tu vnigenito Hijo Iesu Christo mi
Redemptor y intercessor. Amen.*

PRAYER 22 🙰 TERCERA ORACION.

LOS INIVSTOS PEreceran sin quedar ninguno, y el paradero de los malos es perdicion. PSALMVS 37.

O Señor Dios mio y Padre mio, immortales gracias hago à tu diuina Mages-
tad con mi boca, con mi coraçon y con quanto yo soy, por las infinitas mis-
ericordias de que has vsado con migo: que no solamente me has hecho
criatura tuya, hechura de tus manos formada à la imagen y semejança tuya,
me has por la muerte y passion de tu vnico Hijo Iesu Christo reconciliado
con tigo, adoptado me y hecho hija tuya, hermana de Iesu Christo tu pri-
mogenito y de todos aquellos que en ti creen, [Colossians 1:15] en ti esperan
y confian: mas aun porque me has hecho esta tan señalada y tan rara
merced, que siendo yo vna muger de mi naturaleza flaca, timida y delicada,
como lo son todas las demas, me has querido hazer robusta, animosa y
fuerte para resistir a tanta multitud de Idumeos, Ismaelitas, Moabitas,
Agarenos[17] y otra infinidad de gentes y naciones que se auian juntado, con-
jurado, conspirado y hecho liga, contra ti, contra tu hijo y contra todos aque-
llos que confiessan tu nombre y tienen por vnica regla de salud a tu sancta
palabra. O Dios mio, O Padre mio, cuya bondad es infinita y cuya potencia
es immensa, que sueles escoger las cosas flacas deste mundo para confundir
y destruir las fuertes, perseuera, perseuera por la gloria de tu nombre, por la
honra de tu Hijo, por el descanso y quietud de tu yglesia afligida, en dar me
fuerças para que yo como otra Debora, como otra Iudith, como otra Esther[18]
libre à tu pueblo de Israel de las manos de tus enemigos, leuantate Señor
iuzga tu causa. Derrama tu ira sobre las gentes que no te conoscen y sobre
los Reynos que no inuocan tu Nombre. Sea conoscida entre las naciones de-
lante de nuestros ojos la vengança de la sangre de tus sieruos que es derra-
mada. Entre delante tu acatamiento el gemido de los presos, y segun tu gran
potencia reserua los que estan ya deputados para morir. Sean Señor los que
persiguen à tu yglesia auergonçados y conturbados perpetuamente, y sean
confundidos y perezcan. Conoscan que tu, cuyo nombre es IEHOVA, eres
solo el Altissimo sobre toda la tierra. O Señor concede esto à tu yglesia por
aquel vnico intercessor y abogado nuestro que siempre està delante de tu
Magestad intercediendo por ella, que es Iesu Christo tu eterno Hijo: el qual
con tigo y con el Espiritu sancto es vn solo Dios y Señor nuestro. Amen.

17. **Idumeos** Isaiah 34:5; Ezekiel 36:5. **Ismaelitas** Genesis 37:25–28. **Moabitas** Judges
3:28–30; 2 Kings 3:18–27. **Agarenos** 1 Chronicles 5:19–20.
18. **Debora** Judges 5. **Iudith** Judith 13. **Esther** Esther 5–8.

—•—

The Latin Prayers

PRAYER 23 ❧ PRECATIO REGINAE.

Admirabilis est,[19] deus optime Maxime iudiciorum tuorum abyssus. Tu rex regum, Dominator dominantium. Tu imperia quibus visum est aufers et transfers,[20] euellis et plantas, destruis et aedificas. Tu, quae tua est singularis benignitas, ancillam tuam mortis penè filiam liberasti: me, me captiuam in patrio et regali solio collocasti. Tibi igitur gratias ago, tibi laudes et hymnos cano, tuum nomen dies et noctes celebrabo. Per te patriae libertas, doctrinae veritas, ecclesiae tranquillitas restituta sunt. Beneficium tuum, tuum solius[21] fuit, ministerium meum. Onus certè humero muliebri graue, te leuante leue. Adiuua obsecro clementissime pater, nec scelera mea, aut merita parentum, aut populi mei respice, quia mala et infinita sunt: sed misericordiae tuae memineris, quia antiqua et aeterna et omnibus miseris exposita est. Serua regnum, tuere religionem, defende causam tuam, reginam tuam, populum tuum et meum. Dissipentur hostes tui qui bella volunt: qui adorant sculptilia pudefiant et conuertantur. Ne simus praeda gentibus quae te non norunt, et nomen tuum non inuocant. Confirma ô Deus opus quod coepisti, affla spiritum principalem seruulae tuae, et pusillo gregi tuo, vt religionis castitatem cum morum puritate coniungamus, vt vuas non labruscas, [Isaiah 5:2] et fructus dignos resipiscentia,[22] dignos Euangelio proferamus, quò immortali hoc thesauro immortaliter fruamur, quò hic tibi viuentes et morientes regni tui caelestis haereditatem aliquando cernamus, per Christum Iesum Dominum nostrum. Si quidem tuum est regnum, potentia, et gloria in omnem perpetuitatem. Amen.

---

19. **est** es.
20. **aufers et transfers** auferis et transferis.
21. **solius** solium.
22. **resipiscentia** rescipiscenti.

PRAYER 24 ᣟ PRECATIO AD DEUM PRO FOELICI REGNI ADMISTRATIONE ET POPULI INCOLUMITATE.

SVmme rerum opifex et seruator deus, quum hic ad maiestatis tuae pedes humilis iaceo, mecumque seriò reputo quàm indigna sim cui aurem benignus praebeas, vndique suffusa pudore vix audeo ad te oculos attollere. Cum enim iam olim in ipso matris vtero peccati labes me infecisset, ob idque (vt reliqui Adami nepotes) abortu dignissima essem, me tamen hinc tua paterna manus eduxit atque in lucem edi permisit, editam cum Christo mori, et mortuam vt aeterna vita fruerer, renasci. Et tamen (miseram me) iuuentus mea, immo mea incunabula nihil nisi prioris illius vitae fecem spirarunt. Vnde iterum iam me iudicem iratum expectare te debui. At tu pro infinita tua bonitate me indignissimam ab aulicis voluptatibus ad regni tui delitias, per Sanctorum communionem et vocem euangelij tui etiam tum vocasti. Cumque verbis tuis non satis attentè et diligenter auscultarem, etsi me vnà cum alijs huius regni ingratis virga tua percussisti, tamen vicit tua hic quoque bonitas genuinam malitiam. Ecce enim dum me loco filiae, qualem me in Christo adoptaras, detrudere debeat tua iustitia: infinitae clementiae cedens, et nouo me beneficio cumulans, è carcere et custodia, atque adeo è faucibus leonum solutam ad regnum euexisti, aureo diademate immeritum caput cingens, et regali sceptro dextram ornans. Addo et illud (quod ex omnibus non minimum esse censeo) quòd christum ex regno Angliae exulantem, quasi postliminio redeuntem ministerio meo restituendum concesseris. Haec sunt benignissme pater, praecipua tuorum in me beneficiorum capita: quae quanto excellentiora sunt, tanto indignius erga te me gessi, dum vitam meam nouis subinde vitijs corrumpo. Unde fit vt horum consideratione de mea salute planè desperem. Sed rursum cum luculenta tua in Christi sanguine sancta promissa memoria repeto, tota reficior et recreor, et recuperata pristina spe tuum thronum securior accedo, non quidem oblatura aliquid quod meis peccatis expiationi esse possit: sed tantum vt Christi tui oblationem, qua semel perfectos effecit qui sanctificantur, mihi sanctificationem et expiationem esse patiare, supplicatura,[23] meque in tuam clientelam ita suscipias, vt quando ouium adipi[24] obsequium, pecudum carni et sanguini virtutes labiorum an-

---

23. **supplicatura** supplicaturam.

24. **adipi** apparently a derivative of the deponent verb *adipiscor,* "achieve, secure, obtain."

teponis, tuis laudibus efferendis et mandatis tuis exequendis reliquum vitae cursum transigam. Nominatim vero cum me faeminum et imbecillem, et solam ad huius regni gubernacula sedere dignatus sis, et huius administrationis (quae omnium difficillima existit) me coràm Christi tui tribunali rationem reddere oporteat, porrige pater, porrige inquam è sublimi solio filiae tuae, quae illi ad tam arduum munus obeundum necessaria esse iudicas. Dedisti consiliarios, da dextrè eorum vti consilijs: illis autem et piam et aequam et sanam mentem, industriam vero sedulam, vt quae mihi subditoque populo vsui sint,[25] et prouidere sub tuo praesidio, et consulere velint ac queant. Dedisti insuper vt renatus verbo tuo idem populus eodem mecum foueri et ali se patiatur. Da ergo qui eos pascant et fideles pastores, et pios sanosque doctores. Caeterum mercenarios et omne genus luporum ab hoc nostro quantuluscumque[26] est, tibi Christoque dicato grege arce. Quin et gregem ipsum nouis tuis beneficijs ita orna, vt tibi tuum supremum honorem, nobis tua in hac parte vice fungentibus obsequentiam, sibi inter se mutuam charitatem nusquam deneget. Conserua porro tua bonitate mihi partam pacem, et ab omni belli impetu assere patriam et regnum, potissimum ab intestinis et domesticis tumultibus, quibus bona iam orbis Christiani pars quatitur, immunes nos prolege. Et quoniam pauperrimi cuiusque atque abiectissimae conditionis hominis afflictio ad nos qui tui sumus, attinet: etiam afflictorum omnium qui tua opera promptiori egere videntur, vt te misereat supplex oro et obtestor: Idque meritis et nomine filij tui domini nostri Iesu Christi, qui tecum viuit et regnat in omnem aeternitatem. Fiat.

PRAYER 25 ❧ ALIA PRECATIO.

SVmme Deus, qui me iam ab ineunte aetate, et antequam in lucem essem aedita, admirabili potentia, incredibilique prouidentia a capitali humani generis inimico, eiusque sceleratis administris hactenus tutam incolumemque conseruasti: concede itidem vt tua singulari benignitate freta, cum ab omnibus clandestinis insidiis, tum etiam a domesticis exterisque hostibus eripiar, et ea libertate mentisque quieto tranquilloque statu

---

25. **ut quae . . . vsui sint** ut qui . . . usi sint.
26. **quantuluscumque** quantulocumque.

consistam, vt populum regnumque meae fidei ac tututelae²⁷ commenda-
tum, sartum tectum ab omnibus periculis tuearis: et cum ex hac vita inigrauero,²⁸ tecum immortali fruar beatitudine in omnes aeui aeterni-
tates. Amen.

———•———

The Greek Prayers

PRAYER 26 ᘒᔈ᠊ Εὐχὴ ὑπηκόων ὑπὲρ βασιλίσσης.²⁹

ΘΕὸς ὕφιστε, μέγιστε, ὃς πάντα μεν ἔκτισας, καὶ πάντα ἐφορᾶς ἐν
οὐρανῷ, καὶ ἐπὶ τῇ γῇ, κυβερνᾷ τὴν θεράπαιναν σὴν Ε. βασίλισσαν
ἡμετέραν, καὶ ψυχὴν αὐτῆς φώτιζε τῇ αὐγῇ τῆς ἀπειράτου σοφίας
σῆς, ὡς καὶ ἀληθεῖ θρησκείᾳ καὶ εὐσεβείᾳ δι' ὅλον βίον τὸ ὄνομά
σου δοξάζῃ, καὶ ἡμᾶς τὸν λαὸν αὐτῇ ὑποτασσόμενον πιστῶς
καθ' ἡμέραν ποιμαίνουσα διατελῇ·³⁰ μιμνήσκουσα ἀιεὶ οὐκ αὐτῇ
τὴν ἀρχὴν αὐτοκράτειραν εἶναι, ἀλλὰ ὡς διαδόχῳ ἢ μᾶλλον δι-
ακόνῳ τὴν ἐπιμέλειαν ὅλης πολητείας³¹ παρά σου παντοκράτορος
δοθεῖσαν, ἐφ' ᾧτε καὶ σε σέβειν εἰλικρινῶς, καὶ τῶν ἀγαθῶν ὑπ-
ερασπίζειν, κακούς τε καὶ ἀνόμους τιμορεῖν. Δός ἡμῖν ὁμοῦ τοῖς
ὑπηκόοις αὐτῆς, διανοῦμενοις ὡς παρά σου τήν δυναστείαν ἔλαβεν,
οὐ μόνον τῇ ἐξωθὲν δουλείᾳ ἀλλὰ καὶ τῇ ἐντὸς θεραπείᾳ τῶν
καρδιῶν ὑπηκόοις εἶναι, προθύμως τε πρὸς πάντα τὰ ἀπ' αὐτῆς ταχ-
θησόμενα, καὶ ταπεινῶς ἔχειν. Αὐτὴ δὲ, ὡς μᾶλλον ἔτι ἐν πάσῃ
ἀρετῇ, εὐσεβείᾳ, κηδεμονίᾳ τῆς χώρας ταύτης προκοπὴν ποιῇ, τὸν
βίον μακρὸν, μεθ' ὑγιείας σώματος, εἰρήνης, ὄλβου, μεγαλο-

---

27. **tututelae** tutelae. The extra *tu*- syllable resulted from ending a line with *tu*- but then
setting the whole word at the beginning of the following line.

28. **inigrauero** ingravero.

29. The first Greek prayer is the only one in this collection not composed in Elizabeth's
first-person; it may not be her work. But she could have composed devotionally for other
voices; "A prayer for men to say entering into battle" in Queen Katherine Parr's *Prayers or
Meditations* would have furnished a precedent.

30. **διατελῇ** διατελῇ. On the mid-line dot as a punctuation mark, see Prayer 34, note 21,
p. 51, above.

31. **πολητείας** πολιτείας.

πρεπείας δίδοθι, καὶ δύναμιν παρατίθετι κατὰ τῶν ἐχθρῶν, ὥστε νικᾶν τ' αὐτοὺς, καὶ ὑπερέχειν ἁπάντων, καὶ ἀπὸ τῆς πολιτείας πᾶν βλαβερὸν ἀποτρέπειν. Καὶ οὕτω μεν ἐν ἀκατάστατῳ κόσμῳ τούτῳ διάγουσα, τέλος δὲ μετὰ κοινὴν ἀνθρώπων γένει τοῦ βίου ἀπαλλαγὴν τῆς τ' αἰωνίας ζωῆς, καὶ εὐδαιμονίας, κατὰ τό ἐλεός σου τὸ ἀπειρέσιον, λαχέτω, διὰ τὸ αἷμα του υἱοῦ σου μονογενοῦς, ἀρνὸς ἀμολύντου, ὅς ἐπὶ σταυρῷ θνῆσκεν ἵνα ἡμας λυτρώσῃ.³² Ἀμήν.

PRAYER 27 ᎒᎐ Εὐχὴ βασιλίσσης ὑπὲρ ἑαυτῆς καὶ ὑπηκόων.

ΚΎριε ὁ δεὸς³³ ὑψίζυγε, ἀόρατε, ὅς πάντ' ἐποίησας ἐξ οὐδενός, συ μεν ἀδιηγήτω σοφία σῇ.³⁴ καὶ προνοία, καὶ χρηστότητι, τὰ ἐν οὐρανῷ, γῇ, καὶ θαλάσσῃ διοικεῖς, καὶ ἡμῖν τοῖς ἀνθρώποις μηδὲν παρ' αὐτῶν ἰσχύουσι τὰ κτήνη τοῦ πεδίου, τὰ πετεινὰ τοῦ οὐρανοῦ, καὶ τοὺς ἰχθύας θαλάσσης ὑπὸ κάτω τῶν ποδῶν ὑπέταξας, ἐμοὶ δὲ τὸν λαὸν ταύτης τῆς χώρας ὑπηκόον ἔδωκας ἀσθενεῖ καὶ ἀναξίῳ οὔσῃ· ἔμφυε ἱκετεύω σε τὴν ταπεινοφροσύνην ἐν τῇ ψυχῇ μου, ὥστ' ἀναγινώσκουσα καθ' ἑκάστην ἡμέραν, μὴ ἰδιᾳ ἀρετῇ κτήσασθαι τὴν βασιλείαν, ἀλλ' ὡς θεράπαιναν, ἢ διάκονον παρὰ σου εἰληφέναι, δουλεύσω σοι ἐν φόβῳ, καὶ ἀγαλλιάσωμαι ἐν τρόμῳ, πάντα, μὴ πρὸς ἐμὸν κέρδος δρῶσα, ἢ τιμὴν, ἢ βούλησιν, ἀλλὰ πρὸς σὴν δόξαν, καὶ αἶνον, καὶ τοῦ δήμου ἀσφάλειαν, ἐφ' ᾧ ἐν ταύτῃ τάξει κατεστάθην. Καὶ μὴν ἐπειδη οὐδεμία φρόνησις ἰδία παρ' ἐμοῦ οὖσα τυγγάνει, ἐφ' ἣ πεποιθυῖα τοιαύτην ἀρχὴν ἱκανῶς ἰθύνουσα διατελοῖμι, τῆς συνέσεως καὶ σοφίας τοῦ ἁγίου πνεύματος τὸ στῆθος ἐμὸν ἔμπλυθε καὶ φώτιζε ὡς ἐν τῷ φώτι σου τηλαυγεῖ ὁρῶσα φῶς, γινώσκω ἐν τῇ γῇ τὴν ὁδόν σου, καὶ τὴν ἀγνὴν ἀληθῆ τε θρησκείαν σὴν αὐτὴ δι' ὅλου βίου ἀσπάζωμαι, καὶ τῷ ὑποτασσομένῳ ἐμοὶ λαῷ παραδιδῶ, ὡς πάντες τὸ ὄνομα σὸν σεμνότατον μιᾷ φωνῇ, καὶ καρδιῶν ὁμονοίᾳ ὑμνῶμεν. Τὴν ψυχήν μου ποίησον ἀεὶ τῷ θελήματί σου ἁγίῳ· τὸν δὲ δῆμον ἐμοὶ ἐν τῷ αὐτῷ πειθαρχεῖν. τῷ σώματι οὕτω δίδοθι τὴν εὐεξίαν καὶ ὑγίειαν, ὡς ἱκανώτερόν τε πρὸς τὰ ἐπιτηδεύματα, καὶ

---

32. λυτρώσῃ λυτρώσῃ.
33. δεὸς θεὸς.
34. ἀδιηγήτω σοφία σῇ ἀδιηγήτῳ σοφίᾳ σῇ.

μηδέποτ' αὐτὸ λείπειν τὸν ναόν σου, ἁγνὸν καὶ ὅσιον εἶναι. Δὸς
ἐμοὶ πρὸς ἀγαθοὺς τῇ προσηνείᾳ χρῆσθαι, ὡς μᾶλλον ἔτι ἐις τὸ
καθῆκον αὐτοὺς ὀτρύνειν· τοὺς κακοὺς καὶ ἀνάρχους κολάζειν ὡς
ἀπὸ κακίας ἀποτρέπω, καὶ τοῦτο μεν ἰατροῦ δίκην ὡς τὸ σῶμα τῆς
πολιτείας ἐκ νοσεροῦ ὑγιὲς καὶ σόον ἀποτελῶ. Τῶν ἐχθρῶν δὲ
ἡμετέρων μετάβαλλε τὰς ψυχὰς ὥστε τὸ εἰς ἡμᾶς μισος καταπάτειν,
ἢ κατ' αὐτῶν ἐμοί τε καὶ τῶ λαῶ ἐμῶ πόριζε νὴν³⁵ ἰσχὺν, ὡς κατα-
στρέφειν ἐν παση πείρᾳ καὶ νικᾶν ἅπαντας, καὶ αὐτοὺς ἅμα ἐν εἰ-
ρηνῇ ποθεινοτάτη διάγειν. Τελευταῖον γε, σώσας ἐν τῷ νῦν βίῳ τὸν
λαόν σου, καὶ εὐλογήσας τὴν σὴν κληρονομίαν, ἐμέτε, καὶ αὐτὸν,
μετὰ τὴν τῆς ψυχῆς ἐξειρχτὴς³⁶ τοῦ σώματος ἀποχώρησιν, στέψον
στεφάνω τῆς οὐρανίας εὐδαιμονίας ἀσφαλεῖ καί ἀμαράντῳ διὰ Ἰη-
σοῦν Χριστόν υἱὸν σοῦ μονογενῆ, καὶ σωτῆρα ἡμίερον.³⁷ Ἀμὴν.

PRAYER 28 ☙ Εὐχὴ της βασιλίσσῆς πρὸς τὸν θεὸν

Ὑπέρτατε πάτερ, ὃς τὸν κοσμὸν τῷ λόγῳ ἔκτισας, καὶ πνεύματι ἅγιῳ
ἐκόσμησας· καὶ με κατέστησας τῆς βασιλείας βριταννηκὴς μον-
άρχην σοῦ, ἀγαθότητι χαρίζου ἐμοὶ καταφυτεύειν εὐσεβείαν,
ἀσέβειαν ἐχριζοῦν. θρησκείαν ἀσπίζειν θελοθρησκείαν, δεισιδαι-
μονίαν καθ' ἐθελοργίαν ἀφανίζειν, λατρείαν ἐγκεντρίζειν, εἰδω-
λολατρείαν κατασκόπτειν προσέτι τοὺς ἐχθροὺς τῆς θεοσεβείας
ἀπολύειν, καὶ τοὺς ἐμὲ μισοῦντας, καὶ ἀντιχρίστους, καὶ παπι-
φίλους, καὶ ἄθεους, καὶ πάντας, τοὺς σου καὶ ἔμου παρακοούντας.
τὰδε πάντα κύριε παντοκράτωρ χαρίζου ἐμοί. Κὰι μετὰ τὸν θάνατον
τὴν βασιλείαν τῶν οὐρανῶν. Ἀμὴν.

---

35. **τῶ λαῶ ἐμῶ ... νὴν** τῷ λαῷ ἐμω ... νὴν. From this point onward and in the following prayer, the typesetter was evidently in short supply of several letters. He made various
substitutions in varying degrees of frequency, replacing some vowels needing iota subscripts with their ordinary counterparts, sometimes inserting χ (chi) in place of κ (kappa)
and, most often of all, putting μ (mu) in place of ν (nu). To preserve readability, we have
silently inserted missing iota subscripts and replaced each substituted χ or μ with the required κ or ν. The microfilm of *Christian Prayers and Meditations* (STC 6428), sig. Q.q.i r–v,
clearly displays for interested readers the oddities of these texts as originally printed.
36. **ἐξειρχτὴς** ἐξειρχθεισὴ.
37. **ἡμίερον** ἡμέτερον.

POEM 8 ᴂ VERSE EXCHANGE BETWEEN QUEEN ELIZABETH AND
PAUL MELISSUS, POET LAUREATE OF THE COURT OF EMPEROR
MAXIMILIAN II, CIRCA 1577[1]

[Melissus's epigram]

Ad Elisabetham Angliae, Franciae, Hiberniae Reginam

NON solum, Regina, meos tibi sacro libellos,
   Jam quibus imposita est ultima calce manus:
Sive Poësis erit, seu cantio Musica, sive
   Nescio quid melici; scilicet omne tuum est.
Non solos, inquam, tibi dono[2] sacroque libellos: 5
   Ipsum me Genio dedico Diva tuo;
Germanumque hominem Francâque propagine cretum
   Regia me dedo sub juga servitii.
Vtere me servo domina; ingenuoque ministro
   Sis hera, qui laudes incinat usque tuas.   10
Eccui libertas tanti sit, ut esse recuset
   Tantae patronae nobile mancipium?

[Queen Elizabeth's epigram]

Reginae Responsum

GRATA Camena[3] tua est, gratissima dona, Melisse:
   Gratior est animi dulcis imago tui
At quae tanta movet te causa, quis impetus urget,
   Ex homine ingenuo servus ut esse vellis?[4]

---

1. *Source: P. Melissi Mele sive Odae* (Nuremberg, 1580), p. 72. This collection, which includes several other equally adulatory poems addressed by Melissus to Elizabeth, was
brought to modern notice by James E. Phillips, "Elizabeth I as a Latin Poet: An Epigram on
Paul Melissus," *Renaissance News* 16 (1963): 289–98.

2. **dono** do.

3. **Camena** originally, a native Latin name for the Greek Moûsa (Muse); later, by
metonymy, a word for poetry, a poem, a song, as in Horace *Epistulae* 1.11 and *Carmina* 1, 12,
29; Ovid *Epistulae ex Ponto* 4, 13, 33.

4. **Ex homine ingenuo servus ut esse vellis?** (Read "velis.") Roman civil and political life
included the rights of liberty, citizenship, and family (*libertatis, civitatis, familiae*); loss or
deprivation of any of these rights was called *deminutio* (or *minutio*) *capitiis*—the term
which Elizabeth uses in line 6. Such loss of rights had three judicial degrees, among which

Haud nostrum est arctis vates includere septis,   5
Aut vel tantillum deminuisse caput.
Tu potius liber fieres, laxante patrona
Vincula, si famula⁵ conditione fores.
Sed vatum es princeps; ego vati subdita, dum me
Materiam celsi carminis ipse legis.⁶   10
Quem Regum pudeat tantum coluisse Poëtam,
Nos ex semideis qui facit esse deos?

LETTER 43 ෫ QUEEN ELIZABETH TO MONSIEUR, FEBRUARY 14,
1579¹

Monsieur Si l'importune requeste de ce gentilhomme ne me constraig-
noist Ie n'eusse molesté voz yeuz si tost apres mes derniers combres² que
le courage me fust redoublé auoir la bonne acceptacion que les autres eurent pour laquelle m'obligez comme en plusieurs autres endroictz de
plus grande consequence et principallement par ce que vostre retour en
La France n'a este le moins faict pour l'enuie de passer vers moy chose
que ne souhaiterois en doubtant la fin mais desirerois fort autrement si
est ce que par ce l'ententz qu'auez postposé la plus part des conseilz pro-
posez pour suivre le desir que de vous mesmes procede vous assurent
qu'il me desplait infiniement que ceste ingrate multitude vne vraie cahos
doist tant abuse vng tel Prince et pense que dieu si non les hommes en

---

maxima—the greatest—deprived a person of liberty by servitude or condemnation to
death (Justinian, *Institutiones*, bk. 1, chap. 16, sect. 4). It is this extreme treatment which
Melissus professes himself ready to undergo, and which Elizabeth dismisses out of hand.

5. The Latin noun *famula,* meaning "servant" or "attendant," has feminine gender but is
used equally to denote a male or a female.

6. **ego vati subdita, dum me / Materiam celsi carminis ipse legis** The two half-lines—
literally, "I am subjected to a poet, as long as me / You choose for the subject matter of your
lofty verse"—suggest to an English reader a pun on "subject" as one who is subjected and as
subject matter. The pun does not work in Latin; it would work with *subiecta* instead of *subdita,* but *subiecta* breaks the meter. The turn of phrase points to an English-speaking author—Elizabeth herself. Compare Ben Jonson, *Epigrams* 35 and 36, the first of which begins
"Who would not be thy subject, James?" and the second of which refers wittily to James himself as Jonson's "royal subject." We thank Joshua Scodel for this reference.

1. *Source:* PRO, State Papers, France, Elizabeth, 78/3/9, fol. 21r. Copy.

2. **combres** encombres (a self-effacing reference to her letters).

fera sa reuanche et suis tresaise qu'en seurete auez eschappé leurs ini-
quies mains. Et ne doubte nullement qu'ayent passé Silla vous aurez
garde d'entrer en charibdis comme Ie prie monsieur cymier plus au long
discourir[3] et comme aussi pour l'aduis qu'il vous a pleu me demander
protestant que recognoissant ma faulte d'assey bon esprit pour vous in-
struire nonobstant il vous plaira l'accepter comme de telle qui n'aura
Iammais la pensee qui ne se dediera a vostre honneur et qui naguere
vous trayra[4] par ces conseilz, mais les donnera comme si mon ame en de-
pendit comme scait le createur a qui Ie ne cesseray de prier qu'il vous
garde de telz qui ne vous estiment et vous face tout ce que vous sera le
mieulx apres mes trescordielles recommendacions a vous monsieur De
nostre Pallace de westmestre du xivme Iour de fevrier 1578[9]/

LETTER 46 🙰 QUEEN ELIZABETH TO MONSIEUR, CIRCA
DECEMBER 1579–JANUARY 1580[1]

Monsieur quant il me souuient qu'il n'y a debte plus licite que la parolle
du iuste ny chose qui plus lie noz actions que la promesse, Ie m'ou-
blieroys trop en uostre endroyt et a mon honneur si i'ometasse le terme
ordonné pour ma response a la cause que long temps nous auons traisté.
Vous n'ignorez mon trescher que les plus grands retardementes consis-
toyent a faire que nostre peuple le deuoyt congratuler et applauder. A
quoy faire I'ay prins[2] le temps qui communement y faict plus que la raison. Et ayant uzé de tous deux n'ay garde de ne uous declarer rondement
comme Ie cognoys, et uous trouuerez tousiours ueritable. Ie uoyz bien
que plusieurs s'ent vont repentir d'en faire temeraires iudgements au
premier coup, sans auoyr peizé en meilleure balance le fon[3] de leurs
opinions: Ie m'assure que aulcuns auecques hazarde de leur uies propres
souhayttent de n'y estre si sottement gouuernez. Et nonobstant Ie uous
promets sur ma foy qu'encores n'a iamais receu tasche que le public ex-

---

3. **discourir** or "discovrir" (anglicized form of "découvrir"), depending on reading as vocalic or consonantal *u*.
    4. **trayra** trahira.
    1. *Source:* Hatfield House, Cecil Papers, 149/24, no foliation. Copy, with one (and possibly
a second) local insertion in Elizabeth's hand.
    2. **prins** pris.
    3. **fon** fond.

ercice de la Rellligion Romaine adhere tant en leur coeur que Ie ne con-
sentiray iamais que uous ueniez entre telle companie de malcontents
Sans qu'il uous plaize de considerer que les commissionaires relaschent
l'estroytes termes que Monsieur de simièrs nous offryt. Et pour ne
uouloyr que uous les mandastes sans que la cause s'y concluast. Ie uous
supplie en tenir grande consideration comme de choze qui est tant dure
a supporter aux Angloys que ne le pourriez imaginer sans le cognoistre.
De ma part Ie confesse qu'il n'y a prince au monde a qui plus uolontiers
Ie me rende sienne qu'a uous mesme ny a qui Ie me pense plus obligé, ny
auecq qui Ie passeroys les ans de ma uie. Et pour uoz rares uertus et le
doux naturel acompaigné auec tant d'honorables parties que ne puis
reciter pour leur nombre ny en oze faire mention pour la longeur qui
m'y conuiendroyt. Tellement que sil uous plaist considerez comme la
sincerité m'acompaigne en ceste negotiation, du commencement iusques a present Ie ne doubte de comparoistre deuant le siege de uostre
droyct iugement pour me quitter de toute cautele ou dissimulation. Ie me
doubtoys pour noz particuliers accords estant incertaine aultant de ne
complaire comme non assurée que Ie me consentasse. Puis uoyant les
grandes questions qui se faisoyent pour la nation d'ou uous estes puis
pour la mode du gouuernement et plusieurs aultres choses qui ne se
doyuent escrire. Et[4] quelles y ayant uze tant de moyens pour les faire
agreables Ie ne croy d'auoyr faict oeuure de forte mais plustost de grand
oeuurage pour toute la semaine. Et a cest heur Ie ne uous deceuray pour
ne mettre deuant uoz yeux apertement comme Ie treuue la cause et que
l'en pense en laquelle l'ay eu aultant de regard a uostre aize et contentement comme a ma propre uie ou consideration de mon estat qui m'eust
aultrement esmeu a faire aultre response Et pour conclusion Ie ne puis
niy ne ueux que ce negoce uous fasche plus ains que demeurons fideles
amis et assurez en toutes noz actions: S'il ne uous plaize de faire resolution aultre que l'aperte exercice de la Rellligion et qu'il uous semble bon
de m'en escrire ou mander quelque bonne response. Car Ie ne desire rien
qui ne uous contentast. Il'y a encores pour la pension quelque choze a
dire que l'ay donné en charge a ce porteur, de le uous declarer bien a
mieulx comme aultres choses lequel il uous plaira de uostre bonte acous-
tamée ouyr et uous fier comme a[5] fidel comme le cognoyssez. Et Ie l'ay

---

4. This "Et" inserted to begin a new sentence appears to be in Elizabeth's italic.
5. **a** à un.

bien approuué. pour lequel Ie uous doybz⁶ ung million de graces pour l'honneur faueur et liberalité qu'auez uze en son endroyct. pour lequel uous m'obligez bien auant. Ie receuz huict iours a⁷ une lettre qu'il uous a plu me mander par ou Ie uoy que uostre affection ne se diminue pour absence, ny se refroyde par persuasions pour laquelle Ie ne puis rendre qu'une sincere et immuable bonne uolonte / preste a uous seruir en toutes occasions ~~bonnes~~ aduerses⁸ ou mauuaises et telle que Iamais delaissera uostre fortune. mais en prendray ma part. Ie n'ay Iamais ouy de uous nouuells aulcunes ou de france ou des pais bas ou de quelque autre quartiers depuis l'arriuée de Simiers et croy que uous uous doutez trop du silence de femme ou autrement l'entendroys moyns par aultres moyens et plus par uous. Car d'aultre lieu l'entens plus qu'il uous plaist me communiquer Comme Dieu scayt a qui Ie prie uous conseruer en bonne uie et longue auec mes recommendations a ma treschere grenouille /

LETTER 47 ᛤ QUEEN ELIZABETH TO MONSIEUR, JANUARY 17, 1580¹

Mon retarder tant Mon trescher de ne recognoistre l'infiniz modes qui accroissent mes obligations en uostre endroyt me peuuent rendre a bonne raison indigne de traistements si honorables. Mais l'extreme doleur en la gorge ces quinze iours continuels aura puissance l'espere deffacer telle conception. Et a ceste heure me trouuant Vng peu mieux uous presente mes treshumbles graces de nous auoyr monstre ung clair rocher contre lequel les tempestes des faulses persuasions ny l'orage de mauuais langues n'ont eu force de remuer la constance de uostre affection de laquelle Ie me confesse bien indigne pour aucune perfection que Ie retiens et pource me semble tant plus illustre que l'occasion est plus simple. D'une chose Ie me resiouyz que uous estes si bien fourny de bons amiz que uous ne serez ignorant de quelques mes defautz tellement que m'assure de n'estre trouue pire quilz me font desin. Et pourtant estant si bien admonesté uous serez bien resolu ou ne le hazarderez. Et prie a Dieu

---

6. **doybz** dois.

7. The preposition "à" serves as an adverb, "ago."

8. The deletion and the inserted word are possibly in Elizabeth's hand.

1. *Source:* Hatfield House, Cecil Papers, 149/25, no foliation. Copy, with a local correction in Elizabeth's hand. The endorsement reads "the 17 of January to Monsieur."

uous donner la grace de claire ueue pour penetrer l'abisme de leur menées et que Ie ne uiue a estre moyen de uostre mecontentement. Cest si dificile en ce temps de cognoistre la difference entre le sembler et l'estre, que Ie souhaitte la sagesse de Salomon resider en uostre esprit pour separer les fauclez[2] des sinceres et telz qui regardent plus ~~autre~~ oultre[3] en lieu de uous mettre pour but de leur flesches. Ceux sont les plus a estimer qui nous respectent non auecq une meslée de leur grandeur et gouuernement. Mais a cest' heure Ie resue[4] comme les uielles font songents n'ayent bien dormi. l'ay receu nouuelles du Roy que les commissaires s'apprestent ne sachant encores qu'ilz sont. Ie ne pensoys au deuant que la france eust este si mal fourny de princes et personages de grande qualite qu'on fut constraint de me mander ung enfant ou homme de bas lignage. Ie croy qu'ilz le font pour amoindiyr la grandeur de mon honneur ou pour ietter des empeschemens pour n'en mander du tout. l'ay pourtant uzé de rondeur en l'endroyt du Roy Luy mandant dire par son Embassadeur que Ie ne soufriroys que choze de si grand moment prenne disgrace par haine qu'on me porte. Ie n'ay garde de permettre que croniques disent qu'il y aura faute d'estime aux executionaires de si grande feste prometant Ie croy que le Roy en tiendra consideration honorable et pour le lieu que tenez et le renc en que Ie me tiens. pour uoz comissaires Ie tiens pour certain que ferez elite sans changer d'instrument pour finir ce que si bien il commenca. Ie parle de simier de qui ayant ouy tout ce que luy est impozé et ne uoyant raison a le croyre ne preuue a le condemner Ie uous iure mon trescher s'il allast de ma uie, Ie ne uoye occasion de son exil Il est uray que Ie cognoys trop d'idignite[5] usé contre uostre personne par telz que font les gens a croyre qu'estes si presumtible et si remuant quilz uous pourront facilement detourner de uoz plus cheres quand ilz uous ont a part. Et en temps commode Ie ne failliray a le uous monstrer a leur honte, qui en furent l'auteurs[6] Voyez ou me transporte l'amour que uous porte a me faire contre mon naturel (tout au rebours de ceux qui peschent en eaux troubles) de m'ingerer en actions d autruy. Nonobstant Ie ne me puis refrener de uous supplier a mains iointes de uous souuenyr que nous autres princes nous tenants en

2. **fauclez** faulces, faux.

3. The deletion and the inserted word are in Elizabeth's hand, in a different ink.

4. **resue** rêve.

5. **idignite** indignité.

6. **l'auteurs** les auteurs.

hauts lieux sommes asolicitiz aux expositions de plusieurs testes entre lesquelz la plus parte nous accusent comme noz faueurs sattachent a petits filets qui leur font [craindre][7] leur graces entre lesquelz Ie souhaitte que uous soyez exempt. Voyez Monsieur l'imbecillite de mon entendement qui uous escriue de ceste cause en esperance de bonne response poyzant le lieu ou uous uous tenez auecq la compaignie qui y est. Nous pouures habitants de l'isle barbare n'auons garde de comparoistre en iugement ou si ingenieux iuges iuges[8] de nostre scauoyr tiennent si hault lieu au siège de nostre faueur. Mais appellant a Monsieur seul non diuyze Ie ne laisseray mon procez Cy si me feriez donner lestrappade. Ie ne mettray glose a cest texte m'assurent que lentendez que trop bien. Et fin uous supplie de pardonner ceste ceste[9] facheuze lettre et receuez mes treshumbles graces de l'offre que me faittes dordonner la cause de simié comme me semblera mieux. uous assurant que n'ay Iamais garde de uous donner conseil qui uous trahira l honneur plustot Ie mouray. Ie ne suis partial a luy que Ie uous oublie et si fut pour sa fidelite uers uous de qui I'ay eu ma part de preuue, il ne m'est qu'estrangier auecq qui Ie n'ay que faire aucunement comme scayt le createur qui Ie prie uous donner cent ans de uie auecq mes tres affectionez recommendations

Ie uous prie mandez moi uostre bon plaisir par ce porteur lequel retournera en haste /

LETTER 50 ⟨⟩ QUEEN ELIZABETH TO MONSIEUR, CIRCA JUNE 1581[1]

Ie ne puis exprimer Monsieur Le contentement que Ie sens de retz qui sont rompues, et vous si heureusement eschappé de telz Liens, Si Ie ne regretasse trop vos ennuis et ferois sembler inhumaine en adIoustant plus de maulx Ie ne Laisserois a vous condamner pour La source de telz Inconueniences estant bien digne de cuillir telle vendage[2] de si inique moisson. Esloignez Ie vous prie si meschans conseilz de La faueur de uos oreillies et croyez que quelques mauuais merites que aultres vous

---

7. Brackets enclose conjectural restoration of word missing because of a tear in the MS.

8. Repetition in MS.

9. Repetition in MS.

1. *Source:* Hatfield House, Cecil Papers, 149/31, one recto page; no foliation. Copy.

2. **vendage** vendange.

feront. C'est tousiours pour ung Prince de se resembler. Ie vous ay com-
municqué par Somier[3] autant que mon Ignorance vous peult impartir,
Considerez La vraye baze de toutz mes escriptz qui ne tende a autre but
sinon pour vous conseruer en toute seurte et honneur. dieu m'est tes-
moing que Ie n'eusse[4] Iamais de finesses ny stratagemes pour me faire
du bien a voz despens, comme peult estre que plus fines et moins fideles Le font bien souuent. Esprouuez par leurs fruictz La variete et Incer-
titude de telz espritz, et par La assues[5] vostre Iugement, et traictez tellement ceulx qui ne cherchent rien pour bon sinon tout pour vous en
sorte que Leur Ames ne Iectent souspirs par faulte de mielleur salaire, et
que vous ne Leur souhaites quant leur espritz se estourderont en Lieu de
vous vouloir complaire. Ie ne doubte poinct mais que Le Rocher sera asteur[6] assailly de plusieurs orages et de ventz qui souflent de diuers cli-
matz Ie uous souhaitte si bon astronomicque que puissiez Iuger de
L'aduenir, et clairement cognoistre ou Ilz tendent, de peur que euitant
Silla, ne tumbes en Caribdez. Monsieur mon Trescher octroyez pardon
a La paouure vieille qui vous honore autant (I'ose dire) que quelques
Ieune garse que trouuerez Iamais. Ie vous mercy vn milion de fois de
ce que m'escripuez du bord de nostre pays ou La Gouuernante desire
auoir La grace de vous pouuoir seruir en quelque endroict vous assurant que L'Angleterre ne possede rien de bon qui ne vous sera dedie
pourueu que pour telle le traictez. Oyant que dunquirke ne vous concede trop bon ayr Ie vous soubhaite quelque Lieu plus sain, ne doubtant
fort de La continuation de vostre sante que I'entends par du Bexs estre
meilleure que plusieurs autres de vostre train, pour lequel messangier Ie
uous mercye bien humblement estant le premier despuis Baqueville qui
demeura plus d'un demy an chez moy, et Croyez que Ie ne seray faschee
si a chascune heure en receuoise une Lettre elles me sont si cordielles
que vous n'auez scurpule[7] pour Les me mander car autrement Ie me
penseray morte en vostre opinion que Ie meriteray de me conseruer
seure et immaculee Comme dieu scait a qui Ie prie vous conseruer du
tout mal et vous donner cent ans de bonne vie me recommandant mille
fois aux petitz doictz

3. **Somier** a possibly mischievous spelling of "Simier" ("Somier" implies "sleepy").
4. **n'eusse** n'use.
5. **assues** assurez.
6. **asteur** à cette heure.
7. **scurpule** scruple.

LETTER 51 ☙ QUEEN ELIZABETH TO MONSIEUR, MAY 14, 1582[1]

Combien mon trescher que l'heureuze arriue de Monsieur de Baqueville m'ayt si eueillé l'esprit que Ie me suppose auoyr eu la maladie
melancholique qui souuent fait quelqungs de croyre sans teste aultres
depouillé de uue, autres morts du tout. Si ne uous puis Ie cacher les eu-
identes raisons qui me conuoyent de me reputer hors de ce monde.[2]
Car m'assurant de ma part depuis nostre doleureux partement, n'auoyr
manqué a la moindre sillabe que Ie uous auoys promis. Mais plustost
pour lacomplyr me suis rendu eshontée, en mandant et remandant tant
de foys au Roy pour lui faire cler[3] sur quelque petite difficulté. Ceste
cause aresta en luy suppliant de la mieux considerer, comme telle qui ne
l'incommoderoyt trop, s'il eust enuie de la conclurre. A quoy il me re-
spond uoyre ceste derniere semaine en m'assurant qu'il ne pouuoyt plus
faire que ce qu'il promist par sa lettre mandee par pinard Iugez sur ce
mon trescher que puis Ie plus faire uous ayant prins tel estat que uous
auez. Car autrement selon uostre treshonorable offerte uous pouriez de-
laisser la guerre et les pais bas et conclurre uostre pacte nonobstant les
difficultéz de l'accord. comme n'ayant besoing de telle assurance. Mais
acest'heure que ferons nous c'est a uous a en panser Ie uous supplie ne
uous penses d'auoyr faict si perilleux uoyage, pour l'auoyr d'icelle laquelle combien quelle confesse de n'en estre digne du moytie de tel hazard:
Si n'oze Ie iustifier deuant tout le monde qu'il n'a iamais tenu a moy qu'il
ne se concleuast depuis ma derniere promesse que Ie uous fiz sur telles
conditions que uous seul cognoissez lesquelles ainsi que moymesme les
confesse bien difficiles nonobstant selon uostre contentement Ie m'y ac-
cordoys de tresbonne uolonte Et Dieu m'est temoing de n'en estre iamais
eloigne depuis. Et uous iure de ne me uoloyr iamais monstrer indigne de
la faueur d'ung tel prince, n'ayant besoing d'estre ramentue de la moindre grace que l'ay recu de uostre bonté. Et ne doute point que mes
merites ne soyent tousiours tresbons auocatz de mon affection, et constance en uostre endroyt Considerez mon trescher si Ie l'oze dire si tout
l'uniuers ne s'ebahist comment la Roine d'Angleterre ayt tant oblie l'An-

1. *Source:* Hatfield House, Cecil Papers, 149/36, no foliation. Copy. Its endorsement reads
"Coppie of the Quenes letter sent to monsieur bi baqueuilles man from grenwych the Fowr-
tenth of May. 1572 [error for 1582]."
    2. We have interpreted this clause as correlative with "si eueillé l'esprit que" in the opening
line of this letter.
    3. **cler** clair.

gleterre pour amener nouueaux uoisins sur le continent prez de son front. Vostre bon iugement non aueuglé par autre pourra iuger que cest qui depend de telle opinion. Et puis uoyez si de ma part Ie n'ay rien hazardé pour uous m'estant l'amour de ma nation plus cher que la uie, les Roys esants[4] de peu de durée quant cela est eloigné d'eux. pour conclure tout ce que me souhaitterez de faire qui ne me touchera trop l'honeur, Ie le feray en uous rendant treshumbles gráces pour uostre dernièr message aueq la lettre qui m'ont resueillé d'ung treshaut someil, n'ayant iamais ouy mention de ceste cause, depuis nostre separation de corps non d'ames, de quoy Ie m'etonnays d'estrange facon. Ie me resiouys d'enten[5] que uous estes tant honoré de ce peuple qui me semble en auoyr tresiuste cause. Mais Ie ne doutte que ne teniez tousiours en memoire de quel naturel le uulgaire de tous pais est et y mettrez la confiance selon l'occasion que Ie presente, ne desirant rien plus que la continuation de noz contentements, et maudisant (ma charité estant bien froyde en cest'endroyt) tous qui reuercent noz bon desseings. Vous m'entendez en peu de parolles Pour faire fin de ceste lettre uous prie de croyre que si le Roy demande encores une foys a mon ambassadeur ce qui est de mon intention Ie luy donneray en charge de chanter la mesme chanson que deuant, me rougissant de reciter si souuant ce qui sert de si peu

LETTER 52 🙮 QUEEN ELIZABETH TO MONSIEUR, MAY 24, 1582[1]

Mon trescher uous me faittes cognoistre que nonobstant les grandes affaires et importance de uoz negoces, uous ne faillez a me consoler de la uenue de uoz longs escriptz. me confessant uous en estant infiniment obligée de uous en rendre ung million de graces Et en les lizant I'y uoy une masse d'affection, contenantz humeurs de plusieurs qualitez: Et combien que ne suis trop scauante en la pilosophie[2] naturelle ny trop bon medecin pour en faire une droitte distinction. si prendray la hardiesse de uous esclayrcyr la uraye proprieté de quelques parties que

---

4. **esants** estants.

5. **enten** entendre—a hole in the paper has obliterated the word ending.

1. *Source:* Hatfield House, Cecil Papers, 149/38, no foliation. Incomplete copy, with one (and possibly a second) local correction in Elizabeth's hand. The endorsement in Burghley's hand reads "Coppie of the Quenes letter to Monsieur sente from Grenwyche by one of his laqueys xxiiijth of May 1582."

2. **pilosophie** philosophie.

Ie notte au maniement de ma memoirè, Il me semble qu'en commemorant l'hystoyre des traittes entre nous. Il uous plaist me connt longu[3] des hazardz de pertes et machines quauez endure a mon occasion, lesquelz ne puis oblier les ayant engrauez en mon ame, que iusques a la separation du corps Ie ne laisseray a recognoistre. et m'en pesentiray tousiours. Seullement Ie uous supplie de n'oublier[4] que tous ces longeurs n'ont tenu a moy, mes considerations n'ayant esté uuides[5] du respect de nostre plus heureuze demeure en ce pais, n'allant seullement de mon honneur mais aussi bien de uostre sureté. Otez pourtant Monsieur mon trescher quelque pensée que I'en estoys en coulpe, Quant a la patioun de cholere qui uous rend offense, qu'on se doute de uostre constance Ie me quitte de telle doute ne l'ayant iamais dict ny pensé quelque opinion qu'autres en ayent eu. Ie n'ay garde de uous offrir tant d'iniure, Seullement par la forgere[6] Ie me purgoys des Calomnies qu'on m'impoza en france et ailleurs, d'auoyr uze de cautelle ou mutation en ce que uous promettoys. Et tant s'en fallust que I'en fusse en coulpe, que Ie ne laissoys a l'imputer a la personne a qui il tenoyt le plus. Ce que Ie uoy par uoz lettres escriptes a pinard uous a donné argument descrire en mesme facon soubz nostre permission, qui me semble estrange en faizant demonstration que Ie uous pousse a y proceder plus instamment tant pour ma doutte que pour ma haste, O Monsieur combien cela touche a l'honneur, estant dame comme Ie suis. Vous en penserez a uostre bon loysyr qulqungns s'en riront a leur aize. Et Ie men resentz a mon regret qui nonobstant s'amoindroyt quant Ie m'ymagine que la fin tendit a aquerir une fin a noz longs trameaux qui redoublent si auant les serrures de mes liens que personne ne le scaura onques detascher. Vous m'escriuiez de m'auoyr mandé les copies des lettres du Roy et la Reine lesquelles Ie ne uiz encores sinon une lettre a pinard qui fust escritte que le xij^me de May iour bien esloigné du temps de uostre partement de ce Royaume. par ou Ie uoy que uous n'en auiez oncques fait mention, depuis uostre arrivée en flandres. En quoy Ie me puis iustifier quazi de n'y auoyr demeuré impudentement, mon Embassadeur en ayons fait plusieurs fois mention. Et pense que le Roy pour telle me reputera, qui suis la recherchante qui sera tousiours une belle reputation pour une femme. Vous pouuez uoyr s'il uous plait clerement

---

3. **connt longu** conter longuement—the second word breaks off at page edge.
4. This phrase inserted above the line is in Elizabeth's hand, in a different ink.
5. **uuides** vides.
6. **forgere** forgerie—figuratively, "machination."

et[7] facilement lesperance que puis conceuoyr d'ung sincere acomplisse-
ment de la choze qui si difficilement se resoud ou plustost du tout si met
pour le faict de l'argent. Ie suis si mauuais harongeur pour mon profit et
ayme si peu a iouer la mesnagere, que i'en donne la charge a ceux qui
sont plus sages que moy. Lesquelz ont declairé le tout a Marchomont qui
est de ma resolution. A qui l'ay faict requeste de uous en auertyr par-
ticulièrement estant assez importun pour cest'affaire et uous supplie
a mains ioinctes de uouloyr poizer en droittes balances sur quel fondement Ie marche. Et uous uerrez que Ie n'ay moins consideration, de
uostre grandeur et contentation de uoz enterprises que uous mesmes
pouriez souhaytter. Receuant uostre derniere lettre de nouuelles mandez par la Reine de Nauarre Ie uous suis que trop tenué de la grande al-
legresse qu'en prennez. Mais de ma part Ie n'en ay rien entendu par la
derniere audience que mon Embassadeur eust du Roy. qui fut le 6me de
Ce moys, et croyez que mon dernière auertissement se trouuera trop
ueritable, l'ayant receu de bon lieu, m'estonnant bien fort que ne l'ayez
recu encores que le uous ay despeche aussi tost que le uent permettoyt.
Vous me pardonnerez si Ie ne done facilement credit a nouuelles trop
bonnes de peur que la deception ne redouble mon ennuy. Ie me garde
pourtant sans en estre assurée respondre au non[8] / de tel auquel uous me
coniurez / Seullement uous puis Ie dire que telle obligation ne me liera
l'affection, plus que uos merites l'ont desia[9] pour ne pouuoyr receuoyr
l'augmentation. Et feray comparaison a quelque que soyt de uous
affecter non moins que si le petit prestre eust desia faict son office. Ie
feray en sorte que iustement ne me pouvez imputer manquemenz
en uostre endroyt, Ie pourroys dilater la rsponse[10] que uous mande par
Marchomont, Mais Ie l'ay laisse ce trauail uous supliant de croyre que
si nostre mariage se fist Ie n'en prendroys du bien pour l'Angleterre Si
d'auenture Dieu m'ostat de ce monde premier que d'auoyr des enfantz si
onques en auray uous estes sage a penser quel bon tour Ie leur ay faict.
pour leur aquerir si bons uoysins: si dauanture Flandre changast de
maistre, et les francoys y gouuernassent. pardonnez moy ceste franchise.
N'obliez mon coeur. que Ie hazarde ung peu pour uous en cest endroyct
plus que pourrez immaginer mais non plus que Ie sente desia et m'a Ioue

7. An ampersand is inserted above the line in a different ink; it may be in Elizabeth's hand.
8. **non** nom.
9. **desia** déjà.
10. **rsponse** réponse.

d'en taster plus d'ung tel liqueur. Mais quand Ie me souuienne pour qui cest Ie me console si auant que I'en deuienn suporte. pour la commission que nous donnerons Ie ne m'en amuzeray iusques a entendre si le desyr de uous complaire occupa tant l'esprit de la Reine quelle entendist l'intention du Roy resembler a la somme de uostre desir. non du tout l'interpretation que peut estre s'en fera. Quoi entendre &[11]

LETTER 55 ❧ QUEEN ELIZABETH TO MONSIEUR, SEPTEMBER 10, 1583[1]

Monsieur aprez Vne longue attente de receuoyr quelques nouuelles de uous, et uoz affaires monsieur de Reaux me uint uisiter de uostre part, ne portant que lettres toutes plannes d'afection et d'assurance de la Continuance d'icelle a iamais, pour lesquelles Ie uous rends Une infinité de graces, pour en auoyr entendu le soing que prenez de peur de quelque mauuaise impression, que Ie pourroys conceuoyr de uoz actions; puis il me tena[2] language qui me sembla bien fort estrange que desirez scauoyr quelle sera l'ayde que uous donnerez pour la conseruation des pais bas; me disant que uous estez assuré du Roy qu'il uous aydera de mesme que moy. Mondieu monsieur comment estes uous fortené[3] de croÿre que cest le moyen de conseruer uoz amis, de tousiours les debiliter, Quiconque uous en donna le conseil ont creu de faire une tasche en nostre amitie ou du tout la rompre Pour par mesme moyen faire leur desseins et uous reclamer a leur desir, Ne uous souuiont[4] il point Monsieur contre combien d'amis il me faut preparer, doybz[5] Ie tant panser de loing que Ie neglige le plus proche / le Roy nostre frere est il si debil prince qu'il ne uous peust difendre sans Vne autre uoizin qui a asez sur le doz ni si debilité pour ouuryr chemin aux assaillants. Vous ne m'estimerez si indigne de regner que Ie ne me fortifie uoyre des nerfs de la guerre, en attendant tropt

---

11. The copy ends with an ampersand, an abbreviation for "etc."

1. *Source:* Hatfield House, Cecil Papers 149/40, no foliation. Copy. The endorsement reads "Coppie of the Queens letter to Monsieur, sent by Monsieur de Reaux. from Ootelands the xth of September 1583."

2. **tena** tana—from *taner/tenner,* "to tire out or annoy."

3. **fortené** fortuné—meaning *infortuné* in some contexts, as here.

4. **souuiont** souvient. *Souvenir* is intransitive, a now obsolete form—"Does it not come back to your memory at all?"

5. **doybz** dois.

de courtoyzie de ceux qui cherchent ma ruine. Ie m'estonne du Roy nostre frere qui m'a donné la precedence a uous fortifier en si grand besoing, ayant commencé premiere que Luy, et ne luy manquant meillieurs moyens par moins d'incommodite, pardonez moy Ie uous prie a uous dire que que[6] ceste reponse est toute claire qu'il ne uoudroyt rien faire pensant que I'en auroys peu de raison a ne donner, tellement que si le Roy ne parlera et ne fera beaucoup plus que nagueres telle entreprize se rompra bien tost, et si ne soyt pour Luy mesme Ie pense que telle est sa determination Voila mon opinion. Quant auous Monsieur Ie uoy questes si enuironné de contrarionts persuasions et si differantes humeurs, doutant tant et ne s'assurant de rien, que ne scauez ou bonnement uous tourner, Comme en auez assez grande raison plust a Dieu que Ie fusse assez abile de Iugement pour uous impartyr Counseil le meillieur conseil et plus assuré. Et que I'eusse l'entendement, comme en ay la uolonté, Alors plutot Ie le uous porteray que le mander, I'espere entre autres choses qu'il uous souuiendra qu'il est bien digne de tumber qui s'entre ez retz, non seullement prenez auiz durement sentiz, c'est assez. I'entens a mon grand regret que le Roy, Reine mere, uoyre uosmesmes m'impozent la coulpe que Ie n'ay iamais commiz ayant tousiours tenu au Roy de parfaire Ce de qui Ie n'en puis faire plus de mention sinon pour uous supplier de me faire tant de droyt a me purger, uoyre par la sentence de uoz ministres memes qui en scauent mon innocence. Car Ie ne puis supporter telle iniure, quilz mordent et pleurent De mon affection en uostre endroyt I'apelle a l Embassadeur du Roy, a Monsieur la Motte, Marchomant et Baqueuille et combien que Dieu ne permettra tel pacte, si ne laisseray iamais a uous honorer aymer et estimer comme le chien qui estant souuent batu, retourne a son Maistre. Dieu uous garde des conseilz fardez et uous permette suiure ceux qui uous respectent plus qu'eux mesmes.

SPEECH 20 𐑌 QUEEN ELIZABETH'S LATIN SPEECH TO THE HEADS OF OXFORD UNIVERSITY, SEPTEMBER 28, 1592[1]

Merita et gratitudo sic meam rationem captiuam duxerunt, vt facere cogant quae ratio ipsa negat. Curae enim Regnorum tam magna pondera

6. Repetition in MS at transition from recto to verso of page.

1. *Source:* Bodleian Library, University of Oxford, MS Bodley 900; copy in an elegant hand of the period, bound in a fine tooled and gilt limp vellum cover together with Elizabeth's

habent, vt ingenium obtundere quàm memoriam acuere soleant. Addatur etiam huius linguae desuetudo, quae talis et tam frequens fuit, vt in
triginta sex annis, trigesies[2] nec tot vsam fuisse memini. Sed fracta nunc
est glacies, aut inhaerere aut euadere oportet. Non sunt laudes eximiae et
insignes, sed immeritae meae, Non doctrinarum in multis generibus in-
dicationes, narrationes et explicationes, Non orationes multis et varijs
modis eruditè et insignitèr expressae, sed aliud quiddam est multo pre-
tiosius atque praestantius, Amor scilicet, qui nec vnquam auditus nec
scriptus nec memoria hominum notus fuit, cuius exemplo parentes car-
ent, nec inter familiares cadet, imò nec inter amantes, in quorum sortem
non semper fides incidit experientia ipsa docente. Talis est iste vt nec per-
suasiones nec minae nec execrationes delere poterunt, imò in quem tempus gubernationem non habet, quod ferrum consumit, quod scopulos
minuit, id istum separare non potuit. Ista sunt merita, sunt eiusmodi quae
sempiterna futura putarem si et ego aeterna essem. Ob quae si mille pro
vna linguas haberem gratias debitas exprimere non valerem: tantum animus concipere potest quae exprimere nequit. In cuius gratitudinem
accipite tantum votum et Consilium. Ab initio Regni mei gubernationis
summa et praecipua mea sollicitudo cura et vigilia fuit, vt tam ab externis
inimicis quam internis tumultibus seruaretur, vt quod diu et multis se-
culis floruerit, sub meis manibus non debilitaretur. Post enim Animae
meae tutelam in sola mea perpetua sollicitudine collocaui. Quod si totius
tam semper fuerim vigilans, et quòd ipsa Academia pars eius non min-
ima putatur: Quomodo non et in illam extenditur ista cautio, pro qua
tanta diligentia vsura semper sum, vt nullo stimulo opus erit ad excitan-
dam quae ex seipsa prompta est ad promouendam seruandam et deco-
randam illam. Nunc quod ad consilium attinet, tale accipite quod si
sequamini, haud dubito quin erit in Dei gloriam, vestram utilitatem et
meum singulare gaudium. Vt diuturna sit haec Academia, habeatur in-
primis cura vt Deus colatur non more omnium opinionum, non secundum ingenia nimis inquisita et exquisita, sed vt lex diuina iubet et nostra
praecipit. Non enim talem principem habetis quae vobis quicquam pre-
cepit quod contra conscientiam verè Christianam esse deberet. Scitote
me prius morituram quam tale aliquid acturam, aut quicquam iubeam
quod in sacris literis vetatur. Si enim corporum vestrorum semper curam

autograph English translation of Cicero's *Pro Marcello,* and Latin and English versions of
"The Blessed Virgin Mary to the Messenians."

  2. *Trigesies* is a variant spelling of *tricesies,* itself a variant form of *tricies,* "thirty times."

suscepi, deseramne animarum? Vetet Deus. Animarum ego curam neg-
ligam pro quarum neglectu anima mea iudicabitur? Longè absit. Moneo
ergò vt non praecatis³ leges, sed sequamini, ne disputetis num meliora
possunt praescribi, sed obseruetis quae lex Diuina iubet et nostra cogit.
Deinde memineritis vt vnusquisque in gradu suo superiori obediat, non
praescribendo quae esse deberent, sed sequendo quod praescriptum est,
hoc cogitantes, Quod si superiores agere coeperint quae non decet alium
superiorem habebunt a quo regantur qui illos punire et debeat et velit.
Postremò, vt sitis vnanimes, cùm intelligatis vnita robustiora, separata
infirmiora, et citò in ruinam casura.⁴

LETTER 87, VERSION 1 ဢ ELIZABETH TO HENRY IV OF FRANCE,
JULY 1593¹

Ah que douleurs, O quelz regretz, O que gemissementz Ie sentoys en
mon Asme par le sonn de telles Nouuelles que Morlains m'a compté?²
Mon dieu est il possible que mondain respect aulcun deut effacer le
terreur que la crainte Divine nous menace, pouuons nous par raison
mesme attendre bonne sequele d'acte si inique Celuy qui vous ayt
maintes annees conservé par sa main, pouuez vous imaginer qu'il vous
permettat aller seul au plusgrand besoing? Ah c'est dangereux de mal
faire pour en faire du bien: Encore l'espere que plus saine inspiration
vous adviendra. Cependant Ie ne cesseray de vous mettre au premier
reng³ de mes devotions a ce que les mains d'Esau ne gastent la benediction de Iacob.⁴ Et ou me promettes toute amitie et fidelité, Ie confesse
l'auoir cherement merité, et ne m'en penteray,⁵ pour veu que ne chang-
ies du pere, aultrement vous seray Ie que Soeur Bastarde au moins non
de par le Pere. Car l'~~acqueray~~ aymeray⁶ mieulx tousiours le Naturel que

---

3. **praecatis** praecedatis?
4. **casura** cadere (infinitive to follow "intelligatis").
1. *Source:* Hatfield House, Cecil Papers, 133/101, fol. 157r. Copy, with one correction in Elizabeth's hand, and the subscription and initials in a third hand. The endorsement reads
"Minute of her maiesties letter to the French king. Julij 1593."
2. **compté** conté.
3. **reng** renq.
4. See Genesis 27.
5. **penteray** repentirai.
6. This correction appears to be in Elizabeth's italic.

l'adopt. Comme Dieu le mieulx cognoist, qui vous guide au droict chemin du meilleur sentir. /[7]

> Vostre tresasseuree Soeur,
> si ce soit a la Vielle mode,
> auec la nouuelle Ie n'ay que faire.
> E. R.

LETTER 87, VERSION 2 🙰 ELIZABETH TO HENRY IV OF FRANCE, JULY 1593[1]

[Endorsed] Copie de la lettre de la Royne d'Angleterre au Roy.

Ah quelles douleurs! O quelz regretz! O quelz gemissemens Iay senty en mon ame pour le son de telles nouuelles que Morlas m'a contées. Mondieu est il possible qu'aucun mondain respect deust effacer la terreur que la crainte diuine menace. Pouuons nous par raison mesme attendre bonne yssue d'une chose si inique.[2] Celui qui uous a maintenu par sa mercy,[3] pouuez uous imaginer quil uous permit aller seul au plus grand besoin. Or cela est[4] dangereux de mal faire pour en esperer bien.[5] Encor esperay ie que plussaine inspiration uous aduiendra Cependant ne cesseray de uous mettre au premier Renq demes deuotions a ce que les mains dEsau ne gastent les benedictions de Jacob. Et ou uous me promettez toute amytié et fidelité Ie confesse l'auoir chichement[6] merité. Et ne men repentiray[7] pourueu que ne changiez de pere Autrement ne

---

7. **sentir** sentier.

1. *Source:* Paris, Bibliothèque Nationale, MS FR 5045, fol. 408 ("Affaires de France, 1527 à 1605"); copy from the late sixteenth or early seventeenth century, bound immediately following a royal proclamation dated July 25, 1593, in which Henry IV recognizes the Catholic Church as the true Church of God. This version illustrates how a copyist whose native language was French might emend or otherwise alter Elizabeth's grammar and diction. Bibliothèque Nationale, MS FR 17830, fol. 86, shows a later seventeenth-century italic hand performing the same operations; its significant variants are recorded in our notes.

2. **bonne . . . inique** FR 17830 reads "une bonne suite d'vn acte si inique."

3. **par sa mercy** FR 17830 reads "et conserué."

4. **Or cela est** FR 17830 reads "O qu'il est."

5. **bien** FR 17830 reads "du bien."

6. **chichement** meanly, scantily; FR 17830 reads "cherement meritée et conseruée."

7. **repentiray** FR 17830 reads "departiray."

uous seray ie que seur bastarde aumoins de par le pere.[8] Car iaymeray tousiours mieux le naturel que l'adopté comme Dieu mieux le connoit qui uous guide au droit chemin de meilleur sentier. Vostre tres asseurée seur Sire, soit a la vieille mode: Auec la nouuelle ie nay que faire.[9]

LETTER 92 ᘐ᙮ ELIZABETH TO HENRY IV OF FRANCE, CIRCA SEPTEMBER 4, 1596[1]

Mon trescher frere,

Combien que i'ay tousiours estimé que les voluntaires bienvieillauns et non liéés par aultre ligature que l'affection syncere, fussent assez suffisantes pour sure fondement de longue durée: Si est qu'entendant le desir qu'aviez bien grand qu'une ligue se fist publique entre nous deux, ie y suis consenty, et selon les coustumes entre les grands Princes y ay adiousté ma foy et parolle, qui comme elles n'ont iamais encore receu tasche, telles si dieu plaist iay l'ame syncere de les conserver en mesme mode. Et combien que iay advancé la Vielle coustume des Roys pour estre la premiere a commencer le party: Si espere ie que ne me tiendrez pour impudente estant de ma sexe pour commencer la danse d'amour, ne doubtant que me donnerez Vne risée pour telle haste, ains que mesur-erez par la; que ne seray iamais paresseuse a Vous honorer. I'ay reçeu par le Duc de Bouillon voz lettres toutes remplies de protestations de fidel amour en mon endroict, avec vn ardent desir de m'honorer de vostre presence, chose que vous osteroit toute creance de voz ministres qui vous ont abusé Ie doute par tant de louange de ce que quand vous serez l'oculaire iuge vous ne trouuerez nullement respondre au demy de qui vous font a croyre qui me feront vne disgrace en cuydant m'advancer le respect. mais d'vne chose ilz ne se trouueront oncques falsifié, silz vous representent la purité de mon asseurée amitie, et le vif sentiment de quelquun honorable accident qui vous arrive, avec vne promptitude de vous ayder comme mez commoditez me permettront, comme ie ne doute que le Sieur de Bouillon vous representera, a la suffisance duquel

8. **aumoins . . . pere** FR 17830 omits this phrase.

9. **Auec . . . faire** FR 17830 reads "a la nouuelle ie n'en ay que faire."

1. *Source:* Hatfield House, Cecil Papers, vol. 133/153, fol. 236r; copy by Burghley's secretary. The endorsement in Burghley's hand reads "Her Maiestie to the french king. September 1596." The date is taken from the from Hatfield House Calendar of the Cecil Papers.

ie me remetz: suppliant le createur vous conserver en bonne vie et longue, comme desire

Vostre tres affectionée bonne soeur

SPEECH 22 ❦ QUEEN ELIZABETH'S LATIN REBUKE TO THE POLISH AMBASSADOR, PAUL DE JALINE, JULY 25, 1597[1]

Oh quam decepta fui: Expectaui Legationem tu vero querelam, mihi ad-
duxisti, Per literas accepi te esse Legatum, inueni vero Heraldum,[2] Nunquam in vita mea audiui talem orationem; Miror sane, Miror tantam: et
tam insolitam[3] in publico audatiam,[4] Neque possum credere, si Rex tuus
adesset; quod ipse talia verba protulisset, sin vero tale aliquid tibi fortasse; in mandatis comisit, (quod quidem valde dubito) eo tribuendum,
quod cum Rex sit Iuuenis, et non tam Iure sanguinis, quam Iure electio-
nis; ac nouiter electus, non tam perfecte; Inteligat rationem tractandi is-
tiusmodi negotia Cum aliis Principibus; quam vel Maiores illius nobiscum obseruarunt, Vel fortasse obseruabunt alij qui locum eius posthac
tenebunt./

Quod ad te attinet, tu mihi videris libros multos perlegisse; libros
tamen Principum ne attigisse, sed prorsus ignorare, quid inter reges
conueniat, Nam quod Iuris naturae gentiumque tantopere mentionem
facis; hoc scito iuris naturae Gentiumque esse vt cum bellum Inter Reges
intercidit, liceat alteri alterius bellica subsidia; vndecunque allata in-
tercipere et ne ad damnum suum conuertantur precauere; (Hoc inquam) est ius nature et Gentium./

---

1. *Source:* Folger Shakespeare Library, MS V.a.321, fol. 35v; copy in an early seventeenth-
century hand. The heading reads "Her Maiesties Answer to the Polands Ambassador." For a
description of the occasion and of the Polish ambassador's speech which this speech answers, see *CW,* pp. 334–35.

2. **Heraldum** Robert Cecil remarked in the cover note he sent to the earl of Essex, en-
closing a copy of the speech: "I send you this enclosed, not bidden by the Queen, nor for-
bidden. If the Latin be good, I protest to you Her Majesty spake it; but if it be not good Latin
to say *Heraldum* instead of *Foecialem,* I confess that word was none of mine" (Mary Anne
Everett Green, ed., *Calendar of State Papers, Domestic Series, Elizabeth, 1595–1597,* vol. 4
[London: Longmans, Green, Reader, and Dyer, 1869], p. 473).

3. **insolitam** unusual, strange. The seventeenth-century translation in *CW,* p. 333, reads
"insolent."

4. **audatiam** audentiam.

Quod nouam affinitatem Cum domo Austriaca Commemores; quam tanti Iam fieri velis: non te fugiat[5] ex eadem domo non defuisse, qui Regi tuo Polloniae Regnum preripere voluissset./

De caeteris vero quae non sunt huius Loci et temporis cum plura sint, et singilatim Consideranda illud expectabis quod ex quibusdam meis Consiliarijs huic rei designandis, intelliges, Interia vero valeas et quiescas./.

5. **non te fugiat**   The seventeenth-century translation reads "you are not ignorant"—a far less sarcastic locution than Elizabeth's "may it not escape you."

INDEX OF NAMES

Note: Includes only names and identified allusions to personages pre-1700. CW contains a comprehensive index and a full set of reference notes.